TECHNICAL EDUCATION IN KERALA
Emerging Trends

TECHNICAL EDUCATION IN KERALA

Emerging Trends

Edited by

Meera Bai M

SERIALS PUBLICATIONS

NEW DELHI

First Published–2009

ISBN: 978-81-8387-242-3

Published by

SERIALS PUBLICATIONS
4830/24, Prahlad Street, Ansari Road
Darya Ganj, New Delhi-110002 (India)
Phone : 23245225 Fax : 91-11-23272135
E-mail: serials@satyam.net.in

Contents

Preface

Needless to say, science and technology has become the catch word of the day and everything grounded on the above is having encompassing appeal and applause. It is an unbounded truth that the growth and development of science and technology by leaps and bounds has led today into unparalled all round success and all these boil down to the fact that we are on the primary need to concentrate more on and deal with studies on science and technology. It was in this context I ventured to conduct a two day seminar on 'Emerging Trends in Technical Education in Kerala' embracing varied topics on technical education in Kerala. The present edited volume is the outcome of the aforesaid seminar which was funded by the All India Council for Technical Education (AICTE), New Delhi. I express my sincere thanks to the AICTE.

Contributors List

Meera Bai M, Reader, Deptt. of Applied Economics, Cochin University of Science and Technology, Kochi-22.

Bhasi M, Professor, School of Management Studies, Cochin University of Science and Technology, Kochi-22.

Merlie Niemi Kindred, Faculty, Michigan Technical University, Michigan.

Doraipandi Mavoothu, Senior Lecturer, School of Management Studies, Cochin University of Science and Technology, Kochi-22.

Muhammed Aslam, Reader, School of Management Studies, Cochin University of Science and Technology, Kochi-22.

Wilson P R, Professor, School of Management Studies, Cochin University of Science and Technology, Kochi-22.

Moli P Koshi, Reader, School of Management Studies, Cochin University of Science and Technology, Kochi-22.

Mary Joseph, Professor, School of Management Studies, Cochin University of Science and Technology, Kochi-22.

Sreejith P S, Principal, School of Engineering, Cochin University of Science and Technology, Kochi-22.

Mathew Emmannuel, Reader, St. Xaviers College, Vaikom.

Harikumar S, Professor, Deptt. of Applied Economics, Cochin University of Science and Technology, Kochi-22.

Remadevi, Lecturer, Department of Economics, Govt. College, Attingal, Trivandrum.

Sabu Thomas, ICSSR Fellow, Cochin University of Science and Technology, Kochi-22.

Sam Daniel, Faculty, Teacher's Training College, Trivandrum.

Chacko Jose, Faculty, Academic Staff College, Calicut.

Merlin Joseph, Project Fellow (UGC funded Major Research Project), Deptt. of Applied Economics, Cochin University of Science and Technology, Kochi-22.

Dhanalakshmi T, Research Scholar, Deptt. of Applied Economics, Cochin University of Science and Technology, Kochi-22.

Sukumaran Nair M P, Managing Director, Travancore Cochin Chemicals Ltd. , Kochi-01.

Zakariya K A, Senior Lecturer, School of Management Studies, Cohin University of Science and Technology, Kochi-22.

Jagathy Raj V P, Professor, School of Management Studies, Cochin University of Science and Technology, Kochi-22.

Devassia M D, Lecturer (Sl.Gr), Deva Matha College, Kannur

Manoj P K, Lecturer, Deptt. of Applied Economics, Cochin University of Science and Technology, Kochi-22.

Arunachalam P, Reader, Deptt. of Applied Economics, Cochin University of Science and Technology, Kochi-22.

Sangeetha Prathap, Research Scholar, Deptt. of Applied Economics, Cochin University of Science and technology, Kochi-22.

Sajitha, Research Scholar, Deptt. of Applied Economics, Cochin University of Science and technology, Kochi-22.

Bindu George, Research Scholar, Deptt. of Applied Economics, Cochin University of science and Technology, Kochi-22.

Valliammai, Asst. Professor, SWC Department, College of Agricultural Engineering, TNAU, Coimbatore.

PART-1

Meera Bai M

1 Introduction Emerging Trends in Technical Education in Kerala

Since technical education determines the development and socio-economic condition of a nation, there is a greater need for high quality technical education to produce technically skilled manpower in India. A high quality engineer or technician can obviously be created only through high quality engineering and vocational teaching and training. Technical education is imparted at three different levels in Kerala. These are (1) Industrial Training Institutes (ITI) which conduct trade courses for skilled workers; (2) Polytechnic Institutes, which conduct diplomas to produce middle level technicians and (3) Engineering Colleges,which conduct undergraduate and post graduate degree courses in Engineering and Technology.

Technical education offers exciting possibilities for radically enlarging and improving human resource skills. Keralites are competent in its near universal literacy and awareness levels and this can be transformed into economically rewarding and employable skills by deploying the tools offered by technical institutions. Recent trends in convergence of technologies have thrown up new opportunities and new services for the state. Kerala has a large traditional agricultural and industrial sectors and the infusion of technology into this domain would be essential for its survival and growth in the face of imminent international competition. Kerala offers fertile ground for the effective utilization of the new technologies on account of its densely networked communities which possess high awareness and literacy levels, its superior telecom connectivity and its propensity for quick technology absorption. In this background a Two Day National Seminar on 'Emerging Trends in Technical Education in Kerala' was organized by the Department of Applied Economics, Cochin University of Science and Technology on 20th and 21st of January, 2007. This event was sponsored by the All India Council for Technical Education (AICTE), New Delhi. The seminar was expected to bring the universities and institutions, industries and research organizations to evolve policies and programmes to meet the present and future challenges of rapid technological changes and industrial development in India.

The important objectives of the seminar were

1. to understand the extent of awareness on the part of participants about the technical education schemes meant for them and the degree of utilization of such schemes by the people in Kerala
2. to organize a set of concepts, process and systems which are uniquely technological
3. to motivate students to make connection between concepts and real world applications
4. to promote students to use the technical education facilities to design, apply materials, machines, instrumentation processes and technical concepts in an efficient and safe manner and
5. to bring about the network intervention between the institutions and industries to produce technically skilled manpower in Kerala.

The two day national seminar exhaustively discussed various issues like planning, growth and regulation of technical education in India, cost sharing in technical education, SWOT analysis of engineering profession, women and technical education, policy evaluation in technical education, HRD in technical education, industry-academia linkage and R&D, gender and technology, quality assurance in technical education etc.

In the inaugural speech, PK Abdul Azis, the Vice-Chancellor of CUSAT remarked the fascinating trends in which engineering education was increasingly gaining focus. He was of the view that the industry expected technology graduates who could be put on qualitative job directly, without further training from the industry. He indirectly hinted that technical education must be improved in terms of quality and emphasized the need for effective industry-academia partnership for better employability of technology graduates.

During the two day seminar, there were 11 technical sessions, dealing with different topics related with trends in technical education in Kerala.The present volume is a collection of all the papers presented in the two day seminar. The first paper presented in the series of different technical sessions was 'Technical Eucation Expansion: A Bane or Boon for Kerala' by Devassia M. D. The academic, social and economic issues of public expenditure on higher education are discussed in this paper and the author concludes the paper by saying technical higher education has been a boon to the state of Kerala.

In his paper 'Issues in Establishing and Promoting Industry-Institute Partnerships in Kerala' Bhasi M categorically mentions that the industry-institute partnerships have been useful to both the industry as well as the institute. He continues, despite recognizing its importance, most of the institutes have not been able to show much progress in the area. In his paper reasons for the increasing importance of industry-institute partnerships, industry-institute partnerships linkage mechanisms and their suitability to Kerala, the cultural and organizational difficulties in developing such linkages, some guidelines on how institutes should manage the process of development of such linkages are highlighted. Some approaches to managing the finance related issues in such linkages are also discussed.

Merlie Kindred from the Michigan Technological University of the U.S.A argues for eco feminist approaches to communication energy technology. She makes a comparison between America's Keweenaw Peninsula in Michigan and

COSTFORD in Kerala .Kindred throws light on the fact that technology and technical education have been challenged with not only content concerns, but also technical communication in the context of humanist and environmental considerations.

In the paper entitled 'SWOT Analysis of Management Education in India with Special Emphasis on Kerala Situation' the author, Mavoothu emphatically says that among developing countries, India has been going through a process of great change to become a part of the world economy. This requires an active response from corporates and educational institutions, particularly from management institutions (B-Schools). Management education has been playing a significant role in the Indian economy. In India, management education has been imparted by three categories of institutes namely, first-rung institutes (like IIMs), second-rung institutes (mainly the University Management Departments or UMDs) and third-rung institutes (mainly the institutes not affiliated to universities). Top Indian management institutes have proved that India can impart world-class management education. Some of the University Management Departments (UMDs) have also emerged as the top management institutes (e.g. FMS, Bajaj Management Institute, etc.). At the same time, in India, he says third rate B-Schools locate by the side of the top management institute. Quite often it can be seen that world-class management institute and many third-rate management institutes in the same city/town, sometimes in the same road or street locate adjacently. This needs the attention of educational planners, industrialists and politicians who can change this plight. In this context, diagnosing the management education has far-reaching implications for potential students, employers, economy and the society

The paper 'An Introduction to the Problems and Issues of Engineering Education in Kerala' co-authored by Zakariya K A and Jagathy Raj throws light to the fact that the engineering educational system has to under go a drastic change to accommodate the needs of the emerging 'knowledge economy' by providing quality 'knowledge workers'. The authors categorically state that Kerala's engineering education sector needs to be innovated effectively to ensure a high quality education to produce entrepreneurial oriented, industry ready, employable professionals meeting the global employer's requirements.

Muhammed Aslam and Wilson P R point out the problems prevailing in the higher education sector of Kerala. Better prospects for this sector can be assured if the government encourages competition through autonomy and independence from state funding. They are of opinion that institutes must place a stronger emphasis on innovation, R&D and the creation of new knowledge. Universities should be allowed to form alliances with firms for research and funding. Businesses must be consulted in curriculum design and conducting of courses.

With a saying, 'Those who have the will, find the way.......those who do not will find the wayside', Molly P Koshi and Mary Joseph in their paper on 'Management Education-Enhancing the core competencies' firmly assert that the liberalization of the Indian economy has resulted in (a) a highly competitive environment (b) global nature of Indian business (c) great all round emphasis on technology, quality and cost (d) greater concern in society for environmental issues (e) unprecedented development and use of information technology and (f) IT-driven communication, science and emerging economy becoming transitional in nature. Management education plays a significant role in all these. The authors say that the existing management education practices may either emphasis westernised contents or local. Meaningful combination of theories and case materials remain exceptions. Managerial challenges and contextual differences demand more systematic management education solutions.

Manoj P. K. and Meera Bai M. in their paper seek to look into the national as well as international developments having a bearing on the higher education system in India, particularly the technical education system. They try to critically analyze the current scenario of the country in this regard vis-à-vis that of other major economies of the world, particularly in the light of growing pressures of globalization and the impact of General Agreement on Trade in Services (GATS). It made a SWOT analysis of the Indian technical education system with a view to identifying the most appropriate skills to be imparted to the technical students and the desired orientation of the technical graduates and practitioners. Further, an attempt has been made to apprise a few other allied aspects like the imminent need for internationalization of the Indian technical education system, the impact of changing demographics on the skilled manpower, emerging fields in science and technology having the potential to enhance the prospects of country's technical manpower, and after all the necessary policy initiatives to bring about the desired changes. Finally, the paper suggests a few strategies for re-orienting the Indian technical education system so as to make it more effective, dynamic and also in tune with the growing needs of the globalized economy.

Wilson P R and Muhammed Aslam categorically say that Kerala can be an international educational hub. Kerala has a tradition and educational infrastructure suitable for participation in international education. The question is on factors of social justice, equality of opportunities and quality enhancement, so that Kerala would become a favoured destination for transnational education. Their paper entitled ' Kerala-An International Educational Hub'throws light to the fact that internationalized higher education is possible only in an environment and ethos of systematic and result-oriented academic work and other campus operations. A work culture characterized by effective time management and rigorous discipline is essential for an international community to live together and perform together. Impulsive outbursts of campus violence, disruption of studies and closure of institution will have to be totally avoided. There should be a climate of trust between various stakeholders and democratic procedures for settling disputes.

On the second day of the seminar, nine papers were presented. Sreejith P S, in his paper 'Technology and Globalisation' mentioned that Globalization and liberalization of Indian Economy has intensified competition in various sectors such as industry, agriculture and services. However, the educational institutions which cater to the human resources development component of the above sectors have yet to realize the impact of market forces. This paper focused on the importance of globalization of technical education in India.

In his paper entitled 'Problems and Prospects of Entrepreneurship Education in Engineering Colleges and other Technical Institutions in Kerala' Mathew Emmannuel points out the significance of entrepreneurship education in Kerala. Citing the examples of Silicon Valley around Stanford University, The Research Triangle Park in North Carolona and Route 128 in MIT, Boston, Mathew opines that the technical institutions/universities could nucleate the generation of entrepreneurs and employees for the firms and industries and its environment coupled with its expertise and facilities can play a vital role in shaping today's students into tomorrow's entrepreneurs.

Learning should be considered a critical facet of basic development, an alternative medium of capacity-building and a means to people's empowerment. Valliammai A, in her paper entitled 'E- Learning: Emerging Trend in Modern Education- An Overview' states that knowledge and related information, skills, technologies, and attitudes play a key role in the success of modern education. The main objective of e-learning has been to promote the concept of life long learning among the large mass of learners at the faster way in an interactive manner. In 1995, there was no web based online courses, but during 2003, it has been increased to 4 million. So in this electronic era, it is necessary to know about the new technologies in modern education. One of the important technologies has been E learning. The modern world has been undergoing a fundamental transformation as the industrial society of the 20th century rapidly gave way to the information society of the 21st century.

In the combined paper, authors, Manoj P. K. and Arunachalam P focus on the need for saving management education in India from irrelevance. They point out some strategic imperatives. They study systematically the existing management education system in India, to identify the weaknesses and problems of the system as well as the prospects and also make constructive suggestions for improving the system. This paper is divided into four parts. The Evolution of management education in India (including the present status), the weaknesses of management education in India, the prospects of management education in India and suggestions for making Indian management education more relevant to the national realities are dealt with in the paper.

The paper 'Higher Education System in Kerala-An Overview' co-authored by Harikumar S and Remadevi T firmly establishes the fact that the nature of higher education in Kerala has an important role in creating the disequilibrium in the job market of the state. Education planning of the State will become effective only if a restructuring of the educational system without a restructuring of the educational system of the State. They say that it will help both build upon what has already been achieved and to sustain a high rate of growth of the economy.

In his paper entitled 'Influence of Education on the Life long Earnings of Engineers in Kerala', Sam Daniel is of opinion that engineering education in our country plays a significant role in the reconstruction of the nation. He continues engineering education should be viewed as a dynamic process and management of such a process requires formulation of highly progressive objectives, establishment of competitive performance levels, scientific and valid evaluation procedures and appropriate feed-backs and development of self motivating and controlling forces among the students. The demand for engineering education has been increasing in the state.

Chacko Jose is of opinion that attempts for gender mainstreaming have so far seen women merely as consumers and not creators of technology. To get away with such attitudes imparting technical education to women alone will not be enough. Encouraging women to choose and stick on to technical careers have been equally important. For this educating the society to neuter its stereotypical perceptions on gender has been extremely important. Policy measures to provide increased educational opportunities to women are undoubtedly needed. Social and cultural beliefs about the role of women in society and the working world have had a powerful influence on determining the social and economic roles played by women in all societies, as well as determining the opportunities that women have access to. Probably the most important measure to ensure increased participation of women in professional education and careers has been to educate society to neuter its stereotypical gender perceptions, authors mention so in their paper entitled 'Technology and Gender: Promoting Technical Education for Women'.

In their paper 'Technology adoption and Human Resource Development in Tea Plantation Industry of Kerala' Merlin Joseph and Dhanalakshmy argue for the adoption of technology for human resource development through technical education. This has been very relevant in the State for increasing productivity and for solving the crisis in plantation sector. Increasing productivity is required for improving the competitiveness. But huge capital investment is required for replantation and mechanization. Since the companies have been running at a loss quite for some time they are not in a position to make all these huge capital investments. If the government and the companies work in a co-operative manner for fund raising, arranging technical education and training facilities in plantations productivity and better prosperity of industry can be achieved.

Sangeetha, Sajitha and Bindu start their paper 'Quality Assurance and Excellence in Technical Education-An Assessment of Service Quality Perception' with a quote of Aristotle: Quality is a habit, an attitude. But the demand of the time has been to implement, institutionalize and internalize it. In the modern time of globalization, the demand for highly technically qualified persons has been very high. Quality has been the buzzword in every sphere of activities. Adequate emphasis should be given to quality assurance and excellence. In India though agencies like UGC and AICTE do a lot in this regard, still there are miles and miles to go.

Sukumaran Nair M P is of opinion that there has been an urgent need for restructuring technical education in India. Not only the structure of the technical education but also the content and finances of the technical education are to be restructured so as to meet the changing needs of the industry, services, academic, R&D and other sectors and also render it affordable to common people.

Meera Bai M in her paper entitled 'Technical Education and Gender Needs: A Keralite's view' forcefully says technology and technical education have been of paramount importance for women in meeting their gender needs. This is the one among the two papers presented in the seminar with a gender perspective. Through a technology input approach women could attain empowerment at all levels. Investment in women's technical education should not be considered as a waste but wealth. With this idea government and other agencies working in the education field should speak and work for reservation for girls in the technical education institutions and if needed technical institutions only for girls should be started. Special attention should be given to the spread of technical education among women in rural areas. She winds up her paper with a dream of such a level of technical education which could assure high employment, high income, less drudgery and less discrimination in the State.

Irrespective of the institutes they represent, all the contributors say in one accord that there is an urgent need for giving still more priority to technical education in the State.

REFERENCES

Prakash B. A. (1999), Kerala's Economic Development: Issues and Problems, Sage Publications, New Delhi.

Bidanda, Bopaya, Arisoy, Ozlem, and Shuman, Larry J. (2006), "Offshoring Manufacturing: Implications for Engineering Jobs and Education: A Survey and Case Study", *Robotics and Computer-Integrated Manufacturing*, Vol. 22, pp. 576-587. (Available online at *www.sciencedirect.com*).

Prasad, V.V. Durga (2007), "Management Education in India: SWOT Analysis", *University News*, Vol. 45, No. 06, February 05-11, pp. 15-17.

Bhasi M

2 Issues in Establishing and Promoting Industry-Institute Partnerships in Kerala

Governments, have worried about the effectiveness of university-industry links, at least since the 1950s, but this concern has now become almost worldwide, as the long forecast transformation of the industrial scene from labour-intensive manufacture to knowledge-based industry has taken place. There is now a considerable literature about university-industry relations in the new configuration. The literature refers regularly to the "triple helix" of university-industry-government relations and to "mode 2" interdisciplinary research or to concepts of "entrepreneurial science". There is a growing interest in universities' regional impact, universities' role in wealth creation and in the "capitalization of science", and in the effects of globalization and localization. At the same time universities, facing severe reductions in their unit of resource of state funding are becoming much lesser and they are forced to generate non-state resources. Some are also thinking of becoming much more global in their ambitions both in teaching and research.

These changes in the context of university-industry links are having and will have significant impacts on the organizational forms through which they are managed. But to understand these new structures, it is more useful to consider the kind of traditional structures of management, which, at least, in India have been used to maintain links between universities and industry. Under this model universities were funded for teaching and research by the state and looked to industry either because they needed more funding or because industry offered interesting research problems that individual academicians were keen to tackle. Another reason for university interest was that industry often had experimental facilities, equipment or testing facilities not available in university laboratories. Industry, on the other hand, conducted much of its own R&D but recognized the value of out-sourcing a good deal of its more basic research to university laboratories and valued the opportunity of bringing complex problems to universities where leading academics might be found to solve them. The characteristic arrangements were for research contracts to be signed between individual companies and universities to carry out a particular research task or for individual academics to be offered consultancies with companies either for particular projects or to act as a general referral point for problems. Universities appointed industrial liaison officers (ILOs), usually with some industrial backgrounds, to maintain links with industry, facilitate links between academics and companies. R&D was seen as a linear process in which basic research led through applied research into development. Universities did the basic and some of the applied research, and companies did the rest. Relations were essentially one to one, a single company research director with an individual academician. The key was how the former knew of the congruence of academic interest with an industrial problem or how the latter assessed potential industrial interest in the direction of his or her research. In this kind of environment the industrial liaison office was often situated on the periphery of the university campus and provided information brochures, advising individual academics and companies, and visiting companies to enable interaction.

Of course it was not always as simple and tidy as this, and through the 1980s, under the pressure of scarcity of funds, the ILOs became more proactive, more interested in a professional technology transfer role, more concerned with identifying intellectual property, patenting it and licensing it. As Government began to see evidence of industrial collaboration as a performance indicator the role of the ILO was energized and given more central focus. As the scale of industrially-related research grew, the question of the level of overhead charges, or indirect costs, that needed to be levied became more important, especially as state-funding levels declined.

THE GROWTH OF MODE 2 RESEARCH

The linear model of the staging of pure into applied research and then into development has become outdated, in part because of the pressure of competition which compresses the time available for the commercialization of research ideas and in part because commercialization or the development of real products demands an interdisciplinary approach. Mode 2 research is defined as "where discovery and application are more closely integrated". Commercialization, he suggests, "is organized less around the translation of discoveries into new products than in searching for design configurations with the potential for development." Increasingly it is not a problem of generating new discoveries but of making use of the knowledge base that is already available; so the new approaches depend less on basic science and more on the application of knowledge for wealth creation.

THE CHANGING INDUSTRIAL CONTEXT

Single company to university laboratory relationships are being overtaken by pre-competitive consortia or clubs of companies, and sometimes governments, who commit resources and manpower to work with one or more universities on closely targeted R&D, pooling equipment and research expertise. This can involve industrial and university teams working together in the same laboratory or unit with much greater urgency and 'near market' sense of mission than in the past. Under such arrangements "knowledge production is characterized by a closer interaction between scientific, technological and industrial modes of knowledge production, by the weakening of disciplinary and institutional boundaries, by the emergence of more or less cluster of experts, often grouped around large projects of various kinds, and by this sort of world, networking is of critical importance; the days of the single expert or the single point of contact within a university are gone.

THE CHANGING ROLE OF GOVERNMENTS

The recognition of the critical role of the knowledge-based industries for national economies has led to much greater priority being given by governments to what is described as the triple helix of government-industry-and the universities. "Fundamental changes occurring at organizational and institutional levels within and between university, industry and government, constitute a new environment of innovation replacing the linear model. Bilateral government-industry and university-industry ties have expanded into trilateral relationships at the regional, national and multinational levels. Encouraged by government, universities have become a key element in innovation policies throughout the world..." The key collaborations are based on partnerships rather than contractor-research relationships.

THE DEVELOPMENT OF REGIONAL ROLES

Universities are key agents within regional economies, linking with local and regional government and with industry. The growth of science parks, local industrial parks, membership of regional development agencies all bear testimony to the extent to which universities are playing an increasingly significant role in attracting knowledge-based companies to the area or spinning out new companies from amongst their own researchers.

In this context, learning economy, emphasizing the "importance of interactive learning as the basis for innovation and change in modern developed economies" and the concept of "the learning region" are pertinent.

THE RISE OF THE RESEARCH CENTRE IN UNIVERSITIES

These external demands have had an increasing impact on university-academic organization. Where once the academic department reigned supreme, based on a single discipline and, at least in developing countries, teaching a single degree discipline, academics are increasingly grouping themselves in cross-departmental research units or centers in order to tap into the new research markets. They cite intensified competition in fast moving fields and "the realization that a practical or theoretical problem can best be attacked by a group of investigators drawn from several disciplines". However, centres are created by "leaders", academic entrepreneurs, and depend a great deal on their success in generating external funds and industrial contracts. Indeed they often simulate some aspects of industrial research laboratories buying in on a short term basis skills not possessed in the centre, sharing valuable equipment and providing "neutral ground" in which company collaborators can work with university staff. Such centers often offer immediate research access to companies via company subscriptions, industrial clubs and regular seminars for external members.

These external and internal changes are revolutionizing the organizational structures that universities formerly had in place to interface with industry. Inevitably they demand a new range of skills: the ability to build networks, a capacity for brokerage, a wider vision about the university and the economy, strategic skills in identifying and marrying market niches and gaps and university research strengths, legal and intellectual property skills, skills in company formation and a broad appreciation of industrial training requirements. Where you have powerful research centres relating to industrial problems it is likely that the specialist expertise in the research centre far outweighs in effectiveness any liaison skills that can be provided centrally by the university industrial office. Thus, as industrially funded or Mode 2 research expands in universities, research centres take over many of the functions that were previously located in the industrial office in the centre of the university. Inevitably, therefore, the situation becomes much less tidy; more tension can be generated between university central authorities and academic entrepreneurs in academic departments and research centres, and questions of co-ordination, adherence to university regulations, and recognition of success in terms of the allocation of institutional resources or of a financial return to the institution become issues of great sensitivity.

It is not possible to provide easily applicable solutions to these difficulties, especially when university circumstances, funding arrangements and commitment to a particular range of disciplines are so various.

Organizational Issues

It is clear from the above description that the monolithic set of structures that universities previously employed to relate to industry are now no longer relevant and increasingly successful universities are adopting a range of organizational instruments to relate to the industrial world.

Science Parks or Incubator Facilities

The recognition that regional economies need stimulation from knowledge-based companies that academic entrepreneurs, if they are to be loosely retained within a university structure, need independent space and facilities to develop company formations have led to many universities establishing science parks or company incubator units on or adjoining their campuses. A few universities have now established incubator facilities which provide space and support in terms of some common services in order to assist researchers to establish viable businesses based on their research findings. Some universities have, in partnership with external financial bodies, set up venture capital agencies, which will invest in such ventures. One of the advantages of this particular arrangement is that the fund will invest in research, which shows promise of producing a commercial outcome, rather than, as would be the case with a normal private sector venture capital company, only when the research is ready for exploitation.

The importance of a Science Park may be much less as a vehicle for launching university-based companies than in attracting knowledge-based companies to locate on a site adjoining a university and becoming partners with departments, centers or individual researchers in research and development.

Research Office

The traditional university research office deals primarily with research grants and contracts, coming from national research bodies, research councils and foundations. Apart from being passive, research has become more competitive, in positioning an institution and, in a country like the where the Research Assessment Exercise has an important impact on recurrent grants and 'institutions' position, research offices have become more proactive in the new world of university-industry-government, partnerships have begun to play a key role, helping to formulate bids, negotiating with research councils and government and ensuring the contracts are carefully drawn up. However, these offices now tend to sit rather uncomfortably organizationally, when new specialist offices and agencies are springing up.

The Problem of Co-ordination

What has happened is that the university-industrial interface has moved from being one of n university activities, to becoming a central concern. The 'Triple helix' and the "new product of knowledge" have transformed the management of research in universities and have crossed traditional organizational and financial boundaries. Because it has become central to universities success, and because so many schemes demand a significant university investment, the various specialist offices have needed both co-ordination and leadership at something like Pro-\Chancellor, Vice-Rector or vice-presidential levels. However, since the key players are academics and researchers in departments and centres, this role is much less real presentational, diplomatic or motivation. In other words, whatever the policy the universities have towards region, industry or research in general, the implementation of that policy, when it comes to the details, lies within the individual academic staff. Many of the academicians will hold permanent appointments and without their support, such policies can simply remain 'stuck' at level of aspiration. Pro-Vice-chancellors may encourage and motivate, 'putting-up a public face" but they cannot deliver the product. Co-ordination in this area remains a matter of debate, and even, occasionally, one of controversy. At the bureaucratic level, the various offices and activities develop missions of their own, and overlaps in functions can all too easily occur. At the academic level, however, large research centres or departments and highly successful individuals tend to be successful because they follow strategies that rely on their own strengths and interests.

SHORT COURSE UNITS

R&D findings are increasingly conveyed to industrial, as well as to other clients, through short courses, or through modular masters programmes, designed to be taken in employment. Business schools and technologically based academic departments are the most active in this area, and networks created often result in company clubs and consortia to commission research. The provision of such programmes represents a key element in the diffusion of 'the new production of knowledge', and a very important linkage between universities and industry. These programs will be mostly departmentally based, but universities have also created central short course units to assist departments, either in their penetration on the field, or in the management programmes for groups of departments or centers, which co-operatively can offer specialist programmes, sometimes these units are located in Departments of Continuing Education/Lifelong Learning; sometimes they are linked to one of the offices described above. In such circumstances, short course programmes represent powerful tools for bringing universities and industry together.

Financial Issues

It needs to be remembered that one of the stimuli for universities to expand their role in these new markets, is the pressure that is placed on them by the increasing reduction in the resource for university teaching. However, the more universities follow this route, as a way of generating new income, the more at risk they place themselves, as they move away from the comfort of being funded by the state and against student interests. Large research portfolios are not necessarily financially beneficial, and can often be a considerable drain on a university's resources, unless overheads or indirect costs are claimed at an appropriate level. The more a university enters the large research leagues, the firmer its financial control must be, and the more closely its research office must ensure that the terms of the research contracts are being fulfilled. Failure to do so can lead to significant losses of income.

Overheads/Indirect Costs

The question of the level of overheads, or to use the preferred phrase, "indirect costs", that should be charged in respect of externally financed research, is often controversial. Nothing, however, cans be as controversial as to the manner in which, once obtained, they should be divided between the centre of the university, in respect to central costs, and the department or research centre. There are however some principles which should be observed:

(i) A university should not subsidize private industry, by undertaking contract research and failing to charge an appropriately calculated indirect cost rate. Industry will often argue that they pay their taxes and should therefore not be expected to pay a university's running costs twice. However, as we all know, they are not paying twice, because a university is not funded for the additional running costs, which taking on contract research imposes. Also, the market demands that costs be covered.

(ii) The charge should be transparent; i.e., its make up should be described in sufficient detail so as the company may understand what it is paying for. For example, seek a 50% overhead, on research in science and technology, and 25% in the social sciences. These charges are based on a formula that covers the number of staff involved, the space occupied and the overall demands placed on the university by the contract.

(iii) The final authority for the acceptance of the contract and the overheads involved is vested the Finance Officer, or in some other senior officer, who is able to refuse to sign if the figure is not reached. A university should feel able 'to walk away' from a research contract, that does not match up to covering its costs. The individual academic is, only too often, more interested in the contract, for the research involved (or occasionally the individual consultancy that goes with it), than on the level of overhead charged by the institution. Reconciliation, between the respective interests of the researcher and the university, has to take place.

(iv) An element of the indirect costs must be incurred at departmental or research centre level and the sub-division of the lump sum needs to be regulated and transparent. What happens to the departmental share, is a matter the department must deal with, but there are often internal disincentives, where the department takes the entire departmental share and do' not disburse an element to the individual academic's own laboratory or office. Some universities, operate a sliding scale as an incentive to secure the full indirect cost, so that if a contract brings in the full 50 per cent, the department receives a high proportion of the overhead than if it only brings in 40 per cent.

(v) There is no substitute for transparency at all levels, but experience suggests that while this may make the resolution of difficulty easier, nothing will eliminate the possibility of dispute.

Incentives and Motivation

While academic life and research, in particular, depend a great deal on personal motivation, the is no doubt that, in the real world, rewards are important. The most effective rewards are not necessarily financial; public recognition of achievement, granted by the university authorities, well as by one's peers is sufficient. Nevertheless, well managed staff promotion procedures that reward success in research are important stimuli to good and sustained performance, just poorly managed or arbitrary procedures or procedures that seem to prefer age and seniority, talent and success, are important de-motivators.

Resource allocation, whether at the level of university to department/research centre department/research centre, to the individual, provides a crucial reward system. In a department that outperforms the rest in research, but receives the same formulaic allocation of resource based only on the number of students, teachers will rightly feel that their institution is expending its efforts in the wrong way. An individual academic, who is winning large contracts, but who given a norm-based space allocation, or a norm-based allocation of secretarial, or both departmental support, will feel similarly 'de-motivated'.

A university culture that consistently rewards success is difficult to build up and to sustain, be once achieved, it provides the leverage, which encourages individuals, departments and other institution as a whole, to over perform, in comparison with other universities.

Investment

Research is expensive in time, equipment and salaries. In the present highly competitive university world, universities need to build up reserves that can be invested into research areas that match the new research economy. This implies the need to develop a strategic view of research and not simply a reliance on the research interests of individual academics. It is for this, among many reasons, that universities have tended to designate a Pro-Vice-chancellor to take the lead, both in overseeing research offices and other organizational units, and in trying to develop a coherent institutional research strategy. Within the fast moving competitive research market, and in the world of research partnerships and alliances, an essential feature of the 'new production of knowledge', it is essential that a university, at very short notice, is able to make quick decisions and have available funds for effective investment, or for the mobilization of research teams, or facilities. Universities need to be more business-like, if they are going to play their full part in the knowledge based economy.

CONCLUSION

What the foregoing suggests, is that the traditional organization of universities round disciplines, and the traditional university financial structures, need significant adaptation in order to fit in the new environment. Some universities favour significant financial or managerial devolution, to departments/research centres, but this can strip the institution of its overall strategic role. On the other hand, managing a university like a command economy will certainly stifle the entrepreneurial spirit, at the level of the academic unit. Plethora of single function offices can breed bureaucracy, but bundling all these functions into one Research Office can reduce focus on individual lines of activity. Individual universities have to find their own solutions to these problems, depending on their size, disciplinary base and the economy of their region. However, what has become clear is that either the implications of the new industrial environment must become a central element in a university's business, or it will pass it by. If universities allow themselves to be by-passed they will seem increasingly irrelevant to society, and will lose their best staff, either to competitor universities, or to non-university based research and training consortia. The development of knowledge-based industries, and the economy as a whole, would also undoubtedly suffer. Kerala has great potential to develop its Universities in this area because Industry-University Interaction here is at its early stages of development even today.

REFERENCES

Etzkowitz, Henry and Leydesdorff, Loet (1998), "The endless Transition: a 'Triple Helix' of University-industry Government Relations". *Minerva,* Volume XXXVI, No. 3, Autumn.

Etzkowitz, Henry and Webster, Andrew (1998), "Entrepreneurial Science: TheSsecond Academic Revolution", in Capitalizing Knowledge (Etzkowitz, H., Webster A. and Healey, P. (Ed) SUNY Press, Albany.

Gibbons, Michael, Limoges, Camille, Nowotny, Helga, Schwartzman, Simon, Scott, Peter, Trow, Martin (1994), The New Production of Knowledge Sage.

Goddard, John (1999), "How Universities can Thrive Locally in a Global Market" in Universities and Wealth Creation Gray, H (Ed). Open University Press.

Shattock, M.L. (1997), "University-industry Research and Training Partnerships", Industry and Higher Education, June.

Merie Niemi Kindred

3 Eco-feminist Approaches to Communication in Energy Technology

This study generates from the communication challenges stemming from the reality of ever-increasing demand for energy from diminishing, non-renewable sources such as fossil fuels and hazardous materials associated with nuclear power coupled with inattention, lack of knowledge, or denial of issues relating to energy conservation, energy efficiency, and use of renewable energy. Herein is promoted a worldview that posits our responsibility for admitting crises in energy use, transformation of relationships to technologies relating to energy, and advances in commitment to energy consciousness in our residential built environment and the communication challenges at each step.

I perceive advocacy in the arena of energy issues as problematic when it relies primarily on traditional rhetorical forms, which are predominantly patriarchal and hierarchical and not adequately addressing the myriad concerns about responsible, sustainable use of energy. What follows provides rationale for and initial perspectives on energy concerns and introduces ecofeminism in the form of invitational rhetoric (Foss and Foss, 2003) as suited for theorizing alternative rhetorical strategies in seeking transformation of perception and use of energy in the residential built environment with case studies from both in the Keweenaw and Kerala.

ENERGY: THE EXIGENCY

A powerful image of ENERGY, in terms of electrical and political power, appeared in a photograph from America's National Aeronautic and Space Administration (NASA) titled Earth at Night, a composite satellite photo taken 27 November 2000. [*http://antwrp.gsfc.nasa.gE/apod/ap001127.html*].

Portions of continents and countries in the Northern Hemisphere and parts of the coastline of India glow, while vast stretches of entire continents in the Southern Hemisphere, especially South America and Africa, remain darkened. Here is graphic manifestation of ENERGY, electrical energy, and POWER, not only electrical, but linked to political and economic power.

As Earthlings, we are basically confined to this planet with its population expanding beyond 6.5 billion and its natural endowment of resources, especially fossil fuels used for energy production, dwindling and polluting the life-support systems of earth, air, and water. The status quo in any society is perhaps a social force rivaling the physical force of gravity and the challenge of Earth's inhabitants, especially Americans, in these first few years of the 21st century is modifying a way of life dependent on current energy production and use in order not to unduly deplete Earth's resources by its relatively small population (5 percent of the world's total), and destroy ecological systems shared by all. In India, the challenge for its population as one-sixth of the world is how to adopt and adapt Western-style modernization and industrialization selectively in terms of cultural and environmental considerations.

Conservation of energy, increased efficiency of energy use, and employment of renewable energy from sources such as the sun and wind are viable methods for fostering and assisting socially and environmentally responsible energy use. However, technology is not necessarily the prime obstacle in implementing change in energy perception, production, and use; rather, effecting grassroots awareness leading to individual and societal action is a key challenge, which this study explores. Whether we envision ourselves part of all that constitutes Earth or separate from and dominant over it creates different choices about how we conduct ourselves in relation to an unquantifiable and temporally uncertain limits in all global systems: earth, air, and water.

TRADITIONAL RHETORIC

Rhetoric, communication with persuasive intent, has often been judged manipulative since its inception in ancient Greece and the debate continues 2,500 years later. Components of traditional, patriarchal, hierarchical rhetoric of advocacy include clarity of intention and ordering of strategies with an agenda of rhetor-induced confirmation or change in audience response. I am increasingly uneasy serving in the role of a traditional rhetor in my advocacy work relating to energy use because it seems similar to rhetorical practices which are bolstering the status quo and impeding transformation, which is my rationale for questing for alterity of rhetorical strategies that might hold promise for empowering grassroots efforts and eventual governmental action. This study focuses not on the scientific or technological issues relating to change; rather, the concern is identifying and illustrating alternative rhetorical strategies at the grassroots level. Alternative rhetorical strategies are sought to extend rhetorical options when standard practices are either currently ineffectual or negatively affecting environmental concerns relating to ecological balance, particularly relating to energy.

The history and theory of rhetoric and technical communication reveals how torn the world has always been between the positive and negative features of not only rhetoric, but technology. Relating to the latter, anthropologist Peacock (2001) says, "We may have no future, but if we do have one, we are challenged to master it by harnessing science and technology to fight destructive forces themselves derived from science and technology" (pp. 123-124). Rhetoric is part of this struggle. I desire a "feeling mind and thinking heart" (Killingsworth and Palmer, 1995, p. 45) in myself and others with a softening of the polarity of rational and emotional responses as I engage in environmental practice. This is the beginning of my reference to and eventual use of emotion in the elaboration of the development of my study. Foss and Foss (2003) say that although the emphasis on logic in contemporary Western culture often discourages speakers from considering emotions as possible form of elaboration, they can be a powerful way to develop ideas. Human beings respond emotionally-with their feelings-as well as logically to what happens in their lives (p. 77).

This desire leads into the next topic, a turn to the eco-feminist perspective.

ECO-FEMINISM

Researchers Clegg and Barrett (1996) consider "the two most significant 'post-materialist' trends of the late twentieth century [as] the growth of feminist and ecological consciousness" (p. 201). Ecofeminist theorizing, as a combination of these two modes of thought, is a true alternative to traditional rhetoric because it accosts the basic tenets and structure of undue reliance on patriarchal and quantitatively-fixated value systems and modes of operation that have dominated this planet over thousands of years of recorded history. "Ecofeminism, by linking spirituality, ecology and feminism, without insisting on assimilation of their identities, encourages the creation of alternative political spaces" (Bullis and Glaser, 1992, p. 56), which is critical for societal transformation.

Environmental concerns and feminism are emotionally-charged concepts in any society because they question or openly confront the status quo of business-as-usual in patriarchal, corporate-controlled and/or government-controlled versions of "the good life." Grassroots initiatives operate on ecofeminist principles and cooperative, environmentally-sensitive missions help engender "a new sense of the universe, to take humanity forward from the mechanistic orientation of the scientific world and the pathologies of modern industrial society. . . .an exploration about being as well as doing" (Egri, pp. 423, 425). Grassroots efforts have gone global in myriad ways and include a willingness to acknowledge the spiritual elements of mindfully envisioning and constructing societies. These are concerns usually not addressed in a world bedazzled with the wonders of technology and individuals believing unquestioningly that a science-based profession or technical education is the path to a better life through unquestioning adoption of modernity and industrialization.

Sometimes "[scientists] see the pieces clearly, with no feeling for the whole" (Griffin, 1990, p. 88) with scientific objectivity, privileging the rational, serving as a distancing device in the guise of securing truth free of emotional or sensory taint or constraint and organizations supporting this stance by keeping "people from seeing implications and direct consequences of their actions" (Griffin, 1990, p. 93). This observation also often applies to the field of technology and those immersed in technical education. Pieces are often easier to grasp than a complicated, networked, multi-layered, multi-faceted entirety. The Western world's scientific method of analysis can lead to fragmentation with little direction to reconnect or integrate within the larger societal and global context.

Eco-feminism counters the juggernaut thrust of organizations that often ignore or diminish the value of and need for conserving and preserving natural resources such as water, soil, air, and flora and fauna, plus the human resources of this finite orb. My attraction to environmental concerns is awareness of the damaging impact of many conventional architectural practices on the natural world both in terms of material extraction, effects and energy use considerations, and inattention to community building. Ecofeminism might help quell my fear that humankind, in its Western-dominated practices, is merely clever and not wise in its structuring of the world and manipulation of its ecosystems.

Eco-feminism is a means whereby we can view the larger context and while much of the world is at an impasse on the propriety and practicality of social and political action in relation to issues of ecology and economics, peace and justice, ecofeminism calls for deep inward transformation helping manifest outward change, which beckons for alternative rhetorical strategy, the focus of this study.

INVITATIONAL RHETORIC

Rhetorical theorists Sonia Foss and Karen Foss in the early 1990s introduced invitational rhetoric as an alternative rhetorical strategy sharing traits of eco-feminism with conditions of freedom, safety, value, and openness as ways of creating space for transformation as voluntary, co-constructed change. Invitational rhetoric is ecofeminist in nature as it seeks engagement and active participation in mutual construction of the world based on the following tenets:

> (1) the purpose of communication is to gain understanding; (2) the speaker and the audience are equal; (3) different perspectives constitute valuable resources; (4) change happens when people choose to change themselves; and (5) all participants are willing to be changed by the interaction (Foss and Foss, 2003, p. 10).

In invitational rhetoric, mutual understanding based in equality, respect, and self-determination is privileged over persuasion and control, because people usually want to retain agency and therefore dignity by being invited into an experience or learning situation, rather than being simply told or lectured to from a patriarchal, hierarchical perspective. Invitational rhetoric usually occurs in presentational speaking situations, which can be either formal or informal, and inherent in the communication is the preparedness of one person with more information, an opinion, a goal, or in some other way advance thought about the issue or situation, which then seeks free-flowing, respectful communication on the topic under consideration.

Interaction instead of rhetor/audience demarcation is critical in this communication process with the hope of discovery, questioning, rethinking, and possible transformation of all participants to a shared place of change. This transformation can include modifying opinions or values, securing additional information, altering behavior, or generating action. The hallmark of invitational rhetoric is offering, not imposing. "Transformation occurs only through the process of self-change generated by interaction with other perspectives" (Foss and Foss, 2003, p. 266).

Such respectful alternative rhetoric counters the epidemic of traditional rhetoric emerging from rigid, self-righteous belief systems permeating many of the political, religious, economic, and social systems in today's world of often violent interaction and imposition, as reflected in current events. Invitational rhetoric is purposefully nonviolent, in Gandhian mode, and avoids intimidation, humiliation, self-aggrandizement, and competition.

Foss and Foss (2003) declare that "We are privileging change as a condition of our world that is exciting and challenging" (p. 3) with invitational rhetoric as a means of effecting such desired transformation. The fear of change starts dissolving when parties involved in the communication realize that opportunities for learning, growth, and transformation are shared experiences for all participants, including the initiator(s) of the gathering. There are no fixed stances in invitational rhetoric. Instead, there is effort at open communication to come to a mutual understanding of each other's beliefs and values, which may or may not lead to transformative response or action.

Invitational rhetoric is an ecofeminist mode of communication privileging mutual sharing, networking, and cooperation, and deals with power: power-with instead of traditional power-over (Foss and Foss, p. 11), which honors environmental concerns, encourages networking, and makes space for spiritual and intuitive considerations.

How was I going to create conditions for invitational rhetoric to occur in relation to my concerns about energy use in the residential built environment? How was I going to reach into myself and share the emotional, sensual, intuitive essence of my experiences in questing for alternative rhetorical strategies in the Keweenaw and Kerala? My life in the Keweenaw is nearly a decade long, but my experience in India was initially two weeks (2004) and then nine weeks (2005/2006) with a mere month in Kerala. How could I share such varied experiences to engender ecofeminist invitational rhetorical responses?

The purpose of this study is exploration of the strength of ecofeminism and, specifically, invitational rhetoric as a viable alternative rhetorical position and strategy to counter traditional rhetoric in establishing encounters where conditions are established for possible transformation of perception and use of energy in the residential built environment. I acknowledge the tension between attempting not to serve as a traditional rhetor in patriarchal, hierarchical systems, and my struggle to operate from a realm of cooperative, collaborative communication.

I now provide narrative reflection on my nearly nine years of work in the Keweenaw Peninsula promoting passive solar, super-insulated, energy efficient housing in tandem with my late husband, an architect, and our efforts in assisting Copper Country Habitat for Humanity in building houses with even greater efficiency. Storytelling is a universal characteristic of humankind and I engage in narrative reflection, fully acknowledging the fallibility of memory and the inevitability of selection and interpretation in reconstructing events from the archives of the mind.

In India, my experiences are, by comparison, cursory because of temporal constraints, but I share the results as sifted through my sensory and emotional system as recorded in journals for gleanings of insights relating to the study underway. Jottings usually begin as think>write and often morph into write>think.

If I am to break the stranglehold of quantitative, rational-focused data demanded in science and technology, I am determined to accelerate my honed abilities in exploring the often murky depths of emotional and intuitive response to conditions in which I was immersed in both the Keweenaw and Kerala.

THE KEWEENAW

I now focus on a remote area of the United States, the Keweenaw Peninsula in Michigan's Upper Peninsula, the slender finger of land that juts north into Lake Superior and points to Canada. With an average of twenty feet or seven meters of snow a year, the Keweenaw is an unlikely place for designing and building passive solar homes; however, nine years later, over a dozen of these homes serve as rhetors as to the efficacy of passive solar, super-insulated homes. [Note: passive solar=use of available sunlight for daylighting and space heating, not electrical production; super-insulated=2"x 6" walls providing extra insulation for energy savings].

The roots of this study on energy practices stretch back years ago to awareness, even as a youth, that I was immersed in a society whose consumptive practices were well beyond the capacity of this finite planet to endlessly provide for life support with limited resources of earth, air, and water. My awareness grew in focus and depth when I married in the mid-1980s and became business coordinator for Garfield Kindred Associates, P.C., Architects. Skip Kindred was sensitive to issues of energy conservation in design since the inception of his career in the early 1960s. By the 1970s, his interest grew to include extensive research on energy conservation and, when possible, use of renewable energy in the form of passive solar power in his design strategies.

In the early 1990s, with our increasing sensitivity to the exigency of energy availability and use in the world, we made space in our lives for volunteering with Habitat for Humanity International. A journal entry by Skip summarizes his concern:

My feeling is that low income people need energy efficient and functional housing more than others as they have fewer dollars to be squandered on this aspect of their lives. As energy costs increase, more of their limited income will be diverted to heating their houses-properly designed houses will minimize the impact of these increases (21 August 1997).

Often life washes over us with such speed and forcefulness that exact moments of awareness and decision are lost. This is not the case with our decision to ratchet down our architectural practice in suburban Detroit to just the two of us, sell our house, build an energy efficient home in the Upper Peninsula, and re-establish our firm in a small town setting. It happened suddenly in the autumn of 1997 where an entry from my journal reads, "It is time to change, evolve." Exactly a year later we moved into our new home in the Keweenaw.

From the very inception of the idea of moving north, we basically established the conditions of invitational rhetoric. We conceived of the home as providing a sense of welcome for not only family and friends, but especially visitors unknown to us who shared interest in energy concerns. Our carved porch post with a bear's head and sun motif was part of the welcoming gesture and is discussed later. In some ways, we were traditional rhetors seeking to persuade visitors of the importance and possibility of energy efficient living even at such high latitude. However, we also fulfilled the communitarian conditions of invitational rhetoric by letting visitors explore the house in anonymous silence if they so chose, thereby establishing conditions of freedom and safety for them from having to respond to the experience. Mutual value of each other and the condition of openness, especially on our part, was demonstrated by making our home available to visitors and their acceptance of the invitation to tour.

HOUSE AS RHETOR

I've generally considered rhetoric as speaking or writing, but as I become more deeply aware of the scope and depth of eco-feminism, I realize rhetoric can manifest itself even in mute form from the realm of the sensorium, the part of the brain that receives and interprets input from the senses. In this case, the passive solar homes become testaments to energy efficient design and construction. This knowledge gives me great comfort that I don't always have to be saying or doing, as just being with the buildings can be powerful enough. Energy efficient homes also have the potential of having character, displaying the logic of their being, and drawing response from an audience. Rhetoric does not always have to be verbal and the physicality of such homes is an alternative rhetorical manifestation that might be an even more powerful form of invitational rhetoric because there isn't the possible clash of personalities, worldviews, and communicative disjunctions that often detract from personal interaction and transformation.

My home on Crestwood Drive has been quietly speaking for nearly nine years now. It is part of a traditional subdivision with conservatively designed homes lining the street and much of the original woods retained between houses and in yards. As first-time visitors troop up the stairs to the residential level, there are gasps of amazement at the panoramic effect of the living room and the house embraces their imaginations. The deciduous trees wave a leafy hello in the greens of spring and summer, and the reds, yellows, and oranges of autumnal celebration. In winter, the trunks and branches of the sheltering woods. present silhouetted forms against the cloudy grey or clear blue of wintry skies and when the wind blows, there's a slow sway of sensual dancing on display.

The openness of the living space and connection between the house and the world of nature outside is direct and inviting and all visitors are mesmerized by this surprised intimacy. As guests relax into the comfort of the sofa, they gaze outside with comments of rapture: "it's so peaceful," "the woods are almost inside," "it's so quiet," "it's a treehouse." Soon visitors realize that just as the panoramic array brings them closer rapport with nature, the super-insulation of the house quiets the hum of traffic from outside. With indoor air quality an issue in much of the built environment and respiratory conditions such as asthma increasing, guests often go on to mention the quality of the air in the house. Their perception is correct as the heat recovery ventilation system provides a complete air exchange from the outside once every three hours. Breathing eases, stuffiness subsides as people experience a sense of freedom with the spiritual and physical healing attributes of the house. A sense of peace, well-being, and safety is offered by the home's embrace in both visual, auditory, and kinesthetic forms, which constitutes conditions of invitational rhetoric. During frequent house tours, I provide factual and anecdotal information, but it is the very house itself that speaks the loudest in advocating for alternative housing models that are smaller, more energy efficient, and mindful of their natural setting.

Even as my husband and I savored our new home and shared the experience of it with others while entertaining and conducting tours, we also extended our concern for low-income families by volunteering our services to the local affiliate of Habitat for Humanity International. A year after our arrival, Copper Country Habitat for Humanity, which had already been building energy efficient homes was using Skip's designs and building smaller versions of our passive solar house with low-income families.

Since 1995, eighteen families have partnered with CCHFH building seventeen 1,056 square foot (s.f.) houses and one renovated mining-era house. Starting in 1999, twelve of the houses have been passive solar, super-insulated. The CCHFH homes have to be snug and affordable, so they look much like factory-built modular housing as casual glance; however, the significant change is the size of windows on the south side. Sunlight floods into these small homes and provides more than adequate daylighting in summer and equally bright rooms in winter as sunlight reflects off snow. The super-insulated walls and extra insulation above the ceiling and under the floor, plus careful caulking and gasketing, ensure a tight envelope with heating and hot water bills often a tenth of those in previous houses. Habitat housing partners and visitors to their homes are enthralled by not only the economic advantage of their new homes, but also the cheerful ambiance these homes share with their occupants.

The value of the rhetor manifested in these Habitat homes is their compact efficiency, welcoming of sunlight from the south, and a history of neighbors coming together to help build a home for a family in need. The very basis of Habitat for Humanity is rooted in the conditions of invitational rhetoric as low-income citizens are offered the opportunity of participating in what could prove the pivotal acceleration and stabilizing of their standard of living. Citizens of the community are also offered the opportunity to invest time and effort to address poverty housing and the communication is based on ecofeminist principles of cooperation and caring.

The homes become beacons in communities attesting to the possibility of invitational rhetoric's conditions of freedom, safety, value, and openness being manifest in both the practices of Habitat housing partners and volunteers. The homes attest to the reality that small can be beautiful and that perceptions of housing and energy use and more responsible citizenship can be realized even by citizens with modest incomes assisted by citizens who are willing to "give a hand up and not just a hand out" (a slogan of Habitat for Humanity International).

SUMMARY

As a scholar in the humanities, not an architect, scientist, or technologist, I'm concerned with energy use and focusing on what I perceive as the merits of invitational rhetoric as ecofeminist practice with its low-keyed, respectful space for transformation. As I reflect on my nearly nine years in the Keweenaw through the lens of invitational rhetoric, mindful of the abstract nature of its features and realizing it's a process and I'm a metaphoric bridge on the shifting surface of a sandbar, I'm heartened by the exposure and expansiveness of my advocacy efforts. I also recognize I've always had solid partners in my efforts at alternative rhetorical practices: houses as valuable co-rhetors and voices for perceptual transformation.

Next I move to a different venue for studying invitational rhetoric. I maintain my theoretical stance as an eco-feminist positing the conditions of invitational rhetoric and, but I remove myself from my culture of origin in the West and relocate myself in the East, specifically to the Indian state of Kerala where I am audience seeking both manifestations of invitational rhetoric as a viable alternative strategy and assessing its ability to transform me from my Western perceptual base.

KERALA

India represents a diverse mixture of ancient cultures often incongruously abutting cutting-edge modernity. With its kaleidoscopic array of geographic features, traditions, languages, religions, ethnicities, and a population approaching one billion, it forms a vast and dynamic country. I visit this dramatically varied society first casually as a tourist and then return as an ecofeminist researcher questing for manifestations of invitational rhetoric as alternative rhetorical strategy and impacting me immersed in Indian society.

What follows narrates my trip for field research focusing primarily on my month-long stay in the state of Kerala, again using the lens of invitational rhetoric in examining Indian advocacy practices for "a multicultural and diversified global vision of healing for life on Earth" (Diamond and Ornstein, 1990, p. vii). I'm challenging a "masculine consciousness [which has] denigrated and manipulated everything defined as 'other' whether nature, women, or Third World cultures" (Diamond and Ornstein, 1990, pp.ix-x). In visiting India, I am seeking to diminish the sense of other and foreign by letting myself be vulnerable and studying how invitational rhetoric operates in a different culture, and noting how it affects me, and seeing if, indeed, we all "swim in the same interconnected global soup" (Agar, 1980, p. 21). The purpose of study in India is to determine if invitational rhetoric holds promise of alternative rhetorical strategy leading to perceptual change and networked international action in ecofeminist mode.

I note manifestations of being engaged in invitational rhetorical strategies in my encounters with Indian academics, activists, and directors of grassroots cooperative organizations where I am primarily audience and not the instigating rhetor. This involvement of the physical/emotional self in the study process with the goal of being a supporter more than advocate is part of experiencing invitational rhetoric more fully.

SECOND PASSAGE TO INDIA

My first visit to India was the epiphany that led to knowledge that I needed to explore my topic of study from an Eastern as well as a Western stance. Of the nine weeks I was in India on my second visit, I focus on my month in Kerala, which was my longest and deepest encounter in the country as I was studying grassroots organizations, and meeting academics, activists, and ordinary citizens and experiencing their handling of life's challenges in an Indian context. I engaged in some spontaneous interviewing using questions that developed from our interaction, but didn't come equipped with a set agenda because of my nomadic status in the country and willingness to serve as a recipient of conditions of invitational rhetoric. However, writing about Kerala (and India) in relation to invitational rhetoric is very different from the Keweenaw, where I can apply the theory to lived experience with a longer, stronger temporal basis. I submit the caveat that in India I was a novice-audience learning with encounters that are, by comparison, cursory and limited.

Kerala has always been part of a global society with its coastal location at the southern tip of India making it central to the ancient Middle East and China trade and also a confluence of religions. Kerala started on the path of Western-style modernity via German and British missionaries in the 19th century who helped shape the changes that now characterize the state in the areas of education and health. (Cherian).

In the last half-century, Kerala has gained distinction in India and the world for its high standard of living and innovative and successful grassroots efforts in creating a strong, decentralized society. Keralites have:

- Life spans as long as Americans,
- Universal health care
- Nearly 100 percent literacy (at primary school level)
- Relative harmony in matters religious, cultural, and racial
- A high level of political consciousness and participation by the electorate.
- Relatively even distribution of rural and urban populations
- Balanced numbers of females and males
- Narrow differences between the privileged and non-privileged classes (hill tribes and non-scheduled classes or Dalits, formerly the Untouchables) (Tharakan and Cherian, 2005, personal discussions).

Kerala has carefully created a society of justice and equality and a relatively high standard of living based on universal education and health care. However, because of unemployment or underemployment, it is estimated that 1.9 million Keralites in a population of 35 million work abroad and send more than Rs.400 crore (US $88 million) home to their families (Nair, 2005, p. 17). One sad fact: Kerala has the highest suicide rate in India. It is a well-educated, healthy, underemployed or unemployed agrarian society unable to fulfill the expectations of a broader Indian society striving for modernity and industrialization in the Western mode, which is proving a constant source of frustration.

At this point, I share a continuing difficulty with my nine weeks of research in India when I still felt my primary responsibility was to be an active seeker of manifestations of the conditions of invitational rhetoric, both externally and internally. However, as I was primarily an observer of presentations about grassroots organizations and not a participant in the process, I was often left to envision, but not actually experience, invitational rhetorical practice in the Indian context. Only after my return to America did I realize there was another dimension to researching alternative rhetorical strategy: serving as vulnerable, passive, supportive audience in the invitational rhetorical process I was immersed in by the great rhetor, India itself.

What follows is a description of one of Kerala's most impressive grassroots organizations, the Centre for Science and Technology for Rural Development (COSTFORD) and its founder, Laurie Baker.

LAURIE BAKER, ARCHITECT AND COSTFORD

In World War II, Baker was a non-combatant as a Quaker and drove ambulances in China and Burma as part of the war effort. At one point, he met Mahatma Gandhi in Bombay who, in a gesture that could be perhaps construed as invitational rhetoric, invited him to return to India to design affordable housing for the poor. Baker accepted, lived in the north for many years, then moved to Kerala where he and his wife Elizabeth, an Indian physician, raised their family and where he's been designing and building using indigenous materials and designs. Baker has designed over 2,000 homes and public buildings in Kerala alone. Many of the homes were built for ordinary Indians who came to him with whatever money they could save and said, "We only have these rupees to build our house. What can you make for us?" Baker rose to the challenge of designing and physically helping construct houses with severe budgetary constraints.

There are 15,000-20,000 of his buildings throughout India-houses, churches, hospitals, education centers-with innovative design and construction features suited for the subcontinent. Baker, now 89, lives near the capital of Trivandrum with his wife Elizabeth, 90, and his work is being carried on by the next generation of Indian architects, engineers, and builders. For me, Baker was a kindred spirit, and since I didn't meet him, a presence, a rhetor with dirt under his nails with buildings serving as co-rhetors.

However, before seeking Baker's home and office, I visited the headquarters of his non-profit organization, COSTFORD in Thrissur on the central coast of Kerala. This voluntary organization was formed in 1985 by Baker and supporters as an advocacy group for fundamental housing rights. COSTFORD's emphasis is on providing information, and developing and upgrading skills and providing customized, informal programs with people from all over the world who arrive for training. The day we visited, a group of twenty or so youths were learning how to lay locally-made bricks in a training program geared toward developing competency, capability, and creativity. I was fascinated by their careful placing of the bricks in this antiquated, but pragmatic construction mode acknowledging readily-available material(s) and abundance of labor.

Baker was the instigating rhetor because when we're dealing with a physical construct of great complexity (a building), there's practical knowledge that has to be imparted and the work must be supervised. Since Baker is using indigenous materials and design details, he's also been attentive to the builders of this region of the subcontinent who have left artifacts that are hundreds and often thousands of years old. Baker's work displays an openness in communication between Baker and earlier builders, which has led to his distinctive architectural form valuing native Kerala materials and design strategies. Baker, a British-trained architect, has been transformed by his long life in India and now his transformation is being carried onward and extended by Indian colleagues at COSTFORD to the international level.

Spending a few hours at COSTFORD/The Hamlet felt like a homecoming, and transformation and integration of myself into visions of a mode of living more akin to sustainable practices I support. In retrospect, I realize I was relaxing and benefiting as a participant in the invitational rhetorical process. Baker's architecture was an invitation to participate in his vision and helped elaborate on the argument I am making about thoughtful use of space and materials, which inspires and reinforced commitment and ongoing effort toward designing with sustainability as a chief consideration. As I toured Baker buildings, I continued appreciating my role as recipient of invitational advocacy as I basked in the designs, materials, and rhythms of COSTFORD's work.

I had total freedom interacting with architects engaged in COSTFORD's work and sampling many of the buildings. I felt safe in the encounters because nothing was asked of me other than savoring the experiences. Mutual valuation was expressed in my seeking out COSTFORD and the time and attention gifted me for discussion of the firm's activities and tours of the buildings. Openness on all our parts was apparent from the aforementioned manifestations of the other conditions of invitational rhetoric: freedom, safety, and value.

This Indian approach to sustainability energy use and building practices conveyed a strong rhetorical message to me in its parallel emotional tenor, sensory images, and narrative quality with my work in the Keweenaw. Just as dialogue I was engaged in at home in the Keweenaw was often purposefully generated with the conditions of invitational rhetoric and in tandem with houses as co-rhetors, so, too, invitational rhetoric occurred in India

INDIA AND GLOBALIZATION

In many ways, Kerala and India are experiencing yet another economic colonization through globalization and resultant emphasis on an urbanized, industrialized society. Globalization has created a worldwide unified market pitting original culture against strong market forces. Even Communism in Kerala can't resist the onslaught of global consumerism. Newspaper ads contain 30-40 percent content pertaining to the metropolitan, consumer-focused environment. Materialism is being proselytized with missionary zeal and this means an increasing percentage of Kerala's (and India's) life is often globally determined, which has far-reaching cultural, societal, and economic repercussions (Tharakan). Globalization involves marketing and this, to paraphrase Chairman Mao, is simply war by alternate means; this is the war being waged within every country of the world, developed and developing.

Swaraj-living simply-is a primary tenet of Gandhi's teachings. He said "materialism and morality are inversely proportional" and the West's possession of truth was in opposition to what he interpreted at the East's greater interest in the pursuit of truth, however interpreted culturally and this quest is akin to the process orientation of invitational rhetoric. In advocating the return to Indian roots, Gandhi recommended use of local khadi homespun cloth (khadi meaning livelihood) as a symbol and took up his famous discipline of spinning cotton. Gandhi also advocated using materials from a five-mile radius when building a house (a concept used by Laurie Baker). Globalization, with fostering of a marketing culture, counters these teachings and focuses on capitalization, not humanization as advocated by Gandhi.

For me, invitational rhetoric represents a humanizing of rhetorical practice with people-to-people communication and community building. It is about humanization in scale and scope-counter to the omnivorous outlook of globalization. In both the Keweenaw and Kerala, I experienced the familiar challenge of similar problems -- how to establish and maintain satisfying and sustainable life -- and knowing that any descriptor is subject to individual, culturally-based interpretation as well as extra-societal influences.

India was communicating with me every day and every way and my very presence and openness to experiential change was my acceptance of the invitation to change and grow in understanding of why I was drawn to the siren song of India. To experience a deeper understanding of ecofeminist alternative rhetorical strategy meant immersing myself in the processes of invitational rhetoric and letting myself live with the vulnerability that precedes the possibility of transformation.

Finally it became time to leave Kerala amid a super-saturation of sensation, swirl of impressions, and despair at ever being able to translate my India experience into meaningful discourse on alternative rhetorical strategies from an Eastern perspective. The melting of otherness as I journeyed through India and deeper into my knowledge of and responses to the country was invitational rhetoric writ large with me purposefully stepping out of the role of the rhetor and absorbing India through my senses and allowing myself to be transformed and embrace a larger worldview.

"India is rich in poor people." So said my friend Sajan, a civil engineer in Nagpur in central India, and these poor are people without land, fixed homes, or steady livelihoods. As the disparity between rich and poor accelerates in all countries, such richness of poverty will also intensify, thereby further unraveling the fibers of social fabric. Similar tensions exist in America and India regarding the continuing and increasing economic polarization in both societies.

INVITATIONAL RHETORIC AND GANDHI

I continue seeing merit and manifestations of invitational rhetoric and the framing and elaborating devices offered by Foss and Foss (2003) wherever I find myself and I'm increasingly relaxing and melting into the processes as supporter rather than my more practiced role as instigator. I'm encouraging myself to let things happen instead of always struggling to make them happen. Foss and Foss (2003) stress that invitational rhetoric "involves a deliberate exposure to and consideration of diverse voices as beneficial...because every perspective-including your own-is necessarily partial" (p. 12).

FIGURE 1: TWO GANDHI

In listening to Gandhi's grandson, Arun Gandhi, talk about his grandfather's life and work, I realize that Mahatma Gandhi's foundation principles for relationships:

- respect
- understanding
- acceptance
- appreciation

are variations of the conditions of invitational rhetoric as outlined by Foss and Foss:

- freedom
- safety
- value
- openness

However, Gandhi is dealing more with internal conditions manifest by individuals in working to transform the great society. Foss and Foss present conditions of a more external nature-contexts that foster invitational rhetoric in clusters of individuals for communitarian transformation with co-created goals. Nevertheless, both are creating non-threatening and nonviolent rhetorical situations and providing alternatives to the traditional rhetor-based rhetorical modes focused on intention, strategy, and audience analysis. Gandhi and Foss and Foss accentuate balanced relationality by all parties in the communication, which provides the basis for possible experience of transformation of all participants.

However, I still am troubled by the place of the rhetor in both of these constructs. Who and how is the communication initiated? Perhaps it's spontaneous and without leadership, but usually there is an initiator and this person or these persons thereby default to a position of authority, which is perhaps an inevitable and hard-wired feature of rhetorical practice, standard or alternative.

Maybe traditional and alternative rhetorical strategies start with a rhetor and the difference evolves along with the communication when the rhetor in invitational rhetoric lets go of the reins and blends into the general discussion and becomes as interested in being transformed as helping engender transformation. Also, my concerns about an individual rhetor as instigator fade when I remember the impact Indian society, including its artifacts, had on quietly transforming my values and worldview in relation to not only energy concerns in the built environment, but also on myriad issues from large to small. A rhetor can and is more than an individual in human form.

Perhaps the value in seeking to find alternative rhetorical strategies may well be in the very act of questing; means and not the end may be a more worthy goal, which reflects Gandhi's belief in the pursuit rather than the possession as the greater value.

By stepping out of my role as energy rhetor at home, I opened myself to the experience of being transformed in the presence of similarly passionate rhetors in India. I also realize I can't hope for transformation in others unless I'm willing to open myself to experiencing the reality of transformation through lived invitational rhetoric. As Mahatma Gandhi said, "My life is my message."

Invitational rhetoric and grassroots activities are counter forces to traditional rhetorical strategies and patriarchal, hierarchical systems. In particular, the participant involvement in decision-making through open communication is the catalyst that can engender non-coerced transformation, such as the panchayat village councils in Kerala.

CONCLUSION

Despite witnessing and experiencing internally the power of invitational rhetoric as alternative rhetorical strategy, I gradually came to understand the need to formally stretch it further in effecting transformation. My work deals with the physical world and technology-houses and the energy they use in their creation and maintenance-and I feel compelled to push invitational rhetoric forward into the realm of embodiment as demonstrated by both the work of Gandhi and Laurie Baker at COSTFORD and as alluded to earlier in discussions of houses as co-rhetors (material) and personal manifestation (corporeal) using the methods of narrative reflections and journaling. I suggest embodiment as a fifth condition of invitational rhetoric as a way of enhancing its value in providing alternative rhetorical strategies in ecofeminist approaches to communication in energy technology.

REFERENCES

Agar, M.H. (1980), The Professional Stranger: An Informal Introduction to Ethnography, Academic Press, New York.

Bullis, C. and Glaser, H. (1992), "Bureaucratic Discourse and the Goddess: Towards and Ecofeminist Critique and Rearticulation," *Journal of Organizational Change Management*, Vol. 5, pp. 50-60.

Cherian, P. J. (2005, November 28), Director, Kerala Council for Historical Research, Thiruvananthapuram, Kerala, Conversation.

Clegg, S. R., Barrett, M., *et al.* (1996), "Management Knowledge for the Future: Innovation, Embryos and New Paradigms", in Clegg, S. R. and Palmer, G. (Eds.), The Politics of Management Knowledge, Sage Publications, Inc., Thousand Oaks, CA, pp. 190-235.

Diamond, I. and Orenstein, G. F. (1990), Reweaving the World: The Emergence of Ecofeminism, Sierra Book Clubs, San Francisco.

Egri, C. P. (1997), "Spiritual Connections with the Natural Environment," *Organization & Environment*, Vol. 10. No. 4, pp. 407-431.

Foss, S. K. and Foss, K. A. (2003), Inviting Transformation, Second Edition. Prospect Heights, Illinois: Waveland Press, Inc.

Griffin, S. (1990), "Curves Along the Road," Diamond, I. and Orenstein, G. F., Reweaving the World: The Emergence of Ecofeminism, Sierra Book Clubs, San Francisco, pp. 87-99.

Killingsworth, M. J. and Palmer, J. S. (1995), "The Discourse of 'Environmental Hysteria'," Waddell, C. (Ed.), Landmark Essays on Rhetoric and Environment, Hermagoras Press: Davis, CA.

Kindred, G.F. (1997), *Journal entry.*

NASA (2000), "Earth at Night," 27 November, *http://antwrp.gsfc.nasa.gE/apod/ap001127.html.*

Peacock, J. L. (2001), The Anthropological Lens: Harsh Light, Soft Focus, Cambridge University Press, Cambridge, England.

Tharakan, M. (2005, November 25), Former Director, Kerala Institute of Local Administration, Ezhupunna, Kerala, Conversation.

Duraipandi Mavoothu

4 SWOT Analysis of Management Education in India with Special Emphasis on Kerala Situation

The first university level business school was established at Wurttemberg in 1782. In 1852, a B-school was founded in Antwerp(Belgium) which became the prototype for similar institutions in France and Italy (Varghese, 1992). Antwerp's tradition of management education at university level dates back to 1852. 150 years of pioneering, innovation and experience have thus ensured that University of Antwerp Management School's (UAMS) management training is firmly anchored in the local and international business community. The UAMS integrates all postgraduate and executive management programmes of the University of Antwerp (*www.uams.be*).

One of the oldest business schools in Europe is considered to be the Ecole Supérieure de Commerce in Paris(ESCP). ESCP was founded in 1819. Presently it is called as ESCP-EAP(also known as "European School of Management"). In Europe, although the Leipzig Graduate School of Management was founded in 1898, it initially taught at the undergraduate level only.

The MBA designation originated in the United States and became popular all over the world. Business organisations sought out professional approaches in managing their affairs. Master of Business Administration (MBA) is a P.G. degree in business management education. Scheme of studies and syllabi reveal that basically MBA degree is a multi-disciplinary academic programme directed towards professionalisation of management. Completion of MBA degree does not preclude admission to a doctoral programmes primarily catering to another profession, i.e. teaching. However, the main thrust is on the practice of professional management, which involves skills, attitudes and behavioural styles in addition to knowledge in several disciplines.

A business school is a university-level institution that teaches subjects such as accounting, finance, marketing, organisational behavior, HRM, business law, operations management, strategy and quantitative methods in addition to several specialised subjects within each functional or sectoral streams. The institutions imparting management education have different names that include schools of 'business', 'business administration', and 'management'. Most of the B-schools are labelled as 'Institute', 'Faculty', 'College', 'School', 'Department'(within university) or 'Centre' and teach predominantly business courses. The first such 'collegiate business school' was Wharton School founded in 1881 for undergraduate programme in the University of Pennsylvania (initially as an exclusive undergraduate programme specialising in finance). In North America a business school is often understood to be a university graduate school which offers Masters of Business Administration(MBA) or equivalent degree.

Tuck School of Business, a part of Dartmouth College, was the first graduate(MBA) school of management in the world. Founded in 1900, it was the first institution to confer advanced degrees (Masters) in commercial sciences, the forebearer of the modern MBA. Dartmouth College founded in 1769 is the ninth-oldest college in the United States. Harvard University followed suit in 1908, with a programme titled Master in Business Administration. Since then, B-schools in United States have largely dominated management education. The University of Chicago Graduate School of Business was the first business school to offer a Ph.D.(Wikipedia,2006).

In 1881 the Chamber of Commerce and Industry of Paris founded École des Hautes Études Commerciales (HEC) as one of the first business schools in France. In 1969, HEC started the HEC MBA programme. In 1898 the University of St. Gallen was also founded as one of the first business schools in Europe. As the US MBA model emerged at the turn of the 20th century. Europeans developed centres of excellence in business, such as at the universities of London and Manchester. Elsewhere in Europe, companies started management programmes, such as Cass Business School, London, Henley Management College and Ashridge to provide management training for promising employees.

France pioneered one-year MBA programmes, with INSEAD MBA in 1959. University-based French business schools were created since then (mostly in the 1990s) their own 12 to 24-month MBA programmes, but with a much lower emphasis on internationalisation and diversity.

MBA programmes in the UK differ from those in the United States, in that students typically have significantly more work and managerial experience than their American counterparts. Because of this, many full-time MBA programmes in the UK typically last one academic year. London Business School was established in 1965, is an international business school providing postgraduate degrees in finance and management, including MBA (Master of Business Administration) programmes, as well as non-degree courses for business executives.

Few people are aware that South Africa was home to the first MBA outside of the USA. The Graduate School of Management at the University of Pretoria (GSM) was founded in 1949 and two years later, 25 graduates received their MBA degrees-the first to be awarded by a non-American university. In 1968, the Asian Institute of Management was founded in Manila.

In earlier days the focus of business education was more vocational rather than professional. Former businessmen constituted the faculty, and their classes were more about learning from their own stories rather than science based academic theories. As the economy grew more complexes and the demands on business corporations increased, there was a push towards gearing MBAs with more 'science' believed locked in theories and models. Conversely, today, there is criticism that professors teaching MBA courses lack real-world experience in their field of teaching-that their theorems and scientific hypotheses fail to reflect what's demanded in today's market (Ching, 2005).

MBA schools also known as B-schools vary in their orientations, approaches, teaching methodologies and popularity. No wonder that there is considerable competition among the B-schools of today. Rating and ranking have become a popular game among magazine publishers, fuelling a spirit of unhealthy competition among the B-schools. Some MBA programmes are being amended to move with the times. Others are remaining very still. Knowing which is doing what would be a good idea for any potential enrollee (Ching, 2005).

In the United States, by one estimate, the average cost of earning an MBA via an accredited full-time programme (excluding room and board) rose from $124,000 in 1993 to $162,000 in 2001 (Davies and Cline, 2005). The bulk of the cost is in the form of foregone earnings ($109,000 in 1993 and $139,000 in 2001). Accounting for the decrease in expected unemployment as well as the increase in expected wages and expected wage growth, the financial benefits in holding an MBA degree are equivalent to an 18% rate of return on the cost of the degree (Davies and Cline, 2005).

U.S. has currently 1600 B-schools, producing, 1,00,000 MBAs every year. Management education industry is $800 b industry in USA. Economists believe the growth in management education is a barometer of growth in economy (Sinha, 2004). In North America and Europe, the central theme of change in many of the business schools is the internationalisation of management education (Philip,2004). Maldives and Bhutan have recently established Management Development Institute (MDI) but they are yet to establish graduate B-Schools (Sinha, 2004).

MANAGEMENT EDUCATION IN INDIA

Indian management education system is the second largest in the world today, next only to that of U.S. But here again, in terms of number of B-Schools it has already caught up with the U.S., overtaken Europe, and is slowly inching towards catching up with U.S., in terms of MBA production. Its growth in the last 40 years has been phenomenal. Many of us who grew up with the Indian management education system feels proud at its achievement, recognition and popularity (Philip, 2004).

Founded in the early 1960s under the leadership of Prof. A. Dasgupta, The Department of Business Administration of the University of Delhi was the first institute in the country to offer a three year Post Graduate Diploma in Management on a part-time basis for senior and middle level executives. This department has its origin in 1954 in the Delhi School of Economics.Andhra University was the first University in the country to start a full-time Master's Programme in Business Administration(MBA) in 1957 in its Department of Commerce.

The first 'B-School' in India was the Indian Institute of Social Welfare & Business Management (IISWBM), Kolkata (at inception known as All India Institute of Social Welfare and Business Management) was set up in 1958 and headed by Prof.D.K.Sanyal. It was created through a resolution adopted by the Syndicate of the University of Calcutta on April 25, 1953. IISWBM introduced the first programme on management education in India. The foundation stone was laid by Pandit Jawaharlal Nehru, the first Prime Minister of India. It was created in response to a strongly felt need of independent India. The Institute had, as its midwives, the Ministry of Scientific and Cultural Affairs (Government of India), All India Board of Technical Studies in Management (Ministry of Education), Government of West Bengal, Bengal Chamber of Commerce and Industry, Indian Chamber of Commerce, Bharat Chamber of Commerce, and Bengal National Chamber of Commerce and Industry. Initially, IISWBM offered a three year part-time Diploma in Industrial Management (DIM) for employed technical personnel, and a three year part-time Diploma in Business Administration (DBA) for employed non-technical personnel on the recommendation of All India Board of Technical Studies in Management. Now, the institute, apart from Masters in Business Administration (MBA) and Master in Human Resource Management (MHRM), runs courses on Public Systems Management (PSM), P.G.Diploma in Business Management (PGDBM), P.G. Diploma in Sports Management

(PGDSM), P.G. Diploma in Transport Management (PGDTM), P.G. Diploma in Environment Management (PGDEM), P.G. Diploma in Energy management (PGDEM), P.G. Diploma in Hospital management (PGDHM), P.G. Diploma in Travel & Tourism Industry Management (PGDTTIM), P.G. Diploma in Enterprise Software and Management System (PGDESMS), and P.G.Diploma in Bio-Informatics (PGDBI) along with Management Development Programmes (MDPs) and Entrepreneurial Development Programmes (EDPs).

Government of India established the Administrative Staff College of India (ASCI) in Hyderabad in the year 1956 on the recommendation of All India Council for Technical Education. This institute became the first of its kind in the country for training top level officers and managers of India. Ever since it was established in 1956 at the initiative of government and the corporate world, ASCI has synthesised managerial theory and practice to equip corporate managers, administrators, entrepreneurs and academicians to effectively respond to the ever-increasing complexity of managerial issues confronting government, industrial enterprises and non-government organisations, rather than end up as victims of outcomes. For over four and a half decades, ASCI's synergistic blend of management development [training], consultancy and research has set the pace for professionalisation of management in India. Also, it offers a post-graduate training programme in hospital administration in collaboration with Hinduja Foundation and MBA in collaboration with Manchester Business School through distance learning.

In addition to IISWBM, Kolkatta and Delhi University, four universities viz. namely Bajaj Institute of Management(Bombay University), Panjab University, Madras University, and Kerala University(Present SMS, CUSAT) were also given approval for starting the part-time programme in management in their University Management Departments. All these departments were functioning in full swing till these diploma programmes were converted into three-year part-time MBA programme along with two-year full-time MBA programme.

The IIMs were not the pioneers of management education in India; they were preceded by Department of Commerce of

Andhra University (for full-time MBA in 1957), the four metropolitan universities of Bombay(Mumbai), Delhi, Calcutta(Kolkatta) and Madras(Chennai). The best known of these are the Faculty of Management Studies in Delhi University and the Bajaj Institute of Management in Bombay. The Indian Institute of Management Calcutta(IIM-C) was established as the first national institute in November 1961 in collaboration with Alfred P. Sloan School of Management(MIT) and with the supports of Government of West Bengal, The Ford Foundation and Indian industry. The Indian Institute of Management(IIM) was set up at Ahmedabad in 1961 as an autonomous body with the active support of the Government of India, Government of Gujarat, and industry. During its formative years IIM-A had academic collaboration with Harvard Business School. IIM-A, under the influence of HBS, pioneered the case study methodology of teaching in India. The IIM-C and IIM-A started diploma programmes in management with the duration of one year with the intake of experienced candidates as students. Later, the duration of the PGDM programme was made two years, and all graduates were given opportunity for admission after going through the rigorous selection procedure. Other four IIMs–Bangalore (1973), Lucknow (1984), Kozhikode(1996) and Indore (1998)–were started in due course.

Xavier Labour Relations Institute(XLRI) was founded in 1949 by Fr. Quinn Enright, S.J. in the Steel City of Jamshedpur. Over many years XLRI has developed its own identity. It started training programmes for Management personnel and trade unions from 1949 onwards. A two-year full-time course in Industrial Relations and Welfare in 1953, and two- year part-time programme in Business Management in 1966.

Thomas Hill, Warren Haynes and Howard Bomgartel(1973) wrote a book 'Institution Building in India' which evaluated Indo-US collaboration in building management education institutions. The study focused on IIM-A, IIM-C, and ASCI (Sinha, 2004).

Institute of Rural Management, Anand(IRMA) is an autonomous institution with the mandate of contributing to the professional management of rural organisations. It was founded in 1979 at the initiative of the National Dairy

Development Board and, the support of Government of India, Government of Gujarat and Swiss Development Co-operation. Ever since its inception, IRMA has been working closely with Co-operatives, NGOs, Governments, and National and International agencies. It offers Post-Graduate Programme in Rural Management (PRM) along with MDPs and consultancy.

Today, India has nearly 1,400 B-schools offering both MBA and PGDM programmes producing more than 1,00,000 graduates. Institutes offering PGDM programmes are autonomous with freedom to design the courses and examination systems, where as MBA awarding institutions (Universities/Colleges affiliated to universities) do not have such freedom. So, it is quite natural that autonomous PGDM institutions are rated high by the surveys conducted by several agencies. This fact is often ignored by many in the popular ranking/rating exercises conducted by authorised/ unauthorised agencies. However students are often guided by such popular ranking and wide publicity through media by private enterprises in business education. Master's Programme in Management (MBA) was launched by the Banaras Hindu University in 1968. In 1990 it launched the Master of International Business Administration (MIBA) Programme.

MANAGEMENT EDUCATION IN KERALA

School of Management Studies(SMS), under the University of Kerala, Ernakulam Centre, was started in 1964 as one of the management institutes on the recommendations of the Ramaswamy Mudaliar committee of All India Board of Management Studies. The founder Director of the school was Padma Bhushan Emeritus Prof. (Dr.) M.V.Pylee. Initially, P.G. Diploma in Business Management (PGDBM) and P.G. Diploma in Industrial Management (PGDIM) were started for practising mangers only. In 1971, the Ernakulam centre of University of Kerala was converted into University of Cochin comprising of SMS, Dept. of Hindi, Dept. of Law, Dept. of Physics, and Dept. of Marine Sciences. MBA (Full-Time) was started in 1973, and the first batch came out in 1975 under the University of Cochin. SMS was in the forefront among the University Management

Departments(UMDs) during the 70s. During its long history, SMS had introduced innovative academic programmes. Master in Bank Management(MBM) and Entrepreneurial Development Programme(EDP) were the first of its kind in India. SMS was one of the early management institutes like Bajaj, FMS, and UMDs of Madras and Punjab universities.

OTHER UNIVERSITY MANAGEMENT DEPARTMENTS (UMDS) IN KERALA

Department of commerce in University of Calicut was started in 1972. The MBA Programme was started in 1982 by the department and then the name of the Department of Commerce changed as 'Department of Commerce and Management Studies'.

The Institute of Management in Kerala(IMK) was established under the University of Kerala in the year 1991. The Institute is located in the capital city of Kerala, Thiruvananthapuram. The Institute provides Masters as well as Doctoral Programmes in Business Management.

School of Management and Business Studies of Mahatma Gandhi University, Kottayam, was started in 1999 and runs full-time MBA programme.

Department of Management Studies in Kannur University was established in 2000. It runs full-time MBA and research programmes.

OTHER MANAGEMENT INSTITUTES IN KERALA

School of Communication and Management Studies (SCMS) is a business school established in Cochin in the year 1976. The Post Graduate Diploma in Management (PGDM) is offered by SCMS.

The College of Engineering, Thiruvananthapuram, is the pioneering management institution in Kerala University. The MBA programme was started in 1985 as a part time programme to cater to the needs of managers. The department started the full time MBA programme in 2000.

TKM Institute of Management(TIM), Kollam, has been conducting a fully residential, two year MBA programme, affiliated to University of Kerala since 1995.

Rajagiri School of Management(RSOM) was founded in 1995. It runs full-time MBA and MHRM courses.

Berchmans Institute of Management Studies (BIMS) was established in 1996 under St. Berchmans College, Changanacherry, to offer full-time MBA course.

There are more than 20 colleges affiliated to different universities in Kerala offering MBA programmes.

Management education: Current scenario

Management education in the country can roughly be divided into four groups. At the top are the reputed institutes and some university departments, which have maintained the high quality of education. The second rung institutes are those started by industrial houses, which offer some surety of a job after the course. The third rung is university departments which have not been able to impart quality education but can provide jobs in regional industrial groups. The fourth rungs are those institutes, which have neither the advantage of low fees of a university nor the backing of an industrial house. In recent times, a number of academics, retired people, politicians and others have started such institutes which remain essentially money making ventures.

The competition among the top institutes is intense as, everybody wants to do the MBA from one of them. There is no surety of getting in. full-time courses from the most reputed institutions are usually expensive ranging from Rs.50,000 to Rs.2 lakhs per annum approximately. Of course an MBA from an American or European management school would multiply that figure many times so an MBA from India is comparatively cheaper. But working alongside studying for a full-time MBA in India is not possible, though some enterprising students have been able to work out a sponsorship for the programme from a prospective employer.

Usually, the two-year management programmes can be taken up after successful completion of a degree in any discipline. Graduates with a minimum 50 per cent (Some institutes 45 per cent) marks are eligible to apply for admission to management programmes. They have to go through a selection process that includes entrance/admission tests, followed by group discussions and interview of candidates declared successful in the written entrance test.

The aim of the entrance test is to evaluate, under stress, a candidate's general verbal, mathematical and analytical abilities critical for successful completion of MBA programme of studies. The management entrance test calls for a superior command over the English language, as well as quantitative prowess and a sharp, perceptive mind. An MBA admission test is not really a managerial aptitude test. It is rather a test to measure the potentiality of students for successful completion of the MBA programme. However, the group discussion and interview are linked with behaviour competence of future managers, especially relating to communication and leadership skills.

One has to assess the market value of an MBA student as the primary motive of management education is to a managerial position, and to move on to higher positions. If the industry is not aware of the worth of the MBA programme, then the very purpose of such programme is defeated. Specific requirements of specific industries have resulted in a new breed of MBAs. An MBA linking with agriculture, information technology, banking, petro-chemicals, etc. are example. Under-graduation in specific area is also insisted upon for admission to such MBA programmes. All these trends are in addition to the traditional functional specialisation in marketing, finance, HRM, systems and operations.

The wide variety of subjects taught in MBA classroom-economics, psychology, mathematics, statistics, law, IT, sociology, etc-is a true reflection of this 'general approach'. It also may be noted that MBA students are taught as if they are going to be the general managers rather than a specialist in a staff department. It is true that the young MBAs are not likely to be general managers immediately and for immediate placement they need to have specialised knowledge in functional or sectoral area. This is the rationale for the structure of MBA scheme of studies.

Historcally the expansion of MBA is Master in Business Administratin, with more focus on industrial enterprises. But today the concept 'Management' has become more popular with connotation of effectiveness and efficiency for maintenance and growth of all social organisations. 'Post Graduate Dimploma in Management' is now becoming a popular Diploma than the traditional 'Post Graduate Dimploma in Business Administration'.

While the demand for management education will continue to grow with the growth of Indian economy, the quality demanded will undergo a shift. Functional B-schools, sectoral B-schools, condensed MBA for one year or of shorter duration, modular MBA, net based online MBA, executive MBA, etc. will provide new models of higher education in management. It is likely that large corporations and growing industry may ask for customised MBA and B-schools may respond to it. In India steel, power and oil industry have already established excellent executive education centres; they will evolve into promising B-schools (Sinha,2004).

Even after more than five decades of the first management institute being set up in India, most B-schools continue to use American textbooks for practically all the subjects. Philip Kotler's 'Marketing Management' is the best example. Lack of good Indian text books leads to students getting a very 'American view' of management. The lack of appreciation of an Indian context remains one of the biggest banes of management education in India. The American view of management is too bureaucratic, confrontational and rigid-with too much emphasis on the individual. Philip(2004) says that the relevance of what is taught and the methodology used is another critical issue to be looked at. There was a time, particularly in the 60's and 70's that we depended almost exclusively on foreign material and MNC cases. But that has changed substantially. Whether it is textbooks, cases, research studies and other learned articles and publications, we have plenty of such materials in the country. However, in the surge for self reliance, we should not neglect to use foreign material in good measure, recognising the fact, that business management is no more limited by the geographical boundaries of a country, but by the pulls, pressures and developments in the international markets.

Institutions offering MBA programmes must respond to market needs (Baruch and Leeming,1996). Porter and Mckibbin(1988) noted that some B-Schools were not doing enough to develop 'soft skills' among MBA graduates. Prof.Sterling Livington in his classified article 'The Myth of the well Educated Managers' demonstrated the lack of relationship between grades at the Harvard Business School (HBS) and subsequent success in management jobs. He argued that business schools need to access intuitive skills and common sense not just academic ability(Sinha,2004). Herbert Simon, the first management professional to receive Nobel prize, suggested that if you wish to develop a star athlete, you must begin with someone who has the natural endowment, and then through practice, learning and experience, develop that into a mature skill. B-Schools should teach students who are endowed to use them purposefully(Sinha,2004).

The AICTE, which also looks after management education may not be able to do full justice to the discipline. AICTE budget spent for management is only 4%. 99% of its staff is from engineering discipline. AICTE has so far not been able to give significant attention to management education (Sinha,2004). Management is a multi-faculty discipline; AICTE treats it as a single subject. One can't blame the AICTE, which sees technical education, not management, as its core(Sinha,2004). So, it may be prudent to establish an All India Management Council(AIMC) with the sole purpose of enhancing the quality of management education. AIMC, which can take a comprehensive view on the development of the management education(Sinha,2004).

Among developing countries, India is going through a process of great change to become a part of the world economy. This requires an active response from corporates and educational institutions. Management education has a significant role to play in the Indian economy. In this context, diagnosing the management education in India is quite necessary as the trends in management education have far-reaching implications for potential students and employers, economy and the society. Both internal and external factors have to be taken into account while diagnosing the state of affairs in to-day's management education in Indian universities/institutes. Top Indian management institutes have proved that India can impart world-class management education. Some of the University Management Departments (UMDs) have also emerged as top management institutes (e.g. FMS, Bajaj Management Institute, etc.).

In India, we see a third rate B-school located by the side of the top management institute. We see a world-class management institute and many third-rung B-school in the same city/town, sometimes in the same road or street. The same plight we see in Kerala too. This needs the attention of educational planners. Industrialists and politicians who can change this plight. The main objective of this SWOT analysis of management education in India is to develop a framework that tells out B-schools' ability to exploit the opportunities, to weaken the weaknesses and to overcome the threats. When compared to west, our management education has a lot of weaknesses despite the fact that it has strengths too. As the business and business management education are becoming global, it is high time that we should introspect our management education to keep pace with the rest of the world. Till recently our approach was that restricting the number means ensuring the quality, but now the concept is increase the number to create competition among institutes, which, in turn, will ensure the quality. And it is very difficult to say which concept is more effective. But, still one thing is clear that the former created competition among potential candidates (MBA aspirants), and the latter creates competition among B-schools and MBA graduates. It is a well-known fact that the quality of management education is mainly decided by the quality of the potential candidates (MBA aspirants) who come for the programme. Even an excellent B-school can't convert poor quality candidates into good managers within a short period of two years. It is like we can't convert a bullock-cart into a jet plane even if we make some modifications in it to look like a jet. Increasing the number of MBA seats by starting more number of B-schools will not automatically ensure the quality unless the final products are according to the specifications of the final users, the industries. The best technique of quality control in management education is to filter the candidates before their entry rather than after their admission .

After entering the global marketplace, Indian corporates have understood the need for management graduates. But, the irony is that most of the times the best MBAs are joining MNCs and not Indian companies. There is always a shortage for good MBAs for Indian companies. Today, MBAs from B-schools are not accepted y many companies as these MBAs are not matching the requirements of these companies. Many recruiters go back from the campuses without recruiting any MBA graduate or postponing the recruitment to the next year for want of better candidates. In some cases the recruiters, when they see best candidates, recruit more number of graduates than required for the current year fearing that they may not get such students next year. Also, it is true that some other companies select even the junior batch students even for the following years. It is a bitter truth that today the MBA graduates are not able to impress their potential employers. The demand and supply concept has little relevance in management education. If the products are quality ones, then there is a demand. There is an unlimited demand for talented MBAs in Indian market and not for sub-standard ones. In general, there is a feeling that liberalization of management education has reduced the package for MBAs only has come down and strangely enough the compensation for the best MBAs are only increasing manifolds. One of the important changes the liberalization of management education brought is now that MBA graduates bazar has become the buyers' market from sellers' market and the result being the magic letters MBA is now loosing its premium value.

One of the reasons for emerging of under-average B-schools is more demand for MBA admissions just because it is very popular. Thus even people who don't have the aptitude for management come to this programme. Since, the demand for admissions is more, many B-schools don't care to improve the quality by more inputs of infrastructure and academic resources in spite of levying more fees. It is only a matter of time to prove that only the fittest will survive in management education (both institutes and students). Many B-schools started by the reputed universities and national institutes could not succeed due to poor infrastructure, academic politics, indifference to industries and bureaucracy. There are many instances of B-schools going up and then down due to internal weaknesses. Maintenance of quality on a continued basis is a challenge to many B-schools.

Today the companies find it difficult to decide which B-school to visit?, mainly due to more number of B-schools having varying reputation and quality of students. The two main constraints affecting UMDs are, (1) there is no autonomy for selection of faculty and (2) no autonomy for day-to-day functioning of the departments. There is no doubt that an UMD should be treated different from other departments of university due to the special features of management education.

Dharni P. Sinha(2004), in his book "Management Education in India", summarises the following issues in management education in India:

- MBAs are ill-equipped to cope with or meet the challenges of a dynamic global environment
- B-schools faculty lack necessary business experience
- MBA curriculum is largely theoretical
- Over emphasis on quantitative subjects, while development of people skills is neglected
- Linkage between B-schools and major stakeholders like industry is inadequate.
- High cost of management education
- Unemployment among MBAs
- Lack of indigenous contents in curriculum
- Negligible attention to research in management
- Producing graduates more suitable to business and industry, not suited to social sectors such as public system, rural development, education system, etc.

Now, let us see specifically the strengths, weaknesses, opportunities and threats for management education in India.

Strengths

1. Management education programmes are attractive to even exceptionally talented students after their under-graduation. Many bright graduates from engineering, technology, commerce, economics, computer and information technology prefer MBA programme to other prorammes.
2. Management programmes are run by IIMs, IITs, University Management Departments (UMDs), Engineering Colleges, Arts and Science Colleges and recognized private Management Schools, which are having varying standards. These varying institutes cater to the needs of MBA aspirants of different standards. This is very much true in management education in Kerala also.
3. Prevalence of competition among Indian B-schools in maintaining the standard which makes the potential students and recruiters to be brand conscious in choosing a B-school for admission and campus recruitment respectively.
4. Admission into all management programmes are through CAT and MAT, and then through group discussion and interview which ensure a fair-practice in admission.
5. In India, we have a few B-schools which are internationally reputed. For instance, IIM(A) gives world's toughest competition to the candidates.
6. Management departments are well accepted in Indian universities. Many universities have separate faculty for management studies. A few university departments are at par with IIMs. Some university departments have been given autonomous status. Many UMDs have exclusive hostels for MBAs with compulsory residential programmes, exclusive computer laboratories, etc. The department has the complete freedom in students selection. In many respects, some UMDs are getting a differential treatment by the university administration. In Kerala, UMDs are there in Cochin University of Science

and Technology, Calicut University, Kerala University, Mahatma Gandhi University, and Kannur University.

7. MBAs are well accepted by Indian industries. Employers attach a premium tag to MBA graduates. There is an unlimited demand for good MBAs.

Weaknesses

1. There is a lack of indianisation of management theories and principles. It creates a dilemma among MBA managers in applying the western theories and there by indirectly reducing the efficiency of MBAs.
2. Non-availability of actual case studies in Indian B-school. Most of the B-schools don't have tie-ups with premier management schools in India or abroad for getting case materials. So, they use false case studies which are not reflecting the real life situations, particularly from Indian context.
3. No emphasis on business history, law and political science. Law and politics play a major role in business especially in international business. But, unfortunately these areas are not given enough importance in management education.
4. In Indian management education, more emphasis is given on internal system and sub-systems than on external environment. In fact, more emphasis on external environment is essential as the business has become global. B-schools in Kerala are also not exceptional to this weakness.
5. Teaching methods vary greatly among Indian B-schools. IIMs - predominantly use case studies, second-run-B-Schools use both lectures and case studies and third rung B-schools use mainly lectures for preparing the students for examinations. Most of the B-schools in Kerala are affiliated to their regional universities. The affiliating system encourages preparing the students for examination only. The curriculum structure is very rigid, and no innovation is possible in teaching and evaluation.

6. The syllabi(especially in affiliated B-schools) are revised not even once in five years. Rigid process is involved in syllabi revision. Reluctance by teachers to learn new subjects and no new appointment in the new fields are also reasons for lack of upgradation of syllabi. Students with industrial experience say that B-schools are ten years left behind the industries in advancement in various respects. The same is true in affiliated B-schools in Kerala also.
7. Experience is not a must for admission into management programmes. It makes the teacher's job tough in making the students understand the organizational reality. Also, it makes the case study unpleasant. Moreover, the students are not serious in the programme as they are not aware of the reality.
8. MBA graduates don't come for Ph.D programmes, and inter-disciplinary researches are not encouraged. In management education, more emphasis is given for consultancy and project and not for research. The result is lack of enrichment of the courses due to lack of proper feedback through research findings. But, in this regard the situation in Kerala UMDs are much better. A good number of MBAs come for Ph.D programme(mainly under part-time).
9. Large group of class in MBA programmes. Even more than 60 students are admitted in a class. It is not suitable for case studies, continuous evaluation and individual student attention. Also, it creates indisciplinry problems and groupism among the students.
10. No multi-ethic student groups in Indian B-schools. Most of the Indian B-schools, unlike their counterparts in U.S., U.K., Australia and some other European countries, don't have students from different parts of the world to have multi-ethnic cultures. Having multi-ethnic student groups will give a cross-cultural exposure to our students and faculty. B-schools in Kerala are also not able to attract multi-ethnic student groups. This is a serious shortcoming in the globalised era.

11. Though MBAs are well accepted in the industries and society, still they are branded, compared to others, as arrogant, unadaptable, unrealistic, self-centered-egoistics, money oriented, job hoppers, over-confidents, no loyalty, faster career oriented and no people skill.
12. Management education is confined to business organisations only. Management education can be extended even to areas like societal management, community management and economy management. E.g. NGOs, public administration, agriculture, population control, environment management, forestry management, educational management, etc. The scope for extending management education to sectoral management is very high in Kerala especially in plantation, forestry, NGOs, environment, education, hospital,and tourism sectors.
13. Clubbing commerce and information technology disciplines with management departments. It leads to the following:
    (a) each discipline looses its identity,
    (b) growth of each discipline is affected,
    (c) inter-disciplinary conflict,
    (d) teaching methodologies vary, and
    (e) their outlook on management education differ.
14. Lack of attraction for MBAs to teaching profession. The reasons are: salary difference between industry and university, no career growth, no better work-environment, etc. This is a major issue inflicting management education in Kerala. The faculty attrition rate is unreasonably high in B-schools in Kerala especially in young ones. Many B-schools in Kerala find it very very difficult to get even qualified Directors/ Deans to head them.
15. Except IIMs and a few other institutes, the B-schools conduct their own admissions tests. It creates more inconvenience to the candidates. Clash of dates, more travel, more expenses, stress and tensions, etc. to the candidates. Also it is expensive for the B-schools to

conduct their own admission test at regional level or national level. The nature and quality of these tests varies from institute to institute. In this regard the picture in Kerala is not different from the national trend.

16. Only a few B-schools plan the entire courses much before the semester starts. Course plan includes reading materials, case materials, assignments, dates of test, examinations and results. One of the most disgusted flaws in Kerala is that the over all academic environment will never allow the B-schools to follow the academic calendar. This is highly uncondusive for the growth of management education in Kerala.

17. There is no adequate industry-institute interaction in Indian B-schools. The students will become reality-oriented only by personal experience by direct interaction with industry and practicing managers. The institute-industry interface in most of the business schools Kerala is virtually non-existent.

Opportunities

1. More demand for MBA admission from young graduates. Since there is more demand for talented MBAs by industries, more potential candidates are attracted to MBA Programme.
2. Fairly Sufficient number of B-Schools is spread over to all parts of the country to meet the regional demands. For example, B-schools are spread in all the three regions of Kerala viz. Travancore, Cochin, and Malabar.
3. Export potential for Indian management education is very high. Study centres can be set up in Gulf countries for NRIs to conduct regular programmes and distance programmes. Seats to foreign and NRI students can be reserved to augment the revenue. Indian B-schools can have collaboration with B-schools of third world countries to sell the expertise in exchange of money. In this regard B-schools from Kerala have an edge over other B-schools in India.

4. Potential employers demand better finished products from B-Schools due to growing business complexities. So, the B-Schools are forced to produce better MBAs. The competitive environment in business creates a competitive environment among B-Schools also.
5. There are a lot of opportunities for foreign collaboration. B-Schools in abroad, particularly the west, readily accept Indian B-schools' proposal for collaboration because of matching standard of B-schools and students from India to abroad. Presence of Indian origin faculty in the B-schools in abroad also an added advantage in this respect. Exchange programmes of teachers and students are encouraged by Indian and foreign countries for cross-cultural exposure. The prospect for B-schools from Kerala is very high in this area.
6. Management programes for sectoral management: Professionalism has entered into the sectoral areas like plantation, hospital and health care, transportation, SSIs, tourism studies, co-operatives, forestry and hotel. To manage these sectors sector-specific management approach is necessary. Now-a-days hospital management, healthcare management, hotel management, tourism studies, etc. are growing in importance. Unlimited opportunities are available for Kerala B-schools to exploit these sectors.
7. Extension of management to management of society, community management and economy management. Application of management in these sectors will reduce the business complexities to bring efficiency and to boost the employment. Application of management in these sectors will be an ultimation in human development. Peter Drucker says that it is not information technology, but it is the application of management education in society, community and economy that is going to make the world rich.

Threats

1. Commercialisation of management education is the major threat today. Recent times the AICTE has liberalized the

management education. States like Tamil Nadu, Andhra Pradesh, Maharashtra, Karnataka, Delhi, and Kerala have opened the sector to unscrupulous commercial educationists. The result was substandard MBAs coming out of such institutes who are not acceptable even by substandard companies. These sub-standard institutes produce MBAs and not managers. Some colleges and institutes could not fill even half of their MBA seats. Poor qulity of MBAs reduced the premium image of the MBA degree and created educated unemployment. Some companies prefer to wait and even return empty handed rather than pick-up students from B-schools of 'B' & 'C' grades.

2. Another threat is foreign universities giving MBA degree in India. Indian students are fascinated for foreign MBA degrees. These foreign universities are flexible in procedure, time, etc. though charging high fee. These universities are really a challenge for Indian universities running MBA Programmes.

3. The relatively young profession information technology attracts the young talented graduates with the promise of better salary, better career and better work-environment. Because of this a good number of potential candidates for MBA programme are going to I.T. courses. Now-a-days, I.T. content is increasing in MBA curriculum. Many B-schools have integrated the information technology department as part of management department. Many B-schools run MBA, MCA & PGDITM programmes. It is pertinent to note here that the I.T. related specializations are becoming the favourites of MBA students.

4. Lack of inter-action between faculty-industry. There is always a mental block between institutes and industries from interacting. Both feel inadequate in their expertise and also consider each other as a nuisance. Moreover, today, most of the B-schools are located hundreds of miles away from industries and hence practically impossible to have constant

industry-institute interaction. This is a serious lacuna in most of the B-schools in Kerala.

5. There is no entrepreneurship thrust in B-schools. The MBA curriculum makes them to be job seekers rather than job creators. Even students with entrepreneurial aptitude are not nurtured by the curriculum.
6. MBA qualification is not a must for managerial positions. Anybody without any managerial qualification can get entry into managerial position. No professional body, unlike in law and medicine, is having complete control on the intake and practice of management profession inspite of the existence of AICTE and AIMA and other professional associations/bodies.
7. Today, the students choose a specialization not based on interest and personal strengths, but on the basis of compensation packages and market demand. It leads to wrong choice of career and organisation. In long-run it affects not only the individuals, but also the companies.
8. MBAs are not getting their hands dirty. They want to sit at corporate office and take decisions, and not interested to go to the fields. It may be due to the impact of case study method of learning where they are taught only how to take decisions, lack of awareness about the ground realities and most of them come from elite social class.
9. Many MBAs work in positions which are not managerial. It not only reduces the premium image of the MBA degree, but also creates mismatch between the job and the person.
10. Many companies are not impressed by most of the B-schools because of inadequate training to MBAs and also they are not updated. Sometimes, in-house training centres are considered as substitutes for B-schools. The main advantage of in-house training centres is that they can give company-specific training.
11. It is quite evident that there is an English bias in entrance test, group discussion and interview for admission into

MBA programme and also in instruction and placement later. This English bias refuses opportunities to otherwise talented students from rural and weaker sections. Students with urban sophistication are more comfortable in this whole process. This is true to a fair extent in B-schools in Kerala too.

The SWOT analysis shows that management education in India has more weaknesses and threats than strengths and opportunities. While the strengths and opportunities are really great, the weaknesses and threats are unbalancingly serious. It is clear from the analysis that there is no match between the strengths and opportunities, similarly the weaknesses can't withstand to the threats. With the existing strengths we can't exploit the opportunities available. And we can't overcome the weaknesses and the threats unless some urgent corrective measures are taken. Based on the above analysis, some suggestions are given below:

SUGGESTIONS

1. An all India council for management education (AICME) is to be established in the lines of UGC and AICTE in order to develop, promote, regulate and monitor the management education in Indian universities. The recent tendency of considering management education as a part of engineering and technology have done more than good for management education.
2. Commercialisation of management education should be avoided. Students should be selected only on merit criteria. At the very same time higher fees can be charged from the students. Loans and scholarships should be arranged to needy students.
3. Curriculum should give more emphasis on ethics, international business, communications and external environment. It should not be designed as it is today around disciplines to reflect the needs of the business rather around the major management issues and problems.
4. Bilateral and multilateral exchange programmes for faculty and students must be signed between Indian

B-schools and B-schools in abroad. It will help the process of globalizing the management education.

5. Every B-school should have minimum cut-off CAT score for MBA admissions in their institute. Those students who score less than the cut-off score should not be given admission even if there are vacant seats in order to ensure bringing out MBAs with high caliber.
6. At least 50 per cent of the seats must be reserved for working executives. It will, to some extent, bring the business reality to the class-room. Also, it will help to understand the importance of both class-room training and field experience.
7. One of the preconditions of the agency regulating management education in India should be that the B-school is located near the industrial belt. Or the agency should insist that the B-school has a formal tie-up with a few nearby major business organisations for regular on-hand experience of the students as now being done by some of the B-schools like BIM of Trichy.
8. Case studies must be made compulsory in all subjects wherever possible to bring reality in the class room.
9. In order to enrich the discipline, research in management must be encouraged. Practicing MBA managers have to be encouraged to do Ph.D. programmes on topics relevant to their company/industry.
10. More thrust must be given for entrepreneurial studies in MBA curriculum, so that they acquire entrepreneurial talents which are usually not seen in executives, but essential for modern managers.
11. Students from multi-ethnic culture must be admitted in Indian B-schools. It will popularize our B-schools to the world. In this respect B-schools from Kerala can be a pioneer because of its NRI networks, climate and tourist attractions.
12. The regulatory agency for management education has to introduce a special incentive package to attract the best

talented management graduates to the teaching profession in the lines of one introduced by AICTE to engineering graduates to attract them to teaching profession.

13. The present CAT must be streamlined. There can be state level single CAT for all the universities including affiliated colleges as now prevalent in many states. Or all the B-schools have to join the CAT of IIMs or AIMA. It will ensure at least a minimum amount of uniformity.
14. The management departments under the universities should be given academic and financial autonomy.
15. More sectoral management institutes have to be started, as general management programmes cannot cater to the needs of sectoral areas like hospital, healthcare, tourism, co-operation, transportation and plantations.

REFERENCES

Ammannaya, K.K. (1998), "Overhauling Management Education", *Southern Economist*, Vol. 37, No. 14, Nov. 15, p. 17

Baruch,y. and leeming, A. (1999), 'Programming the MBA Programme-Quest for Curriculum', the *Journal of Management Development*, Vol. 15, No. 7.

Chakraborty, S. (1998), "Management Education Why? What? How?, University News, Vol. 36, No. 36, Sep. 7.

Ching, K. M. (2005), 'MBA-What is it Worth?' in *www.jobstreet.com* (Malaysia), December, 26.

Davies,A. and Cline, T. (2005), 'The Roi on the MBA', in *http://www.aacsb.edu/publications/archives/janfeb05/p42-45.pdf.*

Drucker, P. (1998), "Management's New Paradigms", Forbes Global Business & Finance, Oct. 5.

French, R. and Grey, C. (1996), Rethinking Management Education, Sage Publications.

Mahadevan, G. (2004), "B-schools-Time to Wake Up", The Hindu (education plus Kerala), Oct. 5.

Philip, J. (2004), 'Indian Management Education-The Next Wave for Enhancing Competitiveness', in *htttp://www.xime.org/news/newsdetails.asp?*

Porter, I. and Mckibbin, L. (1988), Management Education & Development: Drift or Thrust into the Twenty-First Century, Mcgraw-hill, New York, NY

Rajan,A. and Dhunna, M. (1998), "Globalisation and Management Education", University News, Vol. 36, No. 35, Aug. 31.

Ranganayakulu, K. C. S. (1995), "Management Education in India", *Indian Management*, Aug..

Ranjiniswamy, "Life-impacting Experience of Management Education in India: A Case Study", *http://www.aacsb.edu/resource_centers/value/manav*

Rao,V. S. P. (1998), "Re-engineering Management Education", *University News*, Vol. 36, No. 31, Aug. 3.

Sinha, D. P. (2004), Management Education in India, ICFAI Publications, Hyderabad

The B-school Report (a cover feature), *Business India*, Feb. 9-22, 1998

Gupta, K., "Docs get on the Management Track", *The Economic Times*, Jan. 30, 2006.

Muhammed Aslam M K & Wilson P R

5 Problems and Prospects of Higher Education in Kerala

Today, the ruling principles of globalization and an emerging knowledge economy have propelled intellectual capital to the frontline of a nation's competitive advantage. Consequently, education today has moved from its previously marginal role, to playing a pivotal role in the new economy.

"Our institutes of higher education must stay relevant in a changing world. They must be at the center of the nation's efforts in managing change, and sustaining growth. They must plan an effective role in knowledge creation and innovation; they must help Indian industries face the challenges of a competitive, globalize economy. However, government regulation in our higher education system has limited the ability of our colleges and universities to adapt and change. As a result, we have failed to build world-class institutions in the country.

India is a very young nation. Thirty three per centof Indians (325 million people) are below 25 years of age. This is one and a half times the population of the United States and equal to the entire population of all countries in the European Union. It is imperative for us to have an education system capable of making 10.5 million job seekers eligible for employment each year till 2015. Higher Education has a larger role to play in shaping the future of a nation. Hon'ble Prime Minister, Mr. Manmohan Singh, has said that, we need to focus our higher education system to create "job creators" instead of "job seekers".

HIGHER EDUCATION IN INDIA

There are 329 universities and 203 state Universities in India at present. The Indian higher education system comprises of 18 central universities, 90 Deemed universities, 5 institutions established under state legislative Acts and 13 Institutes of National importance established by Central legislation, and nearly 17000 colleges including around 1800 women's colleges.

The higher education system of Kerala has increased many folds-both in terms of the number of universities and in terms of the number of colleges in comparison to their number at the time of the formation of the State. Kerala's higher education system comprises of 7 universities, and two deemed universities.

Universities in Kerala have now shifted their emphasis from conventional courses to professional and technical job oriented courses through giving sanction to start new courses. Most of the new courses are self-financing.

PROFESSIONAL EDUCATION IN KERALA

Annual intake of Students in Technical Institutions

Table 1
Category-wise Technical Education Institutions in Kerala with its Sanctioned Intake of Students Per Annum

Sl. No.	*Category*	*Institutions*	*Annual intake of students*
1.	Engineering Colleges	87	24526
2.	Vocational Higher Secondary	375	3300
3.	Polytechnics	59	10875
4.	Technical Higher Secondary Schools	44	2085
5.	Industrial Training Institutes, etc;	470	7587
6.	Government Commercial Institutes	17	740
7.	Tailoring & Garments Making	42	1260
8.	Industrial Schools	5	80
9.	Fine Arts Colleges	3	83
10.	Food Craft Institute	12	622

It should be noted that Arts and science colleges still dominate the higher education in Kerala irrespective of the mushrooming of the new generation of professional colleges. The number of arts and science colleges in the government sector is 39 and in the aided sector are 150.

The total number of students enrolled in various arts and science colleges (excluding unaided colleges) under the four general universities during 2005 is 1.77 lakhs as against 1.70 lakhs in 2004. It shows an increase of 0.70 lakhs. Girls student outweigh boys in both years. Out of 1.59 lakhs degree students 34.61 per cent are boys and 65.39 per cent are girls. Their corresponding number is 0.55 lakhs and 1.04 lakhs respectively during 2005.

The Liberalisation, Privatisation and Globalisation process has brought down many changes in the education sector also. As a result there are no national boundaries for education and we can also experience with innovative forms of transnational education like Internet based Distance Learning, Educational Franchising, Off Campus Programs, Global Competition for best students, etc;

Table 2

Distribution of Work Seekers in Kerala According to Education Level

Year (at the end of December)	*Medical Graduates*	*Engg. Graduates*	*Diploma holders in Engg.*	*ITI Certificate Holders*	*Agricultural Graduates*	*Veterinary Graduates*	*Total*
1999	1698	8334	39408	101384	1205	119	152148
2000	2455	9858	42991	109592	1284	21	166201
2001	2691	10349	46377	115736	1496	383	177032
2002	3736	8506	43128	123387	881	480	180118
2003	3567	8116	40660	105221	897	436	158897
2004	3910	9213	42539	118518	1662	796	176638
2005-June	3895	9661	40806	110469	907	637	166375

Source: Directorate of Employment and Training.

PLACEMENTS IN INSTITUTIONS

The first batch of B.Tech students of NIT, Calicut (NIT-C), after its renaming, has also got good placements in this year's campus interview. This year's placements were considered the best the institution had so far. It was established in September 1961. The highest offer, slightly over Rs.3 lakhs a year has come from the multinational company, Google.

Table 3
Placement Activities in Kerala during 2005

Institute	*Placements*	*Average placement per student / salary*
IIM-K	100%	1.62. Average salary: Rs. 7.3 lakhs p.a.
NIT-K	100%	N.A. Average salary Rs.2.43 lakhs
Computer Applications CUSAT	100%	N.A. Salary Rs. 2 to 2.5 lakhs
Ship Technology, CUSAT	100%	N. A. Salary Rs. 2.5 to 3.5 lakhs
SMS, CUSAT	100%	2.1 Salary Rs. 2.5 to 4.0 lakhs

The campus here, CUSAT, has turned out as the favourite haunts for companies who looked for talents in 2005. CUSAT bettered its record in its campus placement this year with more than 250 final year students landing plum jobs in leading companies across the country and 200 of its final year B.Tech students in the year 2004 got placements a year before passing out. (Wipro, Infosys, TCS and Cognizant, Technology Solutions took several students.)

The Computer Application Department also shared laurels with students finding placement. Average salaries were between Rs.2 lakhs and 2.5 lakhs a year. The companies that recruited students include Wipro, TCS, L&T and Infotech. The students were offered salaries ranging from Rs.2.3 lakhs to 2.5 lakhs.

The Department of Ship Technology of CUSAT always had and still has 100 per cent placement before they pass out with salaries ranging from 20,000 per month to 25,000 per month. The School of Management Studies, CUSAT last year had 2.1 placements per student. This year it has improved its record of placements finishing up the process much earlier. The employers include TCS, IDBI, RK Swamy Group, BBDO, HDFC, ICICI, IBS etc. The pay package ranges from 2.5 to 4.0 lakhs per year.

Between February and April (2005) companies recruited 71 students from various streams of polytechnics, Kalamassery, and the Companies that came for campus recruitment include Eicher Motors, Lucent Technology, HCL Infinite Ltd., MRF Industries and V-Guard Industries.

This academic year, College of Engineering, Trivandrum has witnessed a sudden upsurge in campus placement, the global giants like Google joining the recruitment spree, with annual salaries that ran into six figures and plenty of opportunities it has opened. In the case of the TKM College of Engineering, many IT Companies and engineering firms visited their campus during the last few years and placement was offered to the students through tests. The reputed companies that offered placements to their students are Wipro, Infosys, ACDS, HCL, TCS, Ashok Leyland etc.

The last few years had witnessed the flow of recruiters from all over India to the campuses in Kerala. Even arts and science colleges in Kerala like St.Teresas, Ernakulam, St.Alberts, Ernakulam, Sacred Heart, Thevara, M E S Aluva, Mar Ivanios Trivandrum, Mahatma Gandhi College, Trivandrum etc. found lot of recruiters visiting and selecting UG and graduates. Nothing more is to be said about the fact that there are plenty of jobs with very high salary provided the candidates are good.

At a higher level, the IT sector of India, says the following: Indian IT surveys revenue in 2005-06 touched 13.2 billion dollars (32% growth over last year). The most critical issue is human resource. By 2010 the industry will require 2.3 million IT workers but at present there is a short fall of 5 lakhs.

The HR Departments of various companies are publishing different recruiting ads that give a feel as if the age of industrial revolution is back. The demand for engineers from disciplines such as Metallurgy, Instrumentation, Civil, Refractory and Mechanical is booming. Manufacturing industries are offering engineers with 5-7 years experience anything from Rs.5-6 lakhs annually. In the financial sectors, banking, insurance etc. the picture is pretty much the same. What is more, as Indian economy continues to cruise in high gear (Sensex at 13000) global profit equity funds are betting buck on countries, making the financial sector a happy hunting ground for job seekers. Private sector companies are working closely with educational institutions to help to train people at the entry level. People are inducted from college campuses into all functions-R&D, quality operations and production. The demand for scientists at the entry level is increasing.

In financial services, the introduction of new and more sophisticated fields like credit card rating, credit card information bureau and mortgage insurance services will create greater rush for the right talents in the coming years.

In Telecom, with the urban markets largely captured, the next areas of growth will be third generation services and rural area, and that will mean more people at all levels.

And in aviation sector, with more airlines coming in and the privatization of airports finally taking off, seasoned professionals from pilots, engineers and aircraft technicians, not to speak of airport managers will be in great demand. Industry sources believe that 15,000 jobs will be created every year in the first three years as the industry matures.

All it says that there are plenty of job opportunities in front of the students provided the candidates are good. Then what is the problem we are facing? It is nothing other than the employability of our students. The crux of the issue is that our graduates are unemployable and the fact is well admitted by the students themselves while they were interviewed for a S.W.O.T. analysis of Higher Education in Kerala conducted as part of the International Education Meet-2006, Kochi. Let us have a look at the other aspects revealed by the S.W.O.T analysis.

Threats in front of the Higher Education Institutions

- Students look to foreign countries like Australia, US and UK
- Degree in India by foreign universities through distance education
- Education in India is becoming a costly affair.

Opportunities

- India is a fast developing country and there is industry shift to the country due to lower labour cost
- The countries like U K and U S are outsourcing many jobs to India
- English media of higher education in India is advantageous over China

Weaknesses

- Confidence level of the students is poor
- Lack of competitiveness and Team spirit

- Poor communication skill
- Dissatisfaction of employers on the students with regard to their general awareness, attitude, enthusiasm, smartness, practical application of the subject knowledge, etc;

Strengths

- The strength of the state is its cent percentage literacy.`
- Kerala remains as a State exporting qualified manpower.

A lack of market orientation has resulted in colleges focused on outdated curriculum and role learning. Consequently, a large proportion of our educational institutes produce graduates who are ill-equipped to relate their learning with the outside world.

We must realize that world-class educational institutions are created not through government mandate and control, but through academic freedom, innovation, and the pursuit of excellence. We must provide our institutes with the freedom to take risks and foster bold, new initiatives for growth. Higher education in India must be allowed to function as an industry in a free market environment.

The government must encourage competition, through autonomy and independence from state funding. Institutes must place a stronger emphasis on innovation, R&D and the creation of new knowledge. Universities should be allowed to form alliances with firms for research and funding. Businesses must be consulted in curriculum design and conducting of courses.

*(Sources of data are the report submitted to the Government based on the SWOT analysis of higher education in Kerala conducted as a part of the International Education Meet-2006).

Moli P Koshy & Mary Joseph

6 Those Who Have The Will, Find The Way...Those Who Don't, Will Find The Wayside

Globalisation and liberalisation have brought about tremendous changes in the functioning of business organisations in the past decade and the pace with which organizations have to adapt is becoming awesome. The liberalisation of indian economy has resulted in:

- A highly competitive environment
- Indian business going global
- Great all round emphasis on technology, quality and cost
- Greater concern in society for environmental issues
- Unprecedented development and use of information technology
- IT-Driven commerce and services
- Emerging economy becoming transitional in nature.

ROLE OF MANAGEMENT EDUCATION

The growth of management education in India over the past five decades or so presents a mixed picture of islands of excellence surrounded by large numbers of institutes of wide qualitative gradients (Cherunilam, 2007). Although management education started in India in the late 1940s, it took roots in a systematic manner around 1950. The benefits of management education can be summarized as it-

- Transfers theoretical knowledge
- Nurtures managerial talents of enterprises
- Formulates successful business practices
- Influences public policies, and
- Plays a significant role in the development of various countries and regions (Drucker, 1974, 1995).

Existing management education practices may either emphasize westernised contents or local. Meaningful combination of theories and case materials remain exceptions. Managerial challenges and contextual differences demand more systematic management education solutions.

As Khanna and Palepu (1997) point out, several major aspects of the institutional environment in emerging economies, such as the product market, capital market, and labour market, are substantially different from those in developed economies. This contextual gap should be dealt with. Therefore, the following areas are to be considered with due importance:

- Need of managers with an organizational perspective and a global mindset Emerging themes and dimensions of management teaching and research
- Management of technology and innovation towards continued strengthening of relevant core technologies
- Identification and creation of best industry practises across the world in all areas ranging from production, marketing, finance, logistics and R&D
- Extensive use of Business Process Reengineering and TQM (Natarajan, 2005; Naik, 2006).

Management Education in India should Focus on

Developing leaders for–

- Business
- Government
- Self-help groups
- Cooperatives
- Panchayats
- NGOs etc.

Networking arrangements among

- Leading management institutions

- Private management institutions and professional societies
- Industry
- User organizations

Incorporating international orientation in management education.

The significance of increasing global orientation in our management education is very evident as 68 per cent of the Indian population will be in the 22-27 age group by 2020 and the population across US, Europe, China, Canada, Japan and so on is graying due to low child births.

CHALLENGES IN MANAGEMENT EDUCATION

1. Need for region specific theory of management and application.
2. There is a need for continued training and development of business and educators.
3. Need for optimal mixes of theory, applied material, cases and relevant courses. Hybridisation should be done to suit the changing scenario and varieties of business education models (Kostova, 1999: Scott, 1995, Scott, 1995).

Enhancing the core Capabilities

1. Faculty development.

   Diversity approach is required in exposure, perspectives and expertise continuous training and development to equip for the current and emerging trends.
2. Consultancy.

   To understand the problems of the business sector and generate resources.
3. Development of teaching material and case studies in terms of Indian ethos in management.
4. Infrastructure.
5. Upgrade library.
6. Access to online research material and databases and IT Support.

7. A learning environment facilitated by infrastructural support
8. Interactive learning model/programme design curriculam made contemporary by tailoring it to the needs of managers and industry.
9. Brain Circulation (Saxenian, 2002)
10. Reverse brain drain mobility of human talents from location to location develop attractive measures to recruit from 'human resource mobility'
    1. Foreign Collaboration
       Exchange programmes for students and faculty
       International exposure and varied exposure in the industry and academics for the faculty.
    2. Restructuring of postgraduate education
       Functional areas courses in production, marketing and finance etc., to be recast to include relevant IT application as the stress is now upon IT enabled commerce and services.
       Foundation courses should be oriented towards the cultivation of relevant conceptual and application skills.
    3. Industry-Institute partnership
       live projects for students
       Collaborative research and case studies
    4. Specialized MBA courses

Kerala, being at the south end, is at a disadvantage for students at times. Cross regional collaborations and teaching activities would open up the possibility that students will benefit from different ways of thinking, and appreciate different perspectives more.

Such training and education are important for future business leaders if they are to engage successfully in the global settings of business.

REFERENCES

Business India, 2006. October 22

Cherunilam, Francis 2007. Indian Management Education at Cross-Roads. *Erudition* (*journal*) January, 15-24.

Drucker, Peter F. (1974), Management: Tasks, Responsibilities, Practices. Harper & Row, New York.

Drucker, Peter F. (1995), Managing in a Time of Great Change. Penguin Books. New York.

Hariharan, R. (2004), Role of Technical Education in the Interaction between Institute and Industry, University News, 42(46) 145-147.

Kao, J. (1993), The Worldwide Web of Chinese Business. *Harvard Business Review*, 71(2): 24-36.

Khanna, T. and Palepu, K. (1997), Why Focused Strategies may be Wrong for Emerging Markets. *Harvard Business Review*, 75(4): 41-51.

Kostova, T. (1999), Transnational Transfer of Strategic Organizational Practices: A Conceptual Perspective. *Academy of Management Review*, 24: 308-324.

Naik, B. M. (2006), Quality Assuarance System in Higher and Technical Education-Can We Afford to Ignore it, University News, 44 (30), 9-14.

Natarajan, R. (2005), Technology Enabled Learning Initiatives, University News, 43 (45), 15-21.

Porter, M.E. (1998), Clusters and the New Economics of Competition. *Harvard Business Review*, 76 (6): 77-90.

Saxenian, A. (2000), Brain Circulation. The Bookings Review, 20(1): 28-31.

Scott, W. R. (1995), Institutions and Organizations. Thousand Oaks: Sage Publications.

Varghese, Mariamma A. (2005), Strategy Planning-Significant Gap in Management of Higher Education, University News, 43 (52), December 26, 1-6.

Wilson P R & Muhammed Aslam

7 Kerala-International Educational Hub

It is reported that over two million Keralites are living and working in other countries, pursuing a wide range of professions and occupations. Their earnings, savings and remittances enrich Kerala's economy and social life. These non-resident Keralites contribute substantially to the reduction of unemployment, social frustrations and poverty. Many such emigrants are high quality professional in academics, medicine, nursing, engineering, science and technology. The exodus of such a massive population to foreign employment market would not have been possible but for the groundwork done by the schools, colleges and universities of Kerala over a period of two centuries thanks to the missionary pioneers and local educators who built up institutions brick by brick through hard labour and community participation. The farsighted rulers and administrators of the former Kingdoms that constitute the present Kerala assisted in the educational process with much enthusiasm and generosity. We may criticize and berate our educational system on various counts but we have to admit that this imperfect system was the major springboard from which all those who went abroad for employment took their leap. Therefore Kerala has a tradition and educational infrastructure suitable for participation in international education. The question is on factors of social justice, equality of opportunities and quality enhancement, so that Kerala would become a favoured destination for transnational education.

Higher education, whether in the general or the technical stream, must have links with all national goals and endeavours. To this end, a large number of centres for excellence to turn out quality manpower in areas relevant to industry and society need to be established with the triangular partnership of academia, industry and government. These institutes of excellence are essential to make India a knowledge superpower and would help in retaining our competitive edge in the global economy.

To ensure the quality of education, it is necessary to make our accreditation process more transparent, time-bound and free from the regime of controls. Institutions like the NAAC and AICTE should make public the benchmarks as well as other normative standards, which are absolute minimum requirements for starting colleges and institutes of technical education. There is a need to enforce these minimum standards without any dilution or compromise[3]. Modernization of syllabi, examination reforms and greater attention to issues of governance of universities and colleges, all require urgent attention.

SOME SUGGESTIONS FOR POLICY-MAKING FOR INDIAN UNIVERSITIES

(a) The infrastructure facilities of universities and institutions enrolling international students on their campuses should be of international standard not only for theoretical instruction but also in the form of well-equipped laboratories, library resources, special hostel facilities and environment for social and cultural life.

(b) To increase the desirability of exchange of educational contents it would be necessary for universities to have an international context in education and teaching particularly at the post-graduate level. The students from abroad identify more with the respective countries' context. The contents should therefore focus on requirements of the job market and should have provision for some innovative and flexible programmes.

(c) Accredited Indian universities may be allowed to open campuses in other countries with the help of even without going through the nodal agency with the approval of the government of respective countries. However, information about the same needs to be sent to the nodal agency.

(d) The programmes offered by Indian universities should be equivalent to ones offered in India. Additionally it should be recognized by the universities of both countries, ie. provider as well as recipient countries.

(e) The Indian universities may be allowed to offer programmes through twinning, franchise as well as distance mode. Degrees awarded through these modes will have equivalence with formal degrees in terms of credit hours. The evaluation of

(f) students should be on the same standard as that of any similar formal degree programmes.

(g) Foreign exchange regulations may be suitably modifies so as to allow educational institutions to bring foreign exchange in India, and to spend foreign exchange for the development of off-campus facilities abroad. This should be incorporated in the import/ export policy.

ADVANTAGE KERALA

Kerala's higher education should be upgraded to international standards. If done so, the students in Kerala will be in a position to acquire world class education that helps them to be globally competitive and employable. Another advantage of having world class higher education will be the low cost of education when compared to the developed countries in the world. People from abroad will be able to pursue higher education at a low cost which can attract a lot of students from developed and developing economies. Over a period it will help Kerala to become the international hub of higher education in India.

Table 1
Lower Middle Income Countries with over 10,000 Students Abroad
(GNP Per Capita $ 756 and $ 2995)

	Number ofStudents		*Offered Positions*
Country	*Abroad*	*In India 98-99*	*1997-2000*
China	121,372	28	75
Turkey	41,901	8	12
Morocco	36,181	-	-
Iran	26,380	108	30
Algeria	22,253	-	6
Russian Fed.	21,080	7	6
Palestine	17,795	-	-
Thailand	17,093	197	12
Kazakhstan	15,491	9	15
Syria	14,993	16	15
Jordan	14,300	80	14
Tanzania	10,000	38	7

Source: Various Reports

The Table 1 shows the lower middle income countries with over 10,000 students abroad. China having the most number of students studying abroad with 1,21,372 students but number of students studying in India was only 28. Even lower middle income countries like Morocco, Algeria and Palestine too have students who go abroad and study but their number in India is nil in the year 1998-99. The highest number of students who come to India is from Thailand which amounts to 197 which is very low compared to the students studying aboard form Thailand. Hence Kerala has a huge potential to tap students from such countries with its low cost, world class facilities etc.

The Table 2 shows the upper middle income countries with over 10,000 students abroad. Korean Republic had the most number of students studying abroad with 71,749 students and only 19 of whom were in India. The most number of students studying in India from the middle income countries was from Malaysia which was 37 but the number of students studying abroad accounted for 49,413 which is very huge compared to those studying in India. Countries like Brazil and Lebanon had no students where as the number of students studying abroad from these countries were very high indicating the potential that can be tapped from this sector.

Table 2
Upper Middle Income Countries with over 10,000 Student Abroad (GNP per capita # 2,996 and $ 9,265)

Country	Number of Students Abroad	Number of Students In India 98-99	Offered Positions 1997-2000
Korea Rep.	71,749	19	6
Malaysia	49,413	37	-
Poland	13,544	6	24
Brazil	12,092	-	-
Mexico	12,298	3	12
Lebanon	10,274	-	-

Source: Various Reports.

The Table 3 shows the high income countries with over 10,000 students abroad. The highest number of students studying abroad was from Japan which accounted for 64,284 followed by Germany which had 49,876 students but their numbers in India were 38 and 8 respectively which is very low compared to the students studying abroad. Countries like Hong Kong, Ireland, Austria and Sweden have a greater number of students studying abroad but no students come to India for their studies. Even though we have 87 and 26 students from the most developed countries like USA and UK respectively, it is very bleak compared to the potential we can tap out of this sector as most of these students seek low cost and world class facilities.

Table 3
High Income Countries with Over 10,000 Students Abroad (GNP Per Capita # 9,266 or more

Country	Number ofStudents Abroad	Number ofStudents In India 98-99	Offered Positions 1997-2000
Japan	64,284	38	30
Germany	49,876	8	30
Italy	40,663	4	12
France	39,152	14	48
Hong Kong	36,481	-	-
USA	30,359	87	-
Canada	29,643	30	6
Spain	25,596	2	15
UK	25,085	26	6
Ireland	20,159	1	-
Singapore	18,087	7	-
Nether land	13,034	2	9
Austria	10,707	-	-
Sweden	10,571	-	6

Table 4
Countries with 10,000 or more Students Abroad at Tertiary Level

Countries	*Number*	*Number of Students*	
		Abroad	*In India*
High Income	14	413,700	219
Upper Middle Income	6	170,200	65
Lower Middle Income	12	358,800	526
Low Income(excluding India)	4	45,300	116
Total	36	988,00	926

Source: Various Reports.

Table 5
Foreign Students from Different Countries which had 100 or more Students in India in 1998-99 (Source: Various Reports)

Country	*Number of Students Abroad*	*In India 1998-99*	*Maximum*	*Year*
A. Low Income Countries				
Kenya	5,876	639	4268	93-94
Nepal	2,197	574	912	88-89
Bangladesh	5,779	461	1244	95-96
Ethiopia	4,366	403	685	93-94
Sudan	4,396	245	1682	88-89
Uganda	1,617	196	297	94-95
Bhutan	118	115	181	94-95
Indonesia	22,136	106	106	88-89
Yemen	6,060	100	204	94-95
Afghanistan	3,036	100	204	94-95
B. Lower Middle Income Countries				
Sri Lanka	5,118	368	552	89-90
Thailand	17,093	197	226	94-95
Iran	22,136	108	553	88-89
C. Upper Middle Income Countries				
Mauritius	2,284	398	459	97-98

The Table 4 shows the countries with 10,000 or more students abroad at tertiary level. The total numbers of students who come to India for study are from just 36 countries. Other countries do not consider India as a educational center. The maximum number of students come from the higher income group which amounts to 4,13,700 from 14 countries only and followed by 358800 from 12 lower middle income countries. The total number of students studying in India from abroad were 926 which is very low compared to the total number of students studying abroad from different countries that amounts to 98800 (excluding India).

The Table 5 shows the foreign students from different countries which had 100 or more students in India. The maximum number of students studying in India from abroad was from Kenya which was 639 followed by Nepal which was 574 and then Bangladesh which amounted to 461, were as the number of students studying abroad from these countries was much larger than these figures. The maximum number of students studying in India in any year was in the year 93-94 from Kenya which accounted for 4268 students. Among the lower middle income countries Sri Lanka had the maximum number of students studying in India which stood at 368 and the maximum was achieved in the year 1989-90 which amounted to 552 students studying in India.

Twinning Programs with Foreign Universities (Source: Various Reports)

Discipline	*University*
Medicine	University of West Indies, Trinidad Melaka-Manipal Medical College, Malaysia
Engineering	Andrews University, USAMilwaukee School of Engineering, USADeakin University, Australia University of Edinburgh, UK Kathmandu University, Nepal
Management	Ohio University, USA
Physiotherapy (Proposed)	Andrews University USA

Table 6
Estimated Number of Foreign Students and Projected Earnings

	Foreign Students	*Annual Spending Per Student (Rs in Lakhs)*	*Total (Rs. In crore)*
Arts, Science	40,000	1,00,000	400
Commerce, Management	30,000	2,00,000	600
Law	10,000	2,00,000	200
Engineering	15,000	3,00,000	450
Medicine	3,000	6,00,000	180
Agriculture	2,000	1,00,000	20
Computer Science	50,000	1,00,000	500
	Total	1,50,000	2350

The Table 6 shows the estimated number of foreign students and projected earnings. The total number of foreign students estimated is 1,50,000 and projected earnings is 2350 crores. The annual spending per student is highest for medicine and lowest for arts, science, agriculture and computer science. The projected earning for agriculture is the lowest being 20 crores and an estimated number of students of 2000. The highest projected earnings are for commerce and management with 600 crores and estimated intake of 30000 students.

Table 7
Exchange and Academic Visits:
Indo-U.S. Patterns (Source: Various Reports)

Year	*Foreign Students*	*Total US enrolment*	*Foreign %age*
1954-55	34,232	24,99,800	1.4
1964-65	82,045	53,20,000	1.5
1974-75	1,54,580	1,03,21,500	1.5
1984-85	3,43,777	1,23,87,700	2.8
1994-95	4,52,653	1,45,54,016	3.1
1999-2000	5,14,723	1,35,84,000	3.8

The Table 7 shows the Indo-U.S. exchange and academic visit pattern. The number of foreign students have seen a steady increase from the year 1954-55 which increased from 34,232 students to 5,14,723 students in 1999-2000. Similarly the total number of U.S. student enrolment has seen a steep rise from 24,99,800 in the year 1954-55 to about 1,35,84,000 in the year 1999-2000. The foreign percentage has also seen a similar increase from 1.4 in 1954-55 to 3.8 in 1999-2000.

Table 8
Annual Foreign Exchange earnings of MEMG Educational Programs

Program	*Foreign earnings (US $)*
Nepal	3,900,000
Malaysia	9,750,000
West Indies	450,000
Manipal	10,650,000
Total	US $ 24,750,000

Source: Various Reports.

The Table 8 shows the annual foreign exchange earnings of MEMG educational programs of four countries/universities namely Nepal, Malaysia, West Indies and Manipal. Among the listed nations West Indies earns the lowest foreign income in educational program which is US $ 4,50,000. The highest among them is Manipal with foreign earnings of US $ 10,650,000. This is mainly attributed to the low cost of education with world class facilities in the education system, better infrastructure and easy mobility.

RANKING OF INSTITUTIONS

Though it was found that students coming out of professional colleges as well as arts and science colleges in Kerala are not employable on a macro level, at the micro level there were excellent institutions producing excellent students. Hence we have made an attempt to identify such institutions which can be uplifted to the world class standards. These institutions have very clear objectives in their mission statement. They have been well perceived and well implemented. They could be islands of excellence but one cannot deny the existence of such institutions[7].

The process of selecting such institutions was very difficult because, they differed from one another to a very great extent. Their tradition, culture and the process and even pedagogy were different. They had different agencies to evaluate them like UGC, AICTE, etc. A good number of them were outstanding in some of the aspects measured. But we had been looking from the point of view of a total institute which could welcome foreign students[8]. After much deliberation and investigations a methodology evolved which was applied to select the institutes.

(a) Only those institutes/departments/colleges which had been recognized and accredited by national or international agencies were included in the sample. For example, if a college has to be included it should have a five star rating. If a University Department is to be included, it should have come under a scheme like University with Potential to become Centre of Excellence, if it is a business school, it should have all India Business School ranking, if it is an engineering college, it should have the accreditation from AICTE etc.[9].

(b) These selected institutes should be research institutes/departments/colleges accepted by appropriate authority.

(c) Majority of the faculty members of these institutes/departments should hold Ph.D. and should be research guides[10].

(d) The faculty members of these institutes should have sufficient number of publications in referred journals or should have presented papers at national/international seminars.

(e) These institutions should have funding from other agencies like UGC, AICTE, DST, ICSSR, etc.

(f) These institutions should have 100 percentage placements and there should be facilities to equip the students to make them employable (Placement cells, career development cells, etc.).

(g) These institutions should follow the pattern of semester examinations.

(h) These institutions should have internal assessments.

(i) These institutions should have the backing of alumni associations.

(j) These institutions should have a number of vocational/professional courses.

(k) They should have facilities for skill development like language labs, personality development clinics, etc.

(l) These institutions should have hostel facilities.

(m) These institutions should have library, computer labs, banking and telephone facilities, etc.

(n) These institutions should have extension facilities like NSS, NCC, etc.

(o) The pedagogy followed in these institutions should be more learning oriented with training, seminars, paper presentations, group activities, project work, etc.

Institutions were ranked on the basis of the above said points on a five point scale, and it is from these fifteen criteria that the institutions were selected and they are described below in the alphabetic order. This list was then given to the experts for their further analysis and after a series of discussions, these were accepted.

This is no sense means that the rest of the institutions are not up to the mark. It only means, among the equals, these institutions come first.

Institutions Ranked

Amritha Institute of Medical Sciences, Cochin

Aryavaidyasala, Kottakkal

Centre for Development Studies Trivandrum

Department of Electronics, CUSAT

Department of Physics, CUSAT

Department of Ship Technology, CUSAT

International School of Photonics, CUSAT

Kerala Kalamandalam

M.E.S. College, Kuttipuram

Rajagiri School of Social Sciences

S.B. College, Changanacherry

School of Communication and Management Studies

School of legal Studies, CUSAT

School of Management Studies, CUSAT

School of Marine Sciences, CUSAT

Action Plans for Institutions

High quality university institutions in Kerala may start planning the implementation of internationalized education through steps such as the following:

- Modernizing the curricula, teaching methods and evaluation procedures to internationally comparable levels;
- Staff seminar on the subject of international education as a follow up of this conference;
- Setting up an office of international education;
- Drawing up plans for infrastructure development, construction of international hostels, comfortable lecture halls, new methodologies of teaching, ICT

facilities, recreation facilities, health services, etc.

- Making provision for flexibility in academic calendar to suit the requirements of foreign students;
- Establishing institutional linkages with colleges/universities abroad through TWINNING arrangements, Memorandum of Understanding, exchange of students/faculty, etc.
- Setting up websites; and
- Giving training to selected staff members to deal with foreign scholars, especially in communication and counseling skills, cosmopolitan attitudes and ICT competency.

CONCLUSION

Internationalized higher education is possible only in an environment and ethos of systematic and result-oriented academic work and other campus operations. A work culture characterized by effective time management and rigorous discipline is essential for an international community to live together and perform together. Impulsive outbursts of campus violence, disruption of studies and closure of institution will have to be totally avoided. There should be a climate of trust between various stakeholders and democratic procedures for settling disputes.

The knowledge and skills exported or imported by India in any mode should generate goodwill and fellow feeling so that better environment and harmonious international relationships are established among the countries exchanging the knowledge service. There should be a continuous follow-up and dialogue about the information, knowledge support and exchange of information with alumni over a long period.

(This paper is compiled from the report "SWOT Analysis of Higher Education in Kerala" submitted to Govt. of Kerala as a part of International Educational Meet 2006).

NOTES AND REFERENCES

1. Report of the Kerala Education Commission/Kerala Sastra Sahitya Parishad: Kochi, Kerala Sastra Sahitya Parishad, 1999 p. 16.

2. Ancient Indian Education: Brahmanical and Buddhist, Radha Kumud Mookerji, Motilal Banarsidass, 1998, p. 22.
3. The History of Education in Modern India 1757-1998, Suresh ChandraGhosh, orient Longman Ltd, New Delhi, 2000, p. 28.
4. State funding of Higher Education/Power KB Association of Indian Universities, 1998, p. 73.
5. Upanishads on education/V.S. Idaykidath, 2000, p. 160.
6. Report of the Kerala Education Commission/Kerala Sastra Sahitya Parishad: Kochi, Kerala Sastra Sahitya Parishad, 1999. p. 132
7. The world of Learning 2000- 50th ed. London: Europa Publication, 1999, p. 101.
8. Handbook of Educational Technology/Henry Ellington: Fred Percival; Phil Race-3rd ed.-London: Kogan, p. 97
9. Economics & Primary Education/D. Pulla Rao, New Delhi: Rawat, 1998, p. 86.
10. Education and the disprivileged 19th% 20th Century in India/ Editor: Sabyasachi Bhattacharya, Hyderabad, Orient Longman, 2002, p. 109.
11. Problems of Minorities education in India/Shafiquz Zarman-Book Links Co., 2001. p. 121

Sreejith P S

8 Technical Education and Globalisation

There has been a growing concern for raising the standards of services rendered by our educational institutions, by adopting innovative techniques and to bridge the technology gap which exists between institutions in developing countries and developed countries [1]. Countries that are demonstrating economic success today are those which have invested heavily and selectively in the training and development of its human resource [2]. As technologies change rapidly, retraining and updating of the work force continuously are becoming major challenges facing every country today. Especially, the technical institutions are expected to set an example in propagating quality consciousness, teamwork, optimization of productivity and manage the competitive environment and encourage team spirit among all concerned.

In the past two decades, there has been an unprecedented growth of the technical education facilities in India. The number of engineering colleges and also the annual intake of students also have grown up considerably. Nearly two-thirds of these colleges are in the self-financing sector. Most of these institutions, whether in government or private sector, are facing some major issues which need immediate solutions. These include shortage of competent and motivated faculty, lack of funds, obsolete and inadequate equipments and infrastructure, out-dated teaching learning processes, rigid curriculum, ineffective examination system, and an indifferent and inefficient management structure. To compete and do well in the global economy, we need to produce world class human resource from our institutions and this is possible only if we restructure and adequately modify our technical education system.

CHALLENGES OF GLOBALIZATION AND INFORMATION TECHNOLOGY

Globalization has opened up the economy to global players in the industry and service sector. It can have both positive as well as negative effects depending on how we use it. Instead of globalizing India we can Indianise the globe [3]. However, as of now, the effect on India is mixed tilting more towards negative. The manufacturing base has diminished. Jobs in engineering sector have come down except in IT, which will have a major impact on technical education. All landed goods from China are cheaper than the local ones forcing local industries to close and increasing unemployment. Even in rural sectors there is a very tough competition and imported food items are cheaper. Drastic re-orientation of the technical education to produce world class man power is the need of the hour. The products coming out of our technical education institutions should be capable of meeting the challenges of the modern industry. They should be up-to-date in their technical know- how, have the willingness to adapt to the changing environment, have a deep sense of quality, and be conversant with the skills needed to perform well in a job. These skills include:

- Learning to learn skills
- Communication skills
- Problem solving skills
- Negotiation skills
- Interpersonal skills
- Teamwork
- Self-esteem
- Goal setting
- Leadership
- Creative thinking

Many of the foreign universities include development of these skills as the part of their curriculum.

Schemes of foreign universities to offer degrees in India through distance education mode at reasonable cost is yet another challenge to technical educators in India as we should be able to provide the same quality degrees at much reduced cost. Our focus should be to reverse this trend by offering Indian degrees in foreign countries. This will help in resource mobilization and also provide enormous opportunities to develop new expertise in pedagogy and create teaching-learning materials for global use through CD and internet.

IT will have an important bearing on technical education, considering the enormous demand for IT man power. India is fast becoming an IT super-power and the All India Council for Technical Education (AICTE) has already taken steps to increase seats in IT-related courses in engineering colleges. With the bulk of the jobs in IT and limited opportunity in other engineering disciplines, an undesirable unbalance is created, with the students neglecting other disciplines. But the fact remains that, if India has to succeed under globalization and IT environment, our infrastructure such as roads, airports, power, communication, and railways must be of international standards. This requires proper prioritization, resource allocation and manpower training for infrastructure and engineering institutions have a major role to play in this direction. IT can be effectively used for technical education. Focus should be on e-learning encompassing the use of IT for lecture, tutorials, laboratories, library, office automation, databank, institution web-site etc. Since lectures can be delivered through internet online to different locations simultaneously, we can reach technical knowledge to largest audience with minimum cost. Teleconferencing would enhance interaction through interface and major thrust should be given in this direction by employing expert faculties.

As a result of globalization, the qualities expected of technical manpower will be same through out the world. Institutions have to produce manpower not only for the local market, but also for the national and international market as well. There will also be considerable mobility of work-force in future.

REFORMS AND INITIATIVES

Globalization has thrown many challenges for technical education. To adapt to the fast changing environment, it is necessary that certain reforms and initiatives are needed.

AUTONOMY VERSUS AFFILIATION

Autonomy is the freedom to create and implement new ideas, new programmes, new approaches, and offer new services as a part of an overall thrust towards attainment of excellence of the institutions in their different areas of activity. Ideally all institutions must be totally autonomous to bring out their best. However, as on today a very large number of degree colleges are affiliated to various universities and their programme offerings are controlled by the university bodies. Affiliated colleges have to look for decisions from universities for any change to be made in the curricula which is a very time consuming process and tends to lose its importance by the time it is implemented. Decisions on curricular matters made by universities are binding on all affiliated institutions. Bringing changes based on assessed needs due to changing technology are simply impossible for individual institutions under the affiliated system. As a result, even those colleges that have the potential to academic changes of higher standard do not have the freedom to do so or to introduce new methods or reforms in the examination system. Affiliating university system is prevalent in only very few countries like India and the attempts must be made to give autonomy and deemed university status to more institutions every year by a quality control mechanism by AICTE.

INDUSTRY-INSTITUTE LINKAGE

Partnership between employers and institutions should be recognized as the basis for the development of market-responsive, demand-driven institutions that are firmly linked to the economy of the nation. Partnership between industries and colleges should be encouraged and promoted. Such partnerships include industry and stake-holder-led governing councils for the colleges, industry-driven curriculum committees etc.

INTER-INSTITUTIONAL LINKAGE

Synergising a cluster of institutions as regards faculty expertise, laboratories, library, and computing facility is desirable to optimally use the resources. Reputed institutions can help the less endowed institutions in the neighborhood on curriculum planning, establishment of laboratories, general guidance to teachers and students etc. Technical Education Quality Improvement Programme (TEQUIP) initiated by the Ministry of Human Resources Development (MHRD) is focusing on this type of network scheme.

CURRICULUM DEVELOPMENT

Curriculum development for engineering education must be a continuous and regular affair due to fast obsolescence of subjects and need for upgrading. Agencies like AICTE publish model curricula for different degree programmes and can be used as a guideline during curriculum development.

ALUMNI INTERACTION

Every institute should devise effective schemes to increase alumni interaction, which is beneficial to both. The Alumni can help in resource mobilization, lab development, scholarships, library upgrade, sponsoring projects etc.

RESOURCE MOBILIZATION

Fund raising has become an important function of all institutions. Apart from government, major sources of fund are - student fees, alumni, industry, consultancy and sponsored research. Raising fees beyond a point could have negative impact due to poor paying capacity of the parents.

INFRASTRUCTURE

Good quality education demands modern infrastructure. Class rooms should be equipped with the latest audio-visual facilities. Gadgets like OHP, LCD Projector, large screen, microphones etc. are also necessary. Adequate computing facility is also essential in any campus. Fast obsolescence of PCs is a matter of concern and mechanism to recycle PCs must be evolved. Laboratory is also a matter of prime importance. It is not sufficient that new items and components are procured but it is also important that they are properly maintained.

CONCLUSION

The impact of globalization on technical education has been discussed in this paper. Challenges of rapid advancement and development of information technology has also been emphasized. Initiatives and reforms that has to be taken care of are also discussed.

REFERENCES

R. S. Nirjar (2000), Millennium Mantras for Technical Education, *The Indian Journal of Technical Education,* 23, 6-12.

Higher Education in the 21st Century, UNESCO, 1998, Paris.

S. S. Murthy (2001), Some Critical Issues on Shaping Technical Education for the Future, *The Indian Journal of Technical Education,* 24 7-14.

Mathew Emmanuel

9 The Problems and Prospects of Entrepreneurship Education in Engineering Colleges and Other Technical Institutions in Kerala

Modern science whether basic or engineering science is the mother of almost all the ideas and innovations on which the development of modern industry depends. Technical entrepreneurship plays a pivotal role in the process of industrialization. It can make contribution to industrial development through innovations, new product development and improvements in productivity, production processes and systems. Technicians and technocrats can play a role of innovators comparatively with ease because they have characteristics, such as propensity to adopt new knowledge/ technology more rapidly. Recently, a paradigm shift has been observed away from the heavy/traditional industries to computers and information technology. This is attributed to the radical innovations which has become a vital contributor to the radical innovations taking place particularly in the field of information technology which has become a vital contributor to the nation's economy by way of breeding an entire new and accomplished class of techno-entrepreneurs setting up knowledge based industries and new technology based firms in India as well as across the globe. Analysis of the leading companies worldwide reveal that most of the founders of these new technology based firms are highly qualified professionals having sound academic background. The growth and development of Silicon Valley around Stanford University is the finest example of this new trend. The Research Triangle Park in North Carolina and Route 128 in MIT, Boston are also successful examples towards this trend.[1] This clearly indicates that the technical institutions/universities could nucleate the generation of entrepreneurs and employees for the firms and industries and its environment coupled with its expertise and facilities can play a vital role in shaping today's students into tomorrow's entrepreneurs.

The western world especially USA, UK, France and Germany are technologically more advanced countries vis-à-vis other parts of the globe. They have pioneered initiatives to bridge the missing links between technical institutions/ university and the industry. The evolution of science parks/ research parks/technopolies, etc. is the step towards this direction. These parks have shown greater degree of multiplier effect ion the region by way of generation of wealth and employment, technology upgradation, promoting new work culture, quality and sophistication of the product. The rapid development in these parks stems from the fact that the faculty was motivated to start their own business, consultancy/ R&D in the park. The Unite States was pioneer in promotion of the concepts such as Science Parks way back in 1950. Currently, there are about 200 Science Parks in the US and this stimulated the growth of Science Parks in UK in early seventies and today there are around 60 Science Parks set up in almost every university and important technical institutions, most successful being the Cambridge Science Park. It has also been observed that the American parks are designed to attract large multinational companies whereas most of the European and African parks are catering to the small enterprises, Japan is propagating the technopolies movement to develop rural backward region and has so far promoted 26 technologies. Guided by the success of science park movement in the western world the National Science and Technology Entrepreneurship Development Board (NSTEDB) set up by the Government of India in 1982 with a view to evolve new programmees and schemes for converting

S&T persons into job generators rather than job seekers and after having examined various models of science parks technology parks accepted the Science and Technology Entrepreneur Park (STEP) model suggested by Dr. Y. Nayudamma Committee in 1984.

NEED FOR ENTREPRENEURSHIP EDUCATION IN THE AGE OF GLOBALIZATION

Jacques Delors' Commission-the International Commission on Education for the Twenty-First Century in its report to UNESCO entitled Learning: the Treasure Within in 1996 in the form of Outlooks (from the local community to a world society, from social cohesion to democratic participation and from economic growth to human development), Principles (the four pillars of education-learning to know, learning to do, learning t live together and learning to be, learning throughout life), and Directions (educating the global village) has highlighted pivotal components of entire gamut of education significantly in the context of preparing present generation to become meaningful, effective and productive contributors for the noble task of healthy and happier nation-building. It is imperative to note at this stage that the common thread that runs through in all the aforesaid report is about relevance of introduction of entrepreneurship education at all levels of education.

The objectives of Entrepreneurship related Courses are:

- To equip students with preliminary skills in entrepreneurship
- To enable students to prepare a viable project proposal for submission to banks and other financial institutions
- To motivate as well as to give necessary psychological inputs to students in order to enable them to face inter-personal problems on the one hand and problems of the self on the other during their later career as entrepreneurs
- To impart skills to students in searching, locating and obtaining information whether such information pertains to science and technology or business and industry.

Employability is listed as one of the factors of growth. But now the question arises as to where are the jobs for large number of educated youth coming out of the educational institutional institution? Already the educated youths who are registered with the employment exchanges of the State are more than 40 lakhs. Can our government provide jobs to more than 40 lakhs educated unemployed people in its various departments? It is estimated that jobs in the government and Public Sector Undertakings are not more than 15 per cent of total job opportunities in the State. Are our educational institutions turning out really skilled youth, who have a real employment potential, as per the requirement of the private sector organizations? Barring a few institutions rest is not performing the job of developing the needed skills, competencies and attitudes among youth for their immediate employability. Most of the technological advances are of such a nature that manual work is eliminated. Hence the elasticity of job creation to economic growth is declining, i.e., job creation takes place in ever declining proportion to growth. Since the number of jobs, both in the government and private corporate sector, will keep on reducing due to automation and improved technology, there is a need to think of the alternative mode of employability. One such mode is entrepreneurship and self employment. We have to motivate students in the educational institutions continuously to opt for self-employment and entrepreneurship rather than preparing and orienting them for wage employment.

Entrepreneurship may be considered as a process of establishing an enterprise with an innovative idea and risk-bearing attitude. It does not emerge automatically and spontaneously. Its development depends upon the availability of forces of production, social mobility, marginal security, need achievement, withdrawal of status respect, government action etc .In order to develop entrepreneurial zeal among our youth we need to treat entrepreneurship as a discipline like civil engineering, mechanical engineering, electronics engineering computer science and economics rather than treating it as a part of a subject. For this to happen, we need to integrate entrepreneurship in the curricula of all streams of education in general and technical education in particular.

ENTREPRENEURSHIP IN ENGINEERING EDUCATION IN KERALA: PRESENT STATUS

High levels of per capita consumption coupled with lack of entrepreneurship within have made Kerala the happy hunting ground of MNCs and manufacturers from other parts of the country. The entrepreneurs in the State produce only a handful of food and non-food items and most of these are characterized by low technology, low investment, and marginal value-addition. So much so, Kerala, despite its significant achievements in the social sectors, remains poorly equipped to respond positively to the challenges of globalization. Entrepreneurial initiatives of the youth often fail to take off owing to lack of proper technical guidance.

Globalization has changed the face of business and industry. At a time when every significant corporate venture is planned on a large scale, effective managers are needed in every field. Technological professionals without entrepreneurship/ management background often complain and feel that they are not placed at par with their commerce and management peers. What these technological professional studies in their specialized courses has little applicability if they are not supplemented by entrepreneurial and managerial training. Engineers constitute the backbone of science and technology system of a country. However, engineers and technological professionals now feel the need for undertaking studies pertaining to business courses like marketing, accounting, economics, project appraisal, company laws, rules and regulation of stock exchanges, intellectual property rights, etc for their glorious future. The technology-driven world of today is placing new demands and challenges on human resources. Today's competitive environment demands innovative and high quality products, which are based on modern technology and efficient engineering. To drive maximum advantage from these technological advancements it is essential that we introduce entrepreneurship as an additional subject in our technical and engineering colleges so that our new generation of young engineers will be available to serve in own country instead of draining out to technologically advanced countries where they are paid good salaries, perks, etc.

India has in the recent past been witnessing strong stirrings of an industrial renaissance. The resurgence of the country's manufacturing sector has been nearly magical, thronging up promises of an emerging manufacturing power. Reforms of regulations set in motion in 1991 unlocked India's enormous growth potential and unleashed unstoppable entrepreneurial forces. The Indian enterprises have become more confident, competitive, combative and ambitious about their future than ever before. They have, to compete globally, been investing to build scale in critical areas of production, distribution and marketing[2]. Manufacturing creates productive employment, supports agriculture by adding value to its products besides providing the required inputs, sustains the servicing sector and spins a cycle of wealth creation. It is generally reckoned that an investment in manufacturing produces a multiplier effect of four times i.e. every rupee invested adds four rupees to GDP.

India's free market economy has a legal and regulatory framework, especially the one evolved since the process of liberalization was set in motion that rewards free enterprise, entrepreneurship and risk-taking. The legal system supports economic liberalization and modernization when appropriate. IPR, bankruptcy, foreign exchange control, data protection, competition and other laws have been overhauled to boost foreign investor's confidence. Entrepreneurship in Education is essential to stimulate young people and ignite their minds. Ignited young minds, we feel, are a powerful resource. This resource is mightier than any other source on earth, in the sky or under the sea. Entrepreneurial awareness and motivation is essential part of human resource development for all the students in educational mainstreams. Case studies, stories, video films, entrepreneurships camps and motivation lectures may be organized for this purpose.

GOOD RESPONSE TO ENTREPRENEURSHIP DEVELOPMENT CLUBS

The initiative of the Department of Industries and Commerce in establishing in schools and colleges including engineering colleges is evoking a good response in the State. The efforts that began in 2002 have succeeded in inculcating an entrepreneurial culture among youth, something the people lacked. With in a short period of 4 years the Department through KIED established ED Clubs in 181 educational institutions throughout the State. Out of this, 33 ED Clubs were started in Polytechnic colleges and Industrial Training Institutes[3]. Out of 84 engineering colleges (9government, 3 private aided and 72 self-financing) in the State, only 22 engineering colleges started ED Clubs so far[4]. So this is a dark and untapped area in the new generation engineering colleges.

It was with the aim of tapping the unique strength of the State aimed at providing a suitable stimulus for industrial growth that the Department came forward with this innovative idea. The objective of the scheme includes sensitizing students on the real economic and industrial development scenario of the State and making the members aware of the unlimited developmental potential here. It was also aims at motivating the members to venture into the industrial activity of the State. Any college or higher secondary school, government aided or unaided, may set up an EDC with at least 25 interested students with a teacher/ faculty as coordinator. There will be a mentor attached to the Club, who will be a successful entrepreneur. The Government is extending a grant of Rs. 12000 per annum to each Club. A minimum of 10 per cent of estimated project cost is to be contributed by the institution or the Club. The Clubs organize interactive sessions and workshops with successful entrepreneurs from outside as well as with in the State.

SPINNING SUCCESS STORIES IN ENTREPRENEURSHIP

Entrepreneurial initiatives of the youth often fail to take off owing to lack of financial support and proper infrastructure. Sometimes they may collapse midway owing to lack of proper technical guidance. It is in this contest that the Technology Business Incubator (TBI) at the National Institute of Technology, Calicut(NITC) assumes significance. TBIs have been successfully implemented throughout the world. It stimulates the growth of technology based enterprises with the help of technical manpower and infrastructure available at educational and research institutions. The Dept of Science and Technology has helped the NITC, along with 13 other institutions in the country, to set up its own TBI. The TBI-NITC was established at a cost of Rs. 2.5 crores. The Dept of Science and Technology has sanctioned Rs. 1.55 crores for equipment and recurring cost for five years. The rest of the investment comes in the form of land, building and other infrastructure faculties provided by the NITC. The most remarkable advantage is the NIT's brand name. Besides, there would be effective networking with national and international technical institutions and incubators. Once a proposal is submitted, the advisory committee goes through it. They would ask for a business plan once they think that the idea is viable and could be supported by the TBI. They would enter into an agreement.

STRATEGIES FOR THE PROMOTION OF TECHNICAL ENTREPRENEURSHIP IN KERALA

To the State of Kerala and the institutions in the higher education, globalization of higher education poses both a challenge as well as an opportunity. It is true that unless pro-active defense measures are adopted, we may get swamped by the competition from international players. The irreversible globalization will offer immense opportunity for the State in promoting itself to a huge community of students and thereby take advantage. It is imperative to effect a transition in our infrastructure, institutions and administrative and regulatory mechanisms aimed at delivering quality. This repositioning is an attempt at a revolution to modernize the higher education sector to take on the world[5]. The Industrial Policy (2007) of the CPM-led LDF Government wants to improve investment climate through investment protection, decentralization, facilitation and by creation of more growth opportunities, profit-linked incentive schemes, induction of professionals, public-private partnership, joint ventures, special package of fiscal benefits, steps to attract foreign direct investment, special economic zones, industrial townships, a new company to acquire land, and conversion of the state into a world class commercial hub for retail and wholesale services. The Government intention for a paradigm shift from an entrepreneurs supply side to creating entrepreneurs demand side is clear[6]. The technical educational system of our State has remained education oriented emphasizing acquisition of knowledge while underplaying skills and performance. Though there are few exceptions but in most of the cases the technical education has not been relevant to the needs of neither industry nor it has produced individuals who are competent and confident to find out their own ways of fruitful earning rather than depending on wage-employment. Therefore grooming first generation techno-entrepreneurs should be the first priority of our technical educational institutions.

The technological entrepreneurship can be promoted by developing organizational mechanisms, which promote technology trade between small firms. The strategy of industrialization should motivate technically qualified entrepreneurs to take up role of innovators leading to new product development which enhances the competitive position of the State. The component of entrepreneurship development in technical institution can be incorporated by evolving a systematic and integrated approach encompassing following key activities:

SELECTION OF TECHNICAL INSTITUTIONS

State Director of Technical Education in consultation with Technical Teachers' Training Institute and other agencies like KIED, CMD, DICs can identify suitable technical institutions for introducing the EDP. The following criteria for selection are suggested (a) institutions selected should have or be capable of developing good rapport with industries, professional bodies, support agencies and government departments; (b) Institutions selected should be preferably in the vicinity of industrial and commercial activity centers.; (c) The management of the institute should be willing to support these programmes wholeheartedly; Institute should have infrastructure facilities viz, class room, library and learning resources centre.

SETTING UP A SEPARATE DEPARTMENT

The State Directorate of Technical Education can create a separate department to be called "Dept of Entrepreneurship and Management Development".

DIRECTORY OF RESOURCE PERSONS

The centre should prepare a directory of well known resource persons in the field of entrepreneurship and management who can be invited for delivering expert lectures and interaction with students.

SELECTION AND TRAINING OF FACILITY

The Entrepreneurship Training Courses need highly motivated, competent and committed trainer-motivators. The training of trainer-motivators is essential for the success of these programmes.

DEVELOPMENT OF LIBRARY FACILITIES

The technical institutions library should be suitably strengthened by adding books, journals, periodicals, handbooks and directories, films and other teaching and training aids in the field of entrepreneurship development. The library may also procure literature from the support agencies.

PREPARATION OF INSTRUCTIONAL MATERIALS.

For effective implementation of these programmes, it is essential that suitable instructional material be developed. The Kerala Institute for Entrepreneurship Development (KIED) may collaborate with EDII and other resource system for this work.

ESTABLISHMENT OF SCIENCE AND TECHNOLOGICAL PARKS (STEP)

The establishment of STEP in and around academic institution of excellence as an institutional mechanism for fostering interaction among academic and R& D institutions on one hand and industry on the other and also to serve as a launching pad enabling fresh graduates belonging to the S&T stream to start their own enterprises. NITC and CUSAT can be selected as host institution for establishing STEPS like IIT Kharagpur-STEP or NIT Trichi-STEP. Thrust areas electronics, software development, information technology, food technology, rubber technology, chemicals, textiles low-cost housing, multimedia and solar power technology, mechanical and survey instruments, engineering design and environmental engineering.

NOTES AND REFERENCES

1. Naik, B. M. (1998), New Vistas in Technical Education, Vivek Publications, Aurangabad.
2. G. Vijaya Raghavan and V. S. M. Nair (2007), The Great Indian Boom-the Renaissance of Manufacturing, Manorama Year Book, Kottayam.
3. Kerala Institute for Entrepreneurship Development, Cochin.
4. *Economic Review* 2006, State Planning Board, GOK, Trivandrum
5. Kerala Calling, February, 2006, Dept. of Public Relations, GOK, Trivandrum.
6. *The New Indian Express*, Kochi, 11-1-2007.

Harikumar S & Remadevi T

10 Higher Education System in Kerala An Overview

The equilibrium values of the economic system, that is the value for which unemployment is zero can be obtained only if the education sytem grows at a rhythm determined by the economy or if the economy grows at the rhythm determined by the output of the educational system (Correa 1967) While education in all its forms is a vital component for the development of human resources, it is mostly higher education which contributes to the quality of life of the people through the country's economic development. It has been recognized as a 'crucial factor for survival' in the National Policy on Education (1986).

The significance of education as a source of new knowledge, research contribution and man power for all sections of the economy need not be overemphasized. The relevance and importance of higher education has increased several fold with the realization that in the world order based on science and technology it is the quality of higher education that decides the country's pace of social development. In this context it is highly imperative that higher and technical education should be made more purposeful absorbing socioeconomic and political changes and aspirations.

The higher education system in Kerala has an extensive reach and around 10 per cent of those who enter primary school enroll for degree courses of various kinds. The total number of students entering higher education every year is around 100,000 which accounts for about 15 per cent of the relevant age group (Kerala Education Commission, 1999). Despite the extensive coverage and rapid expansion of the system of higher education in Kerala, it is stagnant in the face of global challenges. The Kerala higher education has many problems-both quantitative and qualitative. Quantitatively higher education poses a serious problem of mismatch between supply of and demand for graduates. Qualitatively the standard of higher education is not up to the mark and is gradually declining. The system in recent years does not indicate any healthy sign of expected changes that are envisaged by educational planners and policy makers. The purpose of education is best served when the persons coming out of the institutions find successful areas of employment. But the alarming increase in the number of job seekers with higher qualifications every year indicates the defects in educational planning. There is greater irrelevance of the educational system to the productive sectors of the economy and to the changing conditions in the labour market. The failure to modernize and diversify our system of education comes at a time when the state's economy is getting integrated with the global economy which is becoming increasingly knowledge-driven.

Regarding technical education it is experienced that the demand for courses maintains no relation to the manpower needs of the economy. This has compelled many persons to reveal that though Kerala made impressive progress in literacy and elementary education it has largely neglected higher education and Kerala compares very poorly with respect to several indicators of development of higher education. The system is the victim of some acute ailments such as oversupply of unemployable graduates and post graduates, heavy subsidization, proliferation of substandard institutions, out dated curriculum, disparity in the quality of education, lack of linkage with the labour market etc. Therefore the present paper considers it relevant and imperative to analyse the defects in the education system which contributes towards disequilibrium in the job market and to draw out some remedies in order to improve the linkage between education and the job market for the educated.

The most intractable of the socio economic problems confronting our society is the ever escalating number of graduates and post graduates coming out of general higher education sector. Its chronic character and rising trend with the successive plans is baffling the policy makers. The post independence period witnessed a linear expansion of education in Kerala, both in regard to the number of institutions and enrolment, disregarding the needs of the economy and the dynamic changes around the world. Development of higher education in the state which was in a slow pace till late fifties gathered momentum during the sixties. In the sixties while the enrolment in schools registered an increase of 60 per cent the increase in enrolment for university education was 128 per cent (Manpower studies 1978). The number of arts and science colleges has gone up from 28 in 1956-57 to 186 in 1999. This explains that higher education has expanded without any purpose just as a result of the pressure of expansion in elementary and secondary education and has not brought about the desired socio economic development. The expansion of the educational sector along with sluggish growth of employment opportunities has resulted in severe distortions in the market for educated labour.

The data given above explain that there has been an expansion of institutions in favour of general education. There are 186 Arts and Science colleges accounting for 71.5 per cent. Apart from this there are about 25 unaided institutions imparting general education in the state. This has been the principal cause for a relative over supply of Arts and Science graduates. The growth of arts and science colleges was phenomenal during the third plan period. It is astonishing that about 53 colleges were started during this period. The trend in the growth of arts and science colleges after independence will explain the phenomenon of expansion of education without catering to the needs of economy. The data reveal that the foremost problem facing higher education of the general type is the unabated expansion of higher education both in terms of enrolment and institutions. Also the organizational structure of education is responsible for oversupply of students in higher education.

Table 1
Growth in Higher Educational Institutions in Kerala (General and Technical)

Year	*Univerities*	*General*	*Engineering*
1970-71	4	86	6
1980-81	4	126	6
1990-91	6	133	7
1995-96	7	173	8
1998-99	7	186	25
1999-2000	9	186	32

Source: Selected education statistics 1999 Ministry of Human Resource Development.

Table 2
Growth of Arts and Science Colleges in Kerala

	No. of colleges opened		
Period	*Private*	*General*	*All*
Prior to 1900	2	6	8
1990-1947	11	3	14
1948-1968	89	4	93
1969-1992	31	23	54
1992-2000	15	2	17

Source: 1. E.T. Mathew- Financing of higher education -Sources and uses of funds for Private colleges in India 1991. New Delhi.
2. Economic Review- State Planning Board-various years.

An analysis of the number of higher educational institutions per one million population will also explain the bias in favour of arts and science education. While the institutions of general education accounts for 5.69 it is only 0 .76 regarding engineering colleges, 0.64 in the case of medical colleges and only 0.58 with respect to teacher education centres.

Table 3
No. of Higher Educational Institutions per one million Population

Year	*Universities*	*General*	*Engineering*	*Medical*	*Teacher*	*Total*
1970-71	0.187	4.029	0.281	0.187	0.890	5.575
1980-81	0.157	4.950	0.236	0.157	0.746	0.247
1990-91	0.206	4.571	0.241	0.172	0.653	5.842
1995-96	0.258	5.587	0.258	0.388	0.614	7.105
1998-99	0.276	5.696	0.766	0.643	0.582	7.962

Source: J.B.G. Tilak-Higher Education and Economic Development in India-State Level; Workshop on Higher Education, Kochi, 15th Oct., 2000.

A paradox of higher education in the state is that even though the extent of unemployment among the educated is more among those coming out of institutions of higher education of a general type, the demand for establishing more and more of such institutions is increasing year after year. The paucity of job opportunities at the middle and sub professional levels lead people to pursue education in the expectation that higher levels of education will help them to gain job opportunities. The progress of enrolment of students in Arts and science colleges for different courses in Kerala will be a clear explanation to the gravity of the problem of growing disjuncture between the production of education sector and the pattern of growth of the economy. Scores of economists consider that the time has come to end general purpose education and want the system to be replaced by restructured curricula. The index of growth of enrolment in arts and science colleges during 1956-2000 is shown in Table 4 . It explains steady increase in enrolments.

On the strength of suggestions made by the Education Commission the Govt. started sanctioning private registration for Pre-degree and Degree examinations in 1971. Private registration has its own hand increasing the number of the educated. This has led to the mushrooming growth of parallel colleges in the state. Now Kerala has a unique system of parallel colleges which are only teaching shops floated by private enterprises run more by commercial considerations than by educational reasons. (Oommen-1999). These institutions produce cheap quality graduates adding to the problem of educated unemployment in the state. In the sixties while the enrolment in schools registered an increase of 44per cent the increase in the enrolment for university education was 268 per cent. (Manpower studies Vol. 2, 1978).

The data regarding private registration in the universities of Kerala from 1971 to 1997 as shown in Table 5 will clarify the intensity of the problem.

The index of growth of private registration shows a sharp increase during the period 1971-91. During 1996-97 the index registers a slight decline. The steadily escalating private

Table 4
Index of Growth of Enrolments in Arts and Science Colleges (1956-2000)

Year	*Enrolment*	*Index*
1956-57	22254	100
1961-62	41739	188
1965-66	102841	462
1971-72	153437	689
1976-77	175915	790
1981-82	267639	1203
1986-87	312792	1406
1991-92	369636	1406
1995-96	348804	1567
1999-2000	328652	1477

Source: 1. Selected Educational Statistics–1999. Ministry of Human Resource Development, Govt. of India.
2. Economic Review 2000 (Government of Kerala).

registration contributed towards an over supply of arts and science graduates

The phenomenon of over expansion has resulted in considerable devaluation of education in the state. The greater the devaluation of education greater is the demand to have degrees since degrees serve as a credential mechanism. (Arrow 1973., Spence 1973). The expansion of education has necessarily raised the minimum entry qualification for a number of jobs. The expansion of education therefore does not reflect the desire of the students to learn or educate themselves but merely to seek certification for jobs. Correspondingly, the higher education institutions are performing the task of baby-sitting. The students want an up gradation of credentials because educational levels previously considered sufficient are becoming inadequate for placement. Thus the more university graduates are available the more jobs are upgraded so as to require a university degree. (Blaug. *et. al.* 1967). The tendency to raise the minimum educational requirements for jobs as the available labour force becomes highly educated is some times cited as evidence of conspicuous consumption of educated manpower for reasons of prestige. This is the consequence of a general demand for education as consumption good. (Blaug *et. al* 1967). So it follows that to some extent higher studies can be considered as disguised unemployment. A person may go in for higher studies because he cannot get a job. This leads to inflation of qualification.

Table 5
Growth of Private Registration in the universities of Kerala (1971-1997)

Year	*Pre-degree*	*Degree*	*Post graduate*	*Total*	*Index*
1971	4342 (66.8)	2171 (33.4)	–	6503 (100)	100
1976	22140 (70.3)	6156 (19.6)	3172 (10.1)	31648 (100)	483
1986	66042 (65.4)	21870 (25.5)	7826 (9.1)	85738 (100)	1318.4
1991	119205 (66.6)	46087 (25.8)	13614 (7.6)	178906 (100)	2751.1
1996	94785 (62.9)	44201 (29.3)	11751 (7.8)	150737 (7.8)	2318
1997	85313 (58.6)	45966 (31.6)	14278 (9.8)	14557 (100)	2238.3

Source: Government of Kerala, Economic review (various years)
Figures in parenthesis express percentages.

It has been observed that the expansion in higher education sector is in conformity to national levels. (JBG. Tilak, 2000) Leading educational planners in India have long felt that a restricted expansion of higher levels of the educational system was desirable. The Secondary education Commission(1953) admitted that the expansion in secondary and higher education had never been kept under control and it suggested that it would be necessary in the future to restrict the unplanned and uncontrolled expansion of general secondary and higher education by a policy of selective admissions.

Regarding technical education also there has been tremendous expansion during the last three years. Till the end of the seventh five-year plan there were 8 engineering colleges. By the end of the seventh five year plan it rose to 15 colleges and between 1997 and 2000 the number of engineering colleges have more than doubled and at present there are 32 engineering colleges which includes government, private aided and self financing institutions. Now its strength has gone up to 84 by the end of 2006. In spite of such a miraculous expansion most of the students seek admission outside Kerala after paying hefty capitation fee. In 1988 it was reported that there were 161 private engineering colleges in the country that charge high tuition fees or capitation fee. (Shatrugna 1988). The so called capitation fee colleges charge huge donations and capitation fee and abnormal level of fees. Capitation fee in the colleges presently amount to 1.4 million per student. There cannot be any second opinion on the capitation fee in India that form more than 100 times the fee in Government colleges (Tilak, 1996). The ever-increasing demand for engineering education, even though the employment opportunities within the state are limited has led to grave disequilibrium in the job market for engineering graduates. While the rapid growth of high school and college education reflects an achievement of the state it has become a major challenge because the work opportunities of the type that they seek have certainly not expanded at the same fast pace. So in general it is seen that such blind shot approaches to education on the part of the participants and a readiness of the authorities in keeping an open door at heavily subsidized rates have transformed the universities.

HEAVY SUBSIDISATION

University education in Kerala is subsidized to a considerable extent. On account of subsidization by the government, higher education-both general and technical has become cheap in these days. Meanwhile the contribution of fees in meeting the institutional cost of higher education is only marginal and is declining. The highly subsidised fees and the cross-subsidised transport fares together with the proximity of educational institutions have certainly enhanced the access to education which has contributed to an expansion in the supply of the educated.

A tuition fee in Kerala is fixed at low levels and is kept unaltered for long periods. At the same time the cost per pupil on education has not fallen. It is ironical to note that even at Kinder garten some unaided schools charge a tuition fee which is higher than at collegiate levels. (Mathew, 1997). The present pattern of uniform fees for all students and the present levels of indiscriminate subsidization have contributed to an inappropriation of benefits of higher education leading to a worsening of income distribution (Tilak 1994) Table 6 shows the share of fees in meeting the expenditure on higher education from 1984 to 89.

Table 6
Fees as Percentage of Expenditure on Education

Year	*Amount collected as tuition fees*	*Expenditure in Rs.(Lakhs)*	*Percentage of fees to expenditure*
1984-85	384.85	3760.46	10.23
1985-86	455.97	3966.46	11.50
1986-87	417.56	5119.22	8.16
1987-88	485.00	5814.03	8.34
1988-89	532.89	7329.77	8.42

Source: Report of the Task force on Higher Education VII Plan, Govt. of Kerala Planning Board.

The share of fees in the expenditure on education is a negligible minimum and has decreased over the years. During 1985-86 the percentage of fees to expenditure was 11.5% and it declined to 8.42 in 1988-89. The Task force on education (1990-95) calculated that the tuition fees collected in Kerala in different years from 1984-1985 to 1988-1989 met only a nominal share of expenditure on higher education on the part of the Government. Therefore the Taskforce suggested that as a first step fees for professional courses may be raised to a level comparable to the fee structure in other parts of India. While the revenue expenditure on education in 1989-90 was 623.6 crores the receipt from the sector was only Rs. 18.01 crores, hardly 2.9 per cent of the expenditure on education (Oommen 1994). The High Level Committee on Education and Employment appointed by the Government of Kerala in 1982 admitted that the incredibly low levels of fees was responsible for swelling the number of admission seekers for college courses. (High level committee report 1982).

In order to analyse the trend of government subsidization the institutional cost and fee receipt of the institutions for the period 1976-90 may be considered. The data tell us that during 1976-90 the proportion of fee to institutional cost per student in the engineering colleges declined from 4.5 per cent to 4 per cent

THE COST OF HIGHER EDUCATION IN INDIA

Fee receipts show a declining trend over the years. The government is replacing or substituting the declining fee contribution from its resources with the result that the whole system is being turned into almost a government financed one with all its attendant adverse consequences. (Abdul Salim, 1997) Table 7 indicates that during 1976-'90 the proportion of fee to institutional cost per student in the engineering colleges declined from 4.5 per cent to 4. In the case of general education the share of fees to institutional cost came down from 11.5 per cent to 4.5 per cent during the same period.

Table 7
Total (Gross) Institutional Cost and Fee Receipt per Student (1976-77 to 1989-90)

(in Rupees)

	Technical Education			*General Education*			*Combined*		
Year	*Cost*	*Fee*	*%of Fee to Cost*	*Cost*	*Fee*	*%of Fee to Cost*	*Cost*	*Fee*	*% of Fee to Cost*
1976-77	16480	735	4.5	5098	588	11.5	8294	630	7.6
1977-78	16555	714	4.3	4958	549	11.1	8285	595	7.2
1978-79	16945	765	4.5	5836	566	9.7	9123	624	6.8
1979-80	16687	790	4.7	6023	449	7.4	9218	548	5.9
1980-81	13448	685	5.1	5398	326	6.0	8087	486	6.0
1981-82	11600	747	6.4	4783	303	6.3	7085	453	6.4
1982-83	10356	684	6.6	4978	288	5.8	6680	436	6.5
1983-84	9958	656	6.6	4871	275	5.6	6950	428	6.1
1984-85	10220	663	6.5	4886	265	5.4	7208	425	5.4
1985-86	11262	669	5.9	4832	235	4.9	7377	407	5.5
1986-87	12706	551	4.3	4565	219	4.8	7939	349	4.4
1987-88	12106	526	4.3	4347	215	4.9	7735	338	4.4
1988-89	10879	457	4.2	4255	218	5.1	7324	285	3.9
1989-90	11231	449	4.0	4425	200	4.5	7751	300	4.0

Source: A. Abdul Salim (1997).

The extent of subsidization on general education at different levels is shown in Table 8. A comparison between gross and net private cost of higher education shows that the extent of subsidization is greater in private colleges.

The extent of subsidization for university education is so wide that the private rates of return far exceed the corresponding social rates. The private rate of return measures the relationship between cost and benefits of education for individuals and social rate of return measures the relationship between all social costs of education, that must be borne by the society as a whole and the benefits that are expected to accrue to the society. Heavy subsidies to education can lead to favourable private signals despite unfavorable social signals (Blaug 1973).

Table 8
Gross and Net Private Cost of Higher Education in Kerala (Per Pupil) (in Rupees)

Level of Education	*Academic*	*Incidental*	*Total (gross)*	*Net*	*Extent of Subsidisation*
Govt.	1784	2323	4107	3802	305
Colleges	1456	2554	4010	3848	162
Degree Post	1671	2404	4075	3822	253
Graduates					
Total					
Private	2037	3203	5240	5021	214
Colleges	1570	2733	4303	4141	162
Degree Post	1888	3035	4923	4728	195
Graduates					
Total					
All Colleges	2021	2948	4969	4750	219
Degree Post	1478	2644	4122	3954	168
Graduates	1813	2832	4645	4445	200
Total					

Source: Computed from J B G Tilak (2000)
Note: Academic cost Includes Admission fee in Colleges, Private Tuition, Study tours etc.
Incidental Cost: is the net of Subsidies Received by Students.
The extent of Subsidization: is Gross Private Cost Minus net Private Cost.

A Comparison between the cost per pupil in general and technical education categories in Kerala will prove that the cost is higher with respect to technical education Table 9 shows that annual net cost of education per student in technical education at the degree level is 4.2 times greater than that of general education.

Subsidisation is greater in technical education and in the case of Kerala; experience suggests that the more expensive the type of education, the larger is the subsidy by the govt. (A Salim, 1997) Table 10 brings out the fact that as compared to general education subsidization is greater in technical education in Kerala. Technical education, especially at PG level is heavily subsidized in Kerala. The fact that technical education generates prospects of large private benefits later far outweighing the social benefits causes concern over the present subsidisation policy. The extent of subsidisation is so wide that the private benefits far outweigh the social benefits (A. Salim, 1997).

Table 9
Annual Net Cost of Education per student

Levels	*Technical Education*	*General Education*	*Combined*	*Multiples of Technical Education to General Education*
Degree	9254	2189	5785	4.2
P G	9716	4805	6642	2.0
Combined	9288	2607	5898	3.6

Source: (Salim,1997) The cost of Higher Education in India.

Table 10
Gross and Net Private Cost by Levels of Education (per student)

(in Rupees)

Category	*Academic*	*Incidental*	*Total*	*Subsidy*	*Net*
		Technical Education			
Degree	3025 (52.4)	2742 (47.6) c	5767 (100)	372 (6.45)	5395
PG	2420 (44.5)	2922 (55.5)	5342 (100)	5331 (99.7)	11
Combined	2837 (50.3)	2803 (49.7)	5640 (100)	1903	3737
		General Education			
Degree	2021 (40.7)	2948 (59.3)	4969 (100)	219 (4.4)	4750
PG	1478 (35.8)	2644 (64.2)	4122 (100)	168 (4.07)	3954
Combined	1813 (39.0)	2832 (61.0)	4645 (100)	200 (4.3)	4445

Source: A. Salim, 1997.

The New Economic Policy of 1986 talked of bringing the fee structure closely to the costs of education particularly professional education. The committee held the view that in the case of Indian Institutes of Management revision of fees has taken place and that approach can be expanded to medical colleges, engineering colleges and to other disciplines gradually. The Punnayya Committee Report (1992) recommended for a revision of all tuition fees so as to take care of at least half of the cost per student. While trying to understand what ails the financial aspects of higher education, the committee observed that whereas in the early

1950's, 15-20 per cent of the total expenditure was met from fees, now it has dwindled to 2-3 per cent.

EXPENDITURE ON HIGHER EDUCATION

Spiraling enrolments in higher education have been accompanied by proliferating costs. For the economy of Kerala with a weak resource base, the ever growing expenditure on education remains a knotty problem. Also the experience of Kerala shows that rational calculations have not played a role in the allocation of funds for education as a whole and the distribution among different types and levels of education (Salim, 1997). Within the education sector higher education did not get adequate attention. The state's spending on higher education forms only 14 per cent of the total expenditure on education. Considering near total school enrolment this allocation to higher education is inadequate. Table 11 gives an analysis of the government expenditure on education at various levels.

Table 11
Government Expenditure on Edcation at Various Levels

Stage	*92-93*	*93-94*	*94-95*	*95-96*	*96-97*	*97-98*	*98-99*	*99-00*
Primary	591.12	530.46	660.87	675.10	753.40	817.98	905.30	1234.8
Secondary	273.41	339.10	406.83	451.94	510.70	542.15	602.47	764.5
University and Higher Education	156.62	214.82	212.80	227.02	256.60	286.62	310.63	340.32
Adult Education	0.43	1.60	1.03	0.60	0.63	0.69	5.68	0.50
Language Develop-ment	4.13	4.86	5.40	5.38	7.59	9.05	10.06	15.32
Technical Education	32.61	59.25	62.23	68.53	78.07	90.85	94.75	125.45
Total	1058.32	1150.09	1349.16	1428.57	1606.99	1747.34	1928.89	2480.94

Source: Economic Review 2000 Government of Kerala.

It is proved from the table that expenditure on higher and technical education is low when compared to elementary and secondary education. The expenditure on higher education in 1999-2000 was only 13. per cent of the total expenditure on education. In regard to technical education it was 5.05 per cent Elementary and secondary education accounted for nearly 50per cent and 31 per cent respectively. An analysis of budget expenditure on higher education between 1980-81 and 1996-97 (Table 12) shows that the real growth in public expenditure on higher education in the state was 7 per cent as against 6.8 per cent in the country as a whole.

Table 12
Budget Expenditure on Higher Education

(Crores of Rs)

Year	*Current Prices*		*Constant Prices*	
	Kerala	*All India*	*Kerala*	*All India*
1980-81	22.4	384.9	22.4	384.9
1990-91	93.1	1836.4	40.2	818.9
1991-92	123.0	1948.2	43.7	756.3
1992-93	154.4	2699.9	51.7	967.2
1993-94	208.0	3103.7	67.4	1008.1
1994-95	209.3	2525.3	59.8	1037.6
1995-96	253.6	3871.3	69.0	1054.2
1996-97	252.6	4287.9	65.8	1099.3
1997-98	304.9	6771.2	–	–

Source: J.B.G. Tilak (2000) State Level Workshop on Education.

Growth Rate %
1980-81 to 1996-97

Current Prices		*Constant Prices*	
Kerala	*India*	*Kerala*	*India*
16.34	16.26	6.96	6.78

1990-91to 1996-97

Current Prices		*Constant Prices*	
Kerala	*India*	*Kerala*	*India*
18.09	15.18	8.55	5.03

The analysis of budget expenditure on education on various levels of education in Kerala shows that the increase in the share is nominal and it is not in conformity to the increase in enrolments. Table 13 explains that the expenditure on higher education showed a minimum increase while expenditure on technical education remained more or less the same from 1985-86 to 1995-96.

Table 13
The Percentage Share of Education in the Budget at different Levels from 1980-81 to 1995-96

Year	*Elementary Education*	*Secondary Education*	*University and Higher Education*	*Technical Education*
1980-81	54.2	28.8	10.8	4.2
1985-86	52.0	29.3	13.0	4.7
1990-91	50.0	29.4	13.6	4.7
1995-96	48.6	30.2	15.5	4.7

Source: Computed from the data in Analysis of Budgeted expenditure on Education (Various years) Ministry of Human Resources Development, New Delhi.

The neglect of higher education and technical education can be verified by a careful perusal of the share of NSDP spent on all the four levels. Table 14 compares the share of NSDP spent on elementary, secondary, higher and technical education.

Table 14
The Percentage Share of NSDP Spent on Different Levels on Education in Kerala

Year	*Elementary Education*	*Secondary Education*	*University and Higher Education*	*Technical Education*
1980-81	3.1	1.6	0.6	0.2
1985-86	3.3	1.9	0.8	0.3
1990-91	3.2	1.8	0.8	0.3
1995-96	3.2	2.0	1.0	0.3

Source: Computed from the data in the Estimates of State Domestic Product. (Various years) and Analysis of Budgetary Expenditure on education (Various years) Ministry of Human Resources Development, New Delhi.

This analysis clarifies the neglect of higher and technical education in the educational scene of Kerala. The expenditure per student in Kerala's higher education was the second lowest among the major Indian States in the period 1985-86 to

1991-92. Table 15 gives an estimate of the rate of growth of expenditure per student in different states. With regard to per student expenditure on education Kerala ranks the lowest among the other Indian States. During 1975-85 the rate of growth was 3.2 per cent while it decreased to 1.1 per cent during 1986-92.

Table 15
The Rate of Growth in Real Per Capita Expenditure on Education

State	*1974-75 to 1984-85*	*1985-86 to 1991-92*
Andhra Pradesh	7.3	3.0
Assam	6.3	2.8
Bihar	9.1	7.9
Gujarat	5.8	3.8
Haryana	5.8	4.2
Karnataka	5.7	4.6
Kerala	3.2	1.1
Madhya Pradesh	4.1	6.6
Maharashtra	5.4	5.1
Orissa	4.3	5.8
Punjab	5.2	7.1
Rajasthan	5.1	7.1
Tamil Nadu	5.6	6.1
Uttar Pradesh	4.5	8.3
West Bengal	6.9	5.2

Source: K.K. George and N. Ajith Kumar (2000) What is wrong with Kerala's Education system?

Plan assistance to the higher education sector in Kerala has been very limited during the 90's. More than 90 per cent of the expenditure is covered by non plan expenditure and as a result developmental programmes in the institutions suffered much. Table 16 illustrates the division of educational expenditure between plan and non plan expenditure. The foremost reason for the deterioration in the quality of higher education is the lack of capital investment in this sector. Salaries and pensions account for about 90 per cent of the total expenditure, leaving very little for other academic inputs. As Table 16 indicates, the share of plan expenditure in 1993-94 was only 3.76 per cent as against the national average of 11.4 per cent. None of the Finance Commissions had taken note of qualitative dimensions of Kerala's educational development. With regard to the grants for up gradation of educational services the 8th and 9th Finance Commissions did not provide any grant to Kerala. The up gradation grants provided by the 10th Finance Commission for this sector formed just 0.7 per cent of the total up gradation grants. (George and Kumar, 2001).

Table 16
Plan and Non Plan Expenditure on Education (Percentage)

Year	*Plan*	*Non Plan*	*Total*
1990-91	3.70	96.30	100
1991-92	2.10	97.90	100
1992-93	3.47	96.53	100
1993-94	3.62	96.38	100
1994-95	6.20	93.80	100
1995-96	5.79	94.21	100
1996-97	6.00	94.00	100
1997-98	7.10	92.90	100
1998-99	7.53	92.47	100
1999-2000	N A	N A	100

Source: Analysis of Budget Expenditure on Education.

In terms of financing of education there are three sectors within the educational sector in the state namely the state sector, the aided private sector and the unaided private sector. The institution in the state sector are managed and fully financed by the government, the aided private sector receives grants-in-aid from the government and the unaided private sector does not receive any financial support from the government. In Kerala, higher education expanded through public funding and provision. The private sector did not contribute to the development of educational sector. (. Varghese, 2000) Also regarding physical capital the private sector is keen to pay for its use as well as acquisition. The cost of acquisition has been a public subsidy since the public sector is the source of funding for education. The education sector has not been generating adequate resources on its own. The cost recovery ratios in education in Kerala have always been lower than those of the other states (.K.K George, 2000) Most of the private institutions are 'pseudo private' and the government meets the entire salary and maintenance expenditure. At the same time they retain the rights of appointment of teachers and non teaching staff. The share of private management in the expenditure of colleges had gone down from the already low 2.5per cent in 1972-73 to 1.4 per cent in 1985-86. (K.K. George, 2000) The report of the Taskforce on Higher Education-VIII Five Year plan recommended the introduction of an educational cess for the mobilization of adequate resources for higher education.

The current patterns of expenditure indicate that in publicly funded education, expenditure on improving quality has been limited and has declined. The proportion devoted to higher education has declined from about 14 per cent at the beginning of the nineties while that for secondary education has increased. Real resources for higher education have thus declined in absolute terms which will undoubtedly have substantial effects on quality.

OUTDATED CURRICULUM-IRRELEVANCE TO THE NEEDS OF THE ECONOMY

There is greater wastage in all forms of education in South Asia, much of it is plain malediction-given modernisation and development as the goals, the wrong type of abilities and wrong attitudes are imparted or preserved (Myrdal,1968) This is a clear picture of the Kerala situation regarding higher education. The education system which feeds and serves the economy and constitutes one of its props is usually developed in such a way as to sub serve the needs of the economy. But in Kerala the majority of the courses offered are not relevant to contemporary or emerging needs. There is a mismatch between courses available and courses offered. They have not been designed to meet the growing complexity of various specialization or to facilitate mobility between courses. Further, they do not integrate practical experience with learning process and the course contents are not related to local, regional and national requirements (Kerala Education Commission, 1999).

Regarding the curriculum it can be stated that it is out dated and never adapted to the needs of the Kerala economy. Higher education is often pursued to qualify for employment and employment opportunities have changed significantly in recent years. The undue importance given to general education in Kerala proceeds on the assumption that academic pursuits are carried out for their own sake. The experiment to combine Vocational activity with academic pursuit as was stressed by the Education Commission did not hold good in state. The change in the employment front in the recent decades in favour of technically qualified persons has been widely recognized by the public. The colonial structure of the civil servant, lawyer and teacher has given way to the technical expert, the manager and the executive. (Kerala Education Commission, 1999)

In the absence of planning the state is unable to tackle the major problem of mismatch between the courses available and the courses offered. The courses are not reoriented taking in to account either the developments in the disciplines or the changes in the job market. There have been efforts towards updating of curricula and content. But by and large the system lacks flexibility. It is really unfortunate that the job oriented courses and technical courses already started in the state suffer from lack of employment opportunities within the state. Courses are often started without any reference to their academic relevance or needs of the society.

In technical education also the content of the curriculum is out of the times in the case of some traditional branches of study. Even though an all India pattern exist for undergraduate level in technical education, there is a lot of variation in the system of electives, the weightage for pure/applied science subjects and technical arts, the role assigned to humanities etc. (Kerala Education Commission,1999)) Many of the courses with good potential for employment are not available in Kerala. There is a conspicuous absence of any all India level institution like the IITs, Central Universities and National Research Institutions (George and Kumar 2000).

Technical education in Kerala has a very narrow base. The curriculum does not correspond to the societal needs and aspirations. The field of technology is growing exponentially with the passage of time. The procedure of formulation and revision or upgradation of courses are so elaborate and time consuming that they become obsolete by the time a batch of students complete the course (Kerala Education Commissiom,

1999) About engineering education it can be stated that the rigidity of the system is stifling all creativity and efforts for excellence. Today engineering education has become a second rate science course resembling an applied Physics course and completely devoid of its characteristic features and identity (L.S. Sreenath, 1993). The quality of technical education in the state is getting deteriorated with time. In the employment market some institutions like Govt. Engineering College, Thiruvananthaputam, Regional Engineering College, Kozhikode etc. command a prestigious position while some of the recently started institutions both in the private and public sectors occupy a sympathetic position (Oommen, 2000).

The most distressing malady afflicting Kerala higher education system is its failure to maintain quality. Many of the institutions do not have competent faculty and lack of minimum essential facilities like library, laboratory and the like. (Oommen,2000) To a large extent the deterioration in standards is contributed by the mushrooming growth of parallel colleges which are only tutorial colleges preparing students for university examinations. The inefficiency of the system is reflected in the high drop out rates both for general and technical education at different levels. Dropout rate at the degree level is estimated to be around 30 per cent by the 3rd year of the course. An analysis of the results of examinations conducted by the Kerala university during the five years from 1991-92 to 1995-96 shows the incompetence of the system. Table 17 gives the data regarding failure rates for different levels of education in the general education category during 1991-96.

Table 17
Failure Rates for Different Levels of Education (General) During 1991-96

Levels of Education	*Failure Rates*
PreDegree	60%
B.A.	38%
M.A.	38%
M.Com.	69%

Source: Report of the Kerala education commission, 1999.

The problem of high drop out rate is grave in technical education also. At the Degree level it is 30 per cent and at post graduate level 45 per cent (Kerala Education Commission,1999)

EDUCATION-JOB MARKET LINKAGE

The interface between education and job market is characterized by lack of complementarity. The actual state of affairs of the economy is that of a surplus emerging from educational output and shortages from manpower utilization. Jobs requiring general qualifications are not increasing at the same rate as the availability of manpower. But for many jobs requiring technical competence and manual skills, appropriately trained manpower is not available in sufficient numbers (Mathew E.T. 1997).

The occupational world has certain specific skill demands and people are not simply available to fill vacancies while the educational system is turning out graduates who do not have any skill at all. The content of the job does not require the kind of intellectual skills normally associated with high school or college education. While a rapid growth of high school and college education certainly reflects an achievement of Kerala it has also become a major challenge because the work opportunities of the type that they seek have certainly not exceeded at the same fast pace. The unmotivated, uninvolved student now becomes the unmotivated uninvolved clerk who responds to the formalistic requirement of his job rather than its substantive output goals (Laxmi Devi, 1998). The content of the job may not require the intellectual skill imparted through college education.

The delinking of education from the production sectors of the economy has contributed to the irrelevance of the system. The present system of education is catering to the needs of limited segments of white-collar jobs markets within the state and outside. This has led to a divorce of mental labour from physical labour and has nurtured an obsession with white collar jobs and a general reluctance to manual labour. So a major weakness of Kerala's education is its failure to inculcate rational attitude to labour in the people. In this sense it can be commented that Kerala's education is malediction. It is widely recognized that the demand for labour cannot always be created to suit the characteristics of labour supply. Shortages and surpluses are found to coexist in the labour market due to the mismatch between skill and other requirements of new employment opportunities and the attributes of the available workers.

The lack of proper planning is the main reason for the divergence between education and employment. One of the main reasons why some form of educational planning was adopted in many countries was the desire to achieve a better match between the different levels of education coming from the educational system and the needs and capacities of the job market. The gap between education and the job market is contributed by the slow response of the educational system to changes in the job market. Technology is an important intervening factor in deciding the skill-job linkages but in Kerala the technological development is at a faster rate and our educational system fails to respond to these changes. (Laxmi Devi, 1995). When there is careful and systematic educational planning a suitably trained person would be available for every job to be done and every educated person would find a job appropriate for his education and professional training (NCERT, 1970). But in Kerala the labour market is characterized by fixed relationships and rigidities in both educational and employment practices. A change in the educational system is necessary to allow for greater flexibility in meeting the changing demands of the labour market.

EDUCATIONAL-INDUSTRY LINKAGE

One of the ways of making higher and technical education more purposeful is to build up strong linkages between Universities, Industries and Research and Development (R&D) laboratories. The process of interaction will contribute towards excellence which in turn will contribute towards national development. Industrialization acts as an instrument both for creating capacity to absorb excess labour force and catering for diversification of the market which is required at higher stages of economic development. The need for higher education is based on the demand for the third level manpower which depends essentially on the industrial structure. The structure of labour demand shifts as industrial structure and technology change and then the so far successful educational regime may not be adequate to cope with the future demand structure.

In the earlier years after independence no conscious effort was made by our planners to encourage interaction between University departments catering to science and technology and industries with a view to involve them in our development activities.

(Sudha Rao, 1996). In the state, therefore the higher education sector and the industrial sector are working in isolation from each other. What is done in the university system is not of much relevance to industries. Almost all employers suggest that the graduates of the educational institutions in Kerala do not acquire such knowledge and skill as could be useful in the industrial environment. So unemployment in the state can be equated with unemployability of the educated. Also the industrial activities in the state are conducted in such a manner that the scope for the input of advanced skill and knowledge remains very restricted. The growth of industrial output creates demands only for those persons who have operative skills and not for the manpower possessing the type and form of knowledge provided in the conventional (general) academic institutions. Even if the industry employs the unskilled persons they have to spend some years in training the students so that they can meet their requirements (Sampath, 1994,). In industry Kerala education could have made a greater contribution. However, it did not; not so much due to the fault of education per se, but to the absence of other facilitating factors and environment (Nair, 2000).

The technical education institutions, by and large, function in isolation and the linkages and interaction between technical institutions and user agencies such as industry and Research and Development (R&D) Organizations are not sufficiently strong. The New (Educational policy (1986) has focused on striking proper relationship with the industrial sector so that the students may get in house training. Nothing much has been achieved in this direction. The basic limitation seems to be that the industry has no confidence in the Universities about their credentials. Industry prefers either to depend on its own research and development or to learn on foreign flow of technology. Compatibility between higher education policy and industrial development policy is crucial for techno economic and social well being of a nation. In Kerala because of the lack of a mechanism to make academic and industry mutually supportive, what is taught is not wanted (Naik, 2000) Realising this need, Maharashtra Government has created a new directorate of industry- institute partnership . Germany was the first country in the world to move towards capitalization of knowledge and accordingly it developed well adapted educational institutions and research establishments. U.K. has a unique scheme known as Teaching Company scheme. Under this scheme a scholar does innovation under the joint supervision of an expert from industry and another guide from the university. He is paid scholarship by the industry and the Government pays for equipments. (Naik, 2000)

In Kerala some interaction between university and industry is going on. A study conducted by Association of Indian Universities in seven Universities reveals that the seven universities had 116 interactions. In order to have close interaction between the two the curricula should take into consideration the needs and requirements of the industry. But it is said that barring a few isolated islands of excellence our performance in engineering science has not been up to the mark and unfortunately the interface between science and engineering research and engineering research and engineering industry has been rather poor (. Mashelkar, 1997). The interface is to be created between University-society, University-local Community and University-industry (G. Sreenivasan, 2000).

VOCATIONALISATION OF HIGHER EDUCATION

To make education employable in the industrial sector we have to provide the existing general liberal education with some kind of Vocational or technical education linked with it. Vocationalisation is a distinct stream intended to prepare students for identified occupations. For skill formation focus has to be on vocational education and training. The competitive gains enjoyed by Japan and West Germany has been attributed to their superior vocational training system. (National Commission on Excellence in Education, USA, 1983). The basic requirements of vocational courses is the assessment of the potential and the relevance of courses to the development of the economy. Vocational education is advocated as a cure for unemployment and for the mismatch between educational qualifications and job opportunities. It is stressed on the ground that education which helps to make workers more flexible and adaptable to new technologies is now considered a valuable way of contributing to manpower development just as much as education that prepares them for specific jobs (G. Pscharaplaulose and M. Woodhall, 1985). In Kerala the available evidence suggests that vocational education leads to more unemployment .The number of ITI trained jobseekers in Kerala has reached109408 in 2000 (Economic Review, 2000).

In order to develop professional growth and career advancement opportunities for the students vocationalisation at the degree level is an urgent necessity. Introduction of vocational courses at the degree level strongly comes from the fact that majority of the colleges have general arts, science and commerce courses which are liberal but not utilitarian.. In Kerala the Vocational courses started do not maintain a linkage with the labour market. Consequently there is a lack of social acceptability and the programmes are looked down upon by the society. In the mainstream education when both academic courses and vocational courses are offered, people opt for academic courses. The lack of opportunities for professional higher learning is the keynote of vocationalisation in Kerala. Vocational education works well where educational infra structure is well developed and students have real choices. The vocational courses started with 'little imagination and poor attracting power go against the purpose.(Challenge of Education,1986) This applies to vocationalisation at the degree level in Kerala. Since there are no avenues for further professional growth most of the students who pass out go in for further tertiary level education. So the purpose of vocationalisation itself is lost. In 1994-95 the UGC has launched 30 professional courses at the undergraduate level in about 180 colleges and 19 universities. Although the courses are open to general stream students also, it is expected to provide wider opportunities to vocational graduates. The acceptability of vocational courses is linked with the employability of graduates. The students of vocational courses can find employment if the recruitment rules of the government departments are amended to give preference to the students trained in specific skills. In Kerala the work is going on but our experiments to combine vocational activity with academic pursuits really did not take off as they were out of tune with the dominant middle class concerns of social advancement (K.K. George, 2000) There is a lack of linkage of the system with the industries and there is the non availability of accurate follow up information on vocational pass outs. The New Education Policy(1986) argued that vocationalisation failed in India because of cultural prejudices towards skill oriented education.

MANAGEMENT AND ADMINISTRATION

Problems seem more acute and difficult to remedy in areas of educational management. Rigidity persists in the system as a hurdle for its development and restructuring and its hallmark is red tapism. The keynote of the system of management of educational institutions in Kerala is its highly centralized and hierarchical nature. Every institution is made to lie on the procrustean bed prepared for them by the government and the universities (K.K. george, 2000). In the management of Government colleges there is a diarchy by the government and the university. In the case of private colleges another agency, viz, the management is involved. The existence of multiple layers of authority over the educational system has resulted in lack of accountability for the system. Non governmental agencies played a major role in the expansion of educational sector in Kerala. In 1984-85 , 69.3 per cent of the total number of educational institutions were owned by private agencies. Table 18 gives data regarding the management of colleges.

Table 18
University-Wise and Management-wise Number of Arts and Science Colleges in Kerala

Name of University	*1999* Govt.	Private (Aided)	Total	*2000* Govt.	Private (Aided)
Kerala	9	37	46	9	37
Calicut	16	44	60	16	44
Mahatma Gandhi	7	55	62	7	55
Sanskrit	–	–	–	–	–
Kannur	6	12	18	6	12
	38	148	186	38	148

Source: Economic Review 2000

Now a new breed of private agencies in the name of autonomous institutions- unaided and unregulated by the government have sprung up. In fields of technical education, management education, teacher education etc. a number of such institutions have been established. These institutions charge exorbitant rates of fees which cover not only the recurring cost but also capital cost. It appears that the pendulum has been swinging from one extreme of near total fee subsidy to the other extreme of zero subsidy, unheard of even in the most conservative capitalist countries (K.K. George and N. Ajithkumar, 2000) The self financing institutions are closely related to the 'market friendly' economic reforms started in 1991 with the tacit view that social needs are best reflected as market demands, and that the market will also set a price for meeting such demands. A large number of autonomous institutions sprang up in the field of professional and technical education because these institutions offer the best opportunity for profit oriented entrepreneurs. In the sphere of professional education equity and justice have suffered a retreat. Twenty two out of 34 engineering colleges belong to to the self financing category which offer mostly modern courses like computer, IT, electronics etc. For the modern courses 40 per cent of the seats are reserved for economically forward sections as against 24 per cent for socially and economically backward communities. Only 36 per cent is given on merit. Evidence suggests that 85 per cent of the merit seats are cornered by the affluent 15 per cent of the society. (Field study Report-CSES

1999, Kochi). The difference in the fees charged by regular institutions and autonomous institutions is astonishing.

Table 19
Fees Charged in Autonomous and Regular Institutions-A Comparison

Course	*Fee in regular Institutions (annual)*	*Fee in Autonomous Institutions (annual)*
Engineering	1200	12500
MBA	3000	40000
MCA	4000	15000

Source: Kerala Education Commission 1999

A study conducted by the Mahatma Gandhi University among 640 students of autonomous institutions found that they are forced to meet 100 per cent of the cost. The percentage of fee in the total academic cost of a regular engineering student was only 51 per cent while it was over 90 for a self financing engineering student. This proves the fact that the self financing colleges, even though an easy option to the financial crisis of the education sector, aggravates the entry barriers to higher and technical education. In Kerala the middle and high income groups constitute only 5 per cent of the population as against 14 per cent for the country (NCAER Survey 1996). Also since these institutions can attract talents from only 5 per cent of the households these institutions cannot develop as centres of excellence.

The already elite higher education especially in the professional sector has become super elitist with the introduction of self financing mode of funding. Besides this engineering education turned costly in relation to state's per capita income. The cost varies between 81 per cent in the case of day scholars in regular engineering colleges to 390 per cent in the category of self financing resident scholars (Hindu, Jan. 8, 2002). The socio-economic profile of engineering students shows that a large majority cannot afford to pay higher fees. It is anomalous that 60 per cent of the regular engineering students who pay only Rs. 1200/- as tuition fees are on a par with the self financing stream of students who pay Rs. 35000 along with a deposit of Rs. 1 lakh (*Hindu* Jan 2000).

COMMISSIONS AND COMMITTEES ON EDUCATION SINCE INDEPENDENCE

Our country has seen the appointment of a number of Commissions and Committees on education which have examined several issues on education to meet the emerging needs of the society. Our education is a clear case of a Niagra of reports and a Sahara of action. (I. Ramabrahman and Jhansi Rani 1996). The University Education Commission constituted in 1948 under Dr.Radhakrishnan suggested for improvement of the education system to suit the present and future requirements of the country. The commission noted that there was an urgent need of technicians and for such occupations and skill all over the country which will train a large and growing body of ambitions youth for employment as technicians in various existing industries.

The recommendations of the Radhakrishan Commission were reinforced by the Secondary Education Commission appointed in 1952 with Dr. L.S. Mudaliar as chairman. The Commission suggested the creation of an infrastructure that would procure the large technical manpower and recommended the setting up of technical schools, polytechnics, central technical institutions etc. To deal with all aspects of education and to advise government on the evolution of a national system of education for the country as a whole an Education Commission was appointed under the Chairmanship D.S. Kothari in 1964. Based on the recommendations of the Commission the National Policy on Education 1968 was formulated. After reviewing the development of education in India since independence the Commission came to the conclusion that Indian education needed a drastic reconstruction in order to meet the various problems facing the country. The Kothari Commission recognized the urgent need to transform education to endeavor to relate it to the life, needs and aspirations of the people (Education Commission, 1964). It emphasized the importance of Science education and wanted that work experience should be made an integral part of general education. Regarding vocationalisation of education the Commission recommended that at the lower secondary stage

20 per cent and at secondary stage 50 per cent of the students should be enrolled in vocational courses whereas for higher education 1/3 of the courses should be vocationalised. It observed rigidity and uniformity in the system and suggested change in curricula, teaching methods and training for teachers and administrators. The Kothari Commission considered over expansion of the higher education system as a serious problem and suggested that higher education should be expanded on a selective basis and the output of educational institutions should be broadly related to manpower needs or employment opportunities. The Commission stated that what is needed is a revolution in education which in turn will set in motion the much desired social, economic and cultural revolution For the effective control of education and educational institutions a major development was the constitutional amendment during the emergency to remove education from the state list and place it in the concurrent list in 1976.

The Draft National Policy on Education of 1979 suggested improvement of the quality of secondary education to be both a terminal for those who do not want or cannot proceed for further education and to have a strong academic foundation for higher studies for those who show intelligence and aptitude for that education. Though it recognized the importance of financial inputs it gave more importance to human intellectual contribution and suggested a review. The New Policy on Education (1986) contended that, what requires to be understood is the unfortunate fact that the attempt to evolve a new policy on education was in a sense foredoomed to failure because the exercise was sought to be carried out in isolation from the wider context of restructuring the economy (New Policy on Education, 1986).

The Kerala experience lead one to say that Commissions after commissions have laid base the maladies obtaining in our educational system, but nobody till date has propounded a new scheme to serve as a pattern for development. The present status of education reveals that though much was claimed by the policy makers about the educational development in the post independence period, all the basic problems which formed the main thrusts of the work of Education Commissions are still with us in a somewhat altered condition with some relief but many new dilemmas threatening the economy. Most of the recommendations which are based on an all India pattern prove irrelevant to the situation of Kerala. Because of the inability of the Kerala economy to grapple with those models most of the recommendations remained on paper.

In order to enquire into the problems facing the State's educational system and for suggesting the future policy the Kerala Education Commission was set up by the Shastra Sahitya Parishad in March 1996. The Commission, headed by Ashok Mitra studied the pathetic state of affairs of Kerala Educational scene. Unlike the earlier commissions which concentrated on rationality and management alone, the Kerala Education Commission Report draws on the premise of equity and excellence for the people of Kerala. The report suggested a decentralization of universities and it called for a revision of fees to cover both the maintenance and development expenditure. At the same time it called for increasing the number of scholarships to deserving students. The most important suggestion of the Commission is peoples' education which is an important component of the larger effort to create a humane society capable of realizing its economic cultural and intellectual potential (Kerala Education Commission, 1999).

The analysis of the nature of higher education system in Kerala explains its hold in creating a disequilibrum in the job market and fostering a malutilisation of human capital. Educational planning in Kerala cannot be effective without a restructuring of the educational system of the State. It will not only help to build upon what has already been achieved but also to sustain a high rate of growth of the economy.

REFRENCES

Correa. H. (1967), The Economics of Human Resources; North Holland Publishing Company, Amsterdam.

Ministry of Education (1985), National Policy on Education 1986. New Delhi

Kerala Sastra Sahithya Parishad (1999) Report of the Kerala Education Commission.

Govt. of Kerala, Planning Department (1978), Manpower Studies (Vol. II)

Arrow (1973), Higher Education as a Filter *Journal of Public Economics,* 2 (1973) North Holland; Publishing Company.

Spence, Michael (1973), Job Market Signaling, Quarterly Journal of Economics 1987 (August).

Blaug M. *et. al* (1967), A Cost Benefit Approach to Educational Planning in Developing Countries. World Bank Washington DC.

Blaug, Layard, PRG and Woodhall M. (1969), The Causes of Graduate Unemployment in India, Penguin Books, London.

Tilak, JBG (2000), State Level Workshop on Education, Cochin.

Shatrugna (1988), Privatising Higher Education, *Economic and Political Weekly* 23 (5)

Mathew, E. T. (1997), Employment and Unemployment in Kerala Some Neglected Aspects, Sage. Publications, New Delhi.

Oommen M. A. (1994), The Acute Unemployment Problem of Kerala; Some Explanatory Hypothesis in K. Ramachandran Nair (ed) Education, Employment and Development in India. Classic Publishers, New Delhi.

Report of the High Level Committee on Education and Employment. (1982), Govt. of Kerala.

Report of the Taskforce on Education (1995), Govt. of Kerala.

Abdul Salim A. (1997), The Cost of Higher Education in India. Anmol Publishers, New Delhi.

Blaug M. (1973), An Introduction to Economics of Education. Penguin, London.

Punnayya Committee Report (1992), Govt. of Kerala.

George K. K. and Ajith Kumar N. (2000), What is Wrong with Kerala's Education? CSES, Kochi.

Varghese N. V. (2000), National Conference on Education, 25th December, Thiruvananthapuram.

George K. K. (2000), Paper Presented at National Conference on Education. 25th December, Thiruvananthapuram.

The Report of the Taskforce on Education, Kerala. VIII Plan, Govt. of Kerala.

Myrdal, M. Gunnar (1968), *Asian Drama* Vol. II ,Penguin Books, London

Srinath L. S. (1993), Engineering-a Change, Indian Express April 18.

Oommen M. A. (2000), Paper presented at the National Conference on education December 25th, 2000, Thiruvananthapuram.

Dr. Mashelkar R. A. (1992), Engineering Science in India. Some Issues and Challenges. Current Science, Vol 63. Nos. 9, 10 and 25 Nov. 92.

Sreenivas G. (2000), University-Industry Linkage, *University News*, Vol. 38, Nov. 27.

National Commission on Excellence in Education, (2000), U. S. A.

NCERT (1970), Govt. of India.

Sudha Rao K. (1994), Vocationalisation of Higher Education in India-In Search of Quality, AIU. New Delhi.

Sampath (1994), TimesHigher Education Supplement. Oct., 14.

Gopinathan Nair P. R. (2000), National Conference on Education December, 25th 2000.

Naik B. M. (2000), Industry University Partnership-global Trends and Relevance for India. *University News*, Vol. 38 No. 17 April, 24.

Laxmidevi (1998), Encyclopedia of Educational Development and Planning Series, Laxmidevi (ed) Institute of Sustainable Development. Anmol Publishing Co. New Delhi.

Psacharapanlos and Woodhall (1985), Education for Development. An Analysis of Investment Choice Oxford University Press.

Planning Commission (1973), Report of the Working group on Engineering Manpower, Govt. of India.

CSES (1999), Field Study Report CSES, Kochin.

NCAER (1996), Survey on Technical Education, Govt. of India.

Hindu (2000), Poor Students Hit Hard by Self Financing Courses.

Brahmanandan I. and Jhansi Rani (1996), Regime Changes and Public Policy on Education. Productivity Oct, 96.

Report of the Education Ministry of Education, Commission (1964) Govt. of India. 1964.

Sabu Thomas

11 Administrative Structure and Admission Procedures in the Professional and Technical Institutions in Kerala

Technical Education in Kerala had a humble beginning with the starting of the first Engineering College at Thiruvananthapuram in 1939.The college took shape in the same year with a small batch of 21 students each for the degree and Diploma courses, under the then Travancore University. The college was located in the heart of the city amidst other prestigious establishments. The first Principal was Major T.H Mathewman, an Englishman. Due to the increase in demand of engineers and re-organisation of Technical Education in the State, the diploma courses were transferred to the polytechnics and the college widened the scope for degree courses in Civil, Electrical and Mechanical Engineering.

The Government of Kerala has established the Department of Technical Education (DTE) in 1957. Though the growth of technical institutions in Kerala was very slow compared to other states, the prime objective of constituting this department was to co-ordinate the technical education in the State in the matters of syllabi, standard of examination, prescribe norms for admission of students to degree, diploma and certificate programme and ensure their proper compliance etc. To co-ordinate and exercise the overall control on all technical education institutions in the state and their programmes and activities, the department established a staff structure (see annexure 1). Based on this structural set up, the department is controlling the professional and Technical educational institutions including the institutions having recognition of All India Council of Technical Education (AICTE). The Universities has a different set up in the administrative positions (see annexure 2). The aided and unaided institutions have their own administrative set up. But there is a slight difference in the administrative set up in the private unaided institutions (Annexure 3). The admission procedures in the technical and professional institutions in the state are governed by the rules and regulations formulated by the Government (Annexure 4). The Government and private aided institutions are following the rules and regulations of the Government. The state board of Technical education was constituted with the Hon. Minister for education as the chairman and six members both official and non-official. The board is an apex body to formulate the policy guidelines on all academic matters relating to Technical education in the State.

The self finance colleges in the State started in 2001.The system in the self finance colleges is quite different. After permitting self finance colleges in the state, there was anarchic situation in the state related to the admission matters in the self finance colleges.

ADMINISTRATIVE STRUCTURE IN THE EDUCATIONAL FIELD

Administrative Structure generally means the formation of hierarchic levels of posts of those who are supposed to administer the function of an organization with appropriate rights and authorities. The administrative structure in the educational field is also similar to this general approach.

According to the observation of Professor Iqbal Narain "Administration is an all pervasive concepts" educational administration being no exception, therefore, it covers in vertical terms the entire gamut of educational system from the School to University level. The observation of Professor Iqbal Narain is not always correct as the administrative structure in the educational system has many examples of line and staff relationships and the structures are formulated in such a way in the organization. The concept of line and staff is that they are a matter of relationships. A beautiful example of the line and staff relationship in the educational system is the structure of universities. In the universities there is a vertical relationship between line authorities, eg. the Vice Chancellor and the authorities below to him. In the staff side the function can be divided between academic side which controls the academic matters and advisory role is entrusted with the Syndicate, the Senate and the Academic Council. Also in the educational field other than universities, Line and Staff relationships exist. E.g. in the Professional and Technical Institutions there is a line function in each organization ie. Governing Council, Director and the People lower to them.

Due to the existence of line and staff relationships in the administrative set up in the educational field, the problems can be sorted out at each level. If any problem persists or could not be solved at the lower level, it can be taken to the appropriate level and the problems can be solved then and there. Even then we could not arrive at a conclusion that there are no issues in the admission matters. But comparing the problems in the admission matters the issues in the administrative areas are much less. Therefore, we may examine the problems relating to admission in the Professional and Technical Education in Kerala.

HISTORY OF ADMISSION TEST FOR PROFESSIONAL AND TECHNICAL EDUCATION IN KERALA

During 1981 there were some complaints about manipulation of marks scored by certain students who had passed Pre-Degree examination and got admission to MBBS course in the Kerala University. The University enquired about the complaints and found that it was genuine and the admission of those students was disqualified and the matter was reported to the State. The Government forwarded the complaints to the court and also decided to conduct State level common admission test for professional and technical education. In fact the mark scam in the State was the genesis of entrance test in Kerala. The admission test started in 1982 is continuing every year though the methodology got modified several times. There was not much problem about the admission test so far. Now the question of acceptance of entrance test by unaided (self finance) colleges arose and it is one of the live issues in the State.

PROBLEMS OF ADMISSION IN TECHNICAL EDUCATION IN KERALA

The technical and professional education in Kerala is presently facing umpteen numbers of problems particularly in the matter of admission of students. The admission system was strictly based on the percentage of marks of minimum educational qualification for each course. The admission was based on the criteria of 65 percentage for general candidates and 35 percentage for reserved candidates. The system was also followed in the government aided technical institutions. In 2001 the government of Kerala permitted self finance colleges including Technical and Professional colleges. There was a sudden spurt of new professional and Technical institutions, which are unaided. They were not willing to follow the existing policy of the Government relating to the matters of admission of students on the ground that the new institutions has no support from the Government other than permission to conduct the institutions within Kerala. To substantiate these rights, the management of self financing colleges in Kerala approached the courts several times citing the precedents of admission akin to other States in the country.

To overcome this extra ordinary judicial activism of the managers of self financing institutions in Kerala the State of Kerala passed *The Kerala Professional Colleges Or Institutions (Prohibition Of Capitation Fee-Regulaton Of Admission-Fixation Of Non- Exploitative Fee And Other Measures To Ensure Equity And Excellence In Professional Education) Act 2006.*

The important provisions relating to admission of students in these institutions were;

1. **Method of Admission in Professional Colleges or Institutions (Section 3)**–(1) Notwithstanding anything contained in any other law for the time being in force or

in any judgments, decree or order of any Court or any other authority, admission of students in all professional colleges or institutions to all seats except Non-Resident Indian shall be made through Common Entrance Test conducted by the State followed by centralized counseling through a single window system in the order of merit by the State Commissioner for Entrance Examinations in accordance with such procedure as may be specified by the Government from time to time.

2. **Admission Supervisory Committee (Section 4)–**(1) The Government shall constitute an Admission Supervisory Committee to supervise and guide the process of admission of students to unaided professional colleges or institutions consisting of the following members, namely:
   (i) A retired Judge of the Supreme Court or a High Court: Chairperson
   (ii) The Secretary to Government, Higher Education Department (ex-officio): Member Secretary
   (iii) The Secretary to Government, Health and Family Welfare
   Department (ex-officio): Member
   (iv) The Secretary to Government, Law Department (ex-officio): Member

3. **Collection of capitation fee prohibited (Section 5)–**
   (1) No capitation fee shall be collected by or on behalf of an unaided professional college or institution or by any person who is in charge of or is responsible for the management of such college or institution from or in relation to any candidate in consideration of his or her admission to or continuance in any course of study or his or her promotion to a higher class in such college or institution under the management.
   (2) Where the Admission Supervisory Committee on receipt of any complaint or is otherwise satisfied that the management of an unaided professional college or institution or any person who is in charge of it or is responsible for the management of such college or institution has violated the provisions of sub-section

(1), the Admission Supervisory Committee may after due enquiry recommended to the Government for taking penal action against the management.

(3) The Admission Supervisory Committee shall have the power to regulate its own procedure in all matters arising out of the discharge of its functions, and shall, for the purpose of making any enquiry under this Act, have all the powers of a Civil Court under the Code of Civil Procedure, 1908 (Central Act 5 of 1908) while trying a suit in respect of the following matters, namely:

(a) Summoning and enforcing the attendance of any witness and examining him on oath;

(b) Requiring the discovery and production of any document;

(c) Receiving evidence on affidavit; and

(d) Issuing commissions for the examinations of witnesses and for local inspections and any proceeding before such committee shall be deemed to be a judicial proceeding within the meaning of section 193 and 228 and for the purposes of section 196 of the Indian Penal Code (Central Act 45 of 1860).

4. **Fee Regulatory Committee (Section 6)–**

(1) The Government shall constitute a Committee called the Fee Regulatory Committee for determination of the fee for admission to the unaided professional colleges or institutions consisting of the following members, namely:

(i) A retired Judge of the Supreme Court or High Court: *Chairperson*

(ii) The Secretary to Government either in charge of Health and Family Welfare or Higher Education, as the case may be, depending on the course of study: *Member Secretary*

(iii) A Chartered Accountant nominated by the Government in consultation with the Chairperson: *Member*

(iv) A representative of either the Medical Council of India or the All India Council for Technical Education, as the case may be, depending on the course of study: *Member*

(v) An educational expert nominated by the Government in consultation with the Chairperson: *Member*

(2) The Fee Regulatory Committee shall adopt its own procedure for the conduct of its business.

(3) The terms and conditions of service of the Chairperson and other members of the Fee Regulatory Committee shall be as may be prescribed.

(4) The Fee Regulatory Committee shall have power to:-

(a) Require each unaided professional college or institution to place before the Committee the proposed fee structure of such college or institution with all relevant documents and books of accounts for scrutiny well in advance of the commencement of the academic year i.e., not later than 31st December of the previous academic year;

(b) Verify whether the fee proposed by each college or institution is justified and it does not amount to profiteering or charging of capitation fee;

(c) Approve the fee structure or determine some other fee which can be charged by the college or institution.

(5) The fee determined by the Committee shall be binding on the unaided professional college or institution for a period of three years. The fee so determined shall be applicable to a candidate who is admitted to a college or institution in that academic year and shall not be revised till the completion of his course in the said college or institution. No unaided professional college or institution shall collect a fee amounting to more than one year's fee from a candidate in an academic year. Collection of more than one year's fee in an academic year shall be construed as collecting of capitation fee and shall be liable to be proceeded against.

(6) No person who is associated to any unaided professional college or institution shall be eligible for being a member of the Fee Regulatory Committee.

(7) A member of the Fee Regulatory Committee shall cease to be so if he performs any act, which in the opinion of the Government, is unbecoming of a member of the Committee:

Provided that no such member shall be removed from the Committee without giving him an opportunity of being heard

(8) The Fee Regulatory Committee shall have the power to regulate its own procedure in all matters arising out of the discharge of its function, and shall, for the purpose of making any enquiry under this Act, have all the powers of a Civil Court under the Code of Civil Procedure, 1908 (Central Act 5 of 1908) while trying a suit in respect of the following mattes, namely:

(a) Summoning and enforcing the attendance of any witness and examining him on oath;

(b) Requiring the discovery and production of any document;

(c) Receiving evidence on affidavit; and

(d) Issuing commissions for the examination of witnesses and for local inspections and any proceeding before such Committee shall be deemed to be a judicial proceeding within the meaning of sections 193 and 228 and for the purpose of section 196 of the Indian Penal Code (Central At 45 of 1860).

5. **Factors for Determination of fee (Section 7)**–The Fee Regulatory Committee shall determine and fix the fee or fees to be charged by an unaided professional college or institution taking into consideration the fact, such as -

(a) The obligation on the part of all unaided professional colleges or institutions to provide free ship to a minimum of fifty per cent of the students admitted and the additional expenses, if any, required for the same over and above the excess funds generated from Non-Resident Indians, charity on the part of managements and contribution by the Government for providing free ship for scheduled caste or scheduled tribe students;

(b) The nature of the professional course;

(c) The available infrastructure;

(d) The expenditure on admission and maintenance;

(e) A reasonable surplus required for the growth and development of the college;

(f) Any other factor as the Committee may deem fit.

6. **Determining factors for according recognition and conferring status as unaided minority professional college or institution (Section 8)**–A minority unaided professional college or institution established and maintained by any linguistic or religious minority shall be accorded recognition and conferred status as an unaided minority professional college or institution only if it satisfies all the following conditions of demographic equivalence between the minority community to which the college belongs and the non-minority community of the State, taken as a single unit, namely:

(a) The population of the linguistic or religious minority community in the State which runs the professional college or institution shall be lesser than fifty per cent of the total population of the State.

(b) The number of professional colleges or institutions run by the linguistic or religious minority community in the State to which the college or institution belongs shall be proportionately lesser than the number of professional colleges or institutions run by the non-minority community in the State.

(c) The number of students belonging to the linguistic or religious minority community to which the college or institution belongs undergoing professional education in all professional colleges or institutions in the State shall be proportionately lesser than the number of students belonging to the non-minority community undergoing professional education in all professional colleges or institutions in the State.

7. **Fee not to be collected excessively (Section 9)–**

(1) No unaided professional college or institution shall collect any fee by whatever name called from the candidate for admission over and above the fee determined by the Fee Regulatory Committee and the fee prescribed by the University concerned:

Provided that the Fee Regulatory Committee shall fix the fee for Non-Resident Indian seats and the amount so collected over and above the fee fixed for other students in the college or institution in such seats shall be utilized for providing freeship to socially and economically backward students.

(2) All unaided professional colleges or institutions shall provide freeship to the extent prescribed for a minimum of fifty per cent of the students admitted.

(3) Any officer of the State or Central Government or any other public officer or authority who issues an income certificate which conceals the actual income of the person to whom the certificate is issued and any recipient of such certificate who by making use of the certificate claims any benefit with regard to freeship or scholarship shall be liable for penalty under section 15 of the Act.

(4) Notwithstanding anything contained in any other provisions of this Act, the fixation and levy of fees at the rates fixed by the Committee constituted before the date of coming into force of the Act shall be deemed to be validly collected.

8. **Allotment of Seats (Section 10)–**

(1) In every professional college or institution other than a minority college–

(a) Ten per cent of the total number of sanctioned seats shall be earmarked for the Scheduled Castes and Scheduled Tribes;

(b) Twenty-five per cent of the total number of sanctioned seats to the Other Socially and Educationally Backward Classes;

(c) Three per cent of the total number of sanctioned seats shall be earmarked for physically challenged persons; and

(d) Twelve per cent of the total number of sanctioned seats shall be earmarked for the other sections or society not covered under items (a), (b) and (c) of this sub-section on merit-cum-means basis:

Provided that in an unaided professional college or institution the provisions in item (c) and 9d) shall apply in accordance with the consensus based on mutual agreement arrived at between the unaided professional college or institution and the Government and following such principles and in such manner as may be prescribed:

Provided further that the admissions contemplated in items (b), (c) and (d) above shall be in compliance with the rules as may be prescribed.

(2) In an unaided professional college or institution belonging to both minority and non-minority, up to fifteen per cent of the total number of sanctioned seats may be filled by candidates under the category of Non-Resident Indian seats. Seats not filled up under Non-Resident India seats shall be filled up from general merits seats.

(3) In an unaided professional college or institution belonging to both minority and non-minority community, up to fifteen per cent of the total number of sanctioned seats may be filled by candidates under the category of privilege seats in the manner as may be prescribed. Seats not filled up under privilege seats shall be filled up from general merit seats.

(4) In an unaided non-minority professional college or institution eighteen per cent of the total number of sanctioned seats shall be filled up from general merit seats.

(5) In an unaided non-minority professional college or institution two per cent of the total number of sanctioned seats shall be filled up by students who have made outstanding contribution in the field of culture or sports, on the basis of criteria as may be prescribed. Seats not so filled up shall be filled up from general merit seats.

(6) Where students of specified categories surrender the seats after selection, the same shall be filled by the candidates belonging to the same category from the merit list of the Common Entrance Test.

(7) Where the seats specified for the Scheduled Castes or Scheduled Tribes and other socially and Educationally Backward Classes are left unfilled due to non-availability of candidates from the same category, the seats shall be filled up by rotation from other categories within the specified seats as may be prescribed. Provided that any spillover thereafter arising shall be filled up from the general merit seats.

(8) A minority unaided professional college or institution shall admit not less than fifty per cent of the students from within the State from the minority community to which the college or institution belongs. Fifty per cent of such seats may be filled up from among the socially and economically backward sections from within the minority community or merit cum-means basis with the consent of the minority educational college or institution as prescribed and the rest in the order of merit in accordance with interest merit, both from the rank list prepared by the Commissioner for Entrance Examinations, based on the common application prescribed in the appropriate prospectus published by the State Government.

(9) A minority unaided professional college or institution may surrender up to eighteen per cent of the seats to be filled up by the Commissioner for Entrance Examinations from the specified seats and general merit seats in equal proportion. The first portion shall

be filled up on the basis of merit-cum-means basis as prescribed. The second portion shall be filled up from the general merit seats. Any seats not surrendered shall also be treated as minority seats and filled up as such.

(10) A minority unaided professional college or institution may surrender upto two per cent of the total number of sanctioned seats to be filled up by students who have made outstanding contribution in the field of culture or sports, on the basis of criteria as may be prescribed. Seats not so filled up shall be filled up from general merit seats.

9. **Invalidation of admissions (Section 11)**–Any admission made in violation of the provisions of this Act or the rules made there under shall be invalid.

10. **Power of the Government to issue directions (Section 14)**–

(1) The Government may give such directions to any professional college or institution as in its opinion are necessary or expedient for carrying out the purposes of this Act or give effect to any of the provisions contained therein or in any rules or orders made there under and the management of the college or institution shall comply with every such direction.

(2) The Government may also give such directions to the officers or authorities under its control which in its opinion are necessary or expedient for carrying out the purposes of this Act.

After enacting the act, the self finance college followed the existing admission rules. The admission system in a leading self financing college in Kochi in the admission to MBA, MCA and B.Tech. Courses in 2006-07 (see annexure 4).

A division Bench of the Kerala High Court had declared Section 3, Section 7, Section 8 (b) and (c) and Section 10 of the Act 2006 as invalid.

The management of the self finance colleges was not happy with the Act and they approached the court again and the court found that the government showed undue haste in bringing in the professional colleges or Institutions Act, 2006. The High Court of Kerala declared some of the key position of the Act as invalid.

The court was of the opinion that self financing educational institutions, which were imparting quality education, need to be encouraged. In fact, the state Government was unable to impart quality education to all because of paucity of resources. The court observed that unnecessary regulations on such colleges would be counter productive. Day to-day monitoring of the institution and chocking them financially might result in their closure. Regulatory measures would do more harm than good. The endeavor of the State Government was to take over these institutions.

The court held that unaided minority or non-minority institutions had a fundamental right under Article19 (1) (g) and 30(1) of the constitution to run educational institutions. The admission could be regulated for ensuring the triple test of fairness, transparency and non-exploitative procedure in the matter of admission. The court said there was no need to frame Section 3 arrogating to itself the complete right of admission and the procedure Section 4 (supervisory Committee) prescribed foolproof procedure for the triple test. This was 'nationalization of the education" and was "wholly impermissible"

While formulating the Act, the interest of the Government was to provide for regulating the admission, allotment of seat to selected castes, selected Tribes and other socially and economically backward classes. But the decision of the High court in fact nullified the common entrance test, introduced in the State in 1983 after elaborate discussions and deliberations, in respect of admission to self finance colleges.

I do not know what was in the mind of Government while enacting the rule fixing proportion of the number of professional colleges or institutions and number of students of minority community and non- minority community(see Section 8).

After quashing Section 3 and Section 10 the court reinstated the right of the management of self financing colleges to provide admission to the students they have selected according to their whims and fancies even without considering common admission test and reservation policies. The interest of the government to protect the quality of education and protection to socially and economy backward community was hampered by permitting free hand, to the management of self financing colleges to run educational institution based on the fundamental right under Article 19(1)(g) and 30(1) of the constitution. It may be noticed that there cannot be any right which is injurious to the community as a whole. If people were given complete and absolute liberty without any social control the result would be ruin(Willis: Constitutional Law and the United States,477). For the liberty of one must not offend the liberty of others. Patanjalli Shastri, J., in A.K Gopalan's case observed that " man as a rational being desires to do many things, but in a civil society his desires have to be controlled, regulated and reconciled with the exercise of similar desires by other individuals. The guarantee of each of the above rights is, therefore, restricted by the Constitution itself by conferring upon the State a power to impose by law reasonable restrictions as may be necessary in the larger interest of the community. The restrictions on these freedoms are provided in clauses to 6 of Article 19 of the constitution (A.K. Gopalan v. State of Madras, AIR 1951, SC 21).

Right of Minorities to establish and manage Educational Institutions (Article 30(1)–Guarantees to all linquistic and religious minorities the "right to establish and 'right to administer' educational institutions of their own choice. But the right conferred on the religious and linguistic minorities to administer educational institutions of their own choice is not an absolute right. This right is not free from regulation. Just as regulatory measures are necessary for maintaining educational character and content of minority institutions, regulatory measures are necessary for ensuring orderly, efficient and sound administration. The right to administer is not the right to maladministration. The right to administer implies a correlative duty to good administration (St. Xaviers College v. State of Gujarat, AIR 1974 SC 1389).

The above two observations of the Supreme court may question the decision of the High Court of Kerala invalidating Section 3, Section 8 (b) and (c) of the High Court of Kerala.

CONCLUSION AND SUGGESTIONS

The administrative structure of the professional and technical institutions has to be framed on the basis of the changes in the development in the educational field in the State. The Department of Technical Education (DTE) shall work as a model for framing the administrative structure of all the professional and Technical institutions in the State. A clear participatory nature should be shown in the sample structure of DTE. The DTE can advise the institutions to follow the system. The basic principle of the administrative structure should be that the system shall have a participatory nature in the approach and all the staff members shall have a responsible role in the work entitled him/her.

The admission system in the pressional and Technical Institutions was almost acceptable in the State till 2000. There was not much clash in the matter of admission as there was adequate provision for the Government aided private colleges for admitting some students under management quota. The management was also happy due to the freehand provision for appointment of teaching and non-teaching staff in the colleges. If the Government was controlled this provision (eg. appointment) earlier / the management of the aided colleges were challenged the admission procedures much earlier. Though some managements of aided colleges following the quality aspect in the appointment of teaching staff. It is high time to implement the procedures of appointment of staff members as per the system of Public Service Commission (PSC) to promote quality education in the State.

If the Government could control the aided professional and Technical education institution, both in the matter of admission of student and appointment of staff members, may be fair by giving freehand to self finance colleges as many self finance colleges in the neighboring States was closed down due to low quality of the institutions.

It is not possible to control the quality by enacting Act alone, it has to be come from inside. What the government can do is to monitor the system with appropriate authority.

The objective of the Government through enacting the Act to control the self finance colleges was a move in the right direction considering many aspects in the educated field in the state and neighboring states. But a piece of suspicion in the hasty decision of government and the Act could be more public supporting one, if the importance of the provision invalided by the High Court of Kerala. Whatever be the aftermath of the enactment of the Act and consequent invalidation, the government should publicise the importance of the provision which are invalidated and other provision which are valid now.

DEFINITIONS

1. ***'Capitation Fees'*** *means any amount by whatever name called whether in cash or in kind paid or collected or received directly or indirectly in addition to the fees determined under this Act;*
2. ***'Common Entrance Test'*** *means the entrance test conducted for determination of merit of the candidates followed by centralized counseling for the purpose of merit based admission to professional colleges or institutions through a single window procedure by the State Commissioner for Entrance Examinations;*
3. ***'Professional College or Institution'*** *means a college or institution aided or unaided imparting professional courses in any of the following disciplines, namely:-*
   (a) Engineering and Technology;
   (b) Medicine, Dentistry, Pharmacy, Ayurveda, Homeopathy, Siddha and Nursing;
   (c) Teacher education or any other discipline as may be declared by the Government by notification in the Gazette;
4. ***'Unaided Professional College or Institution'*** *means professional college or institution which is not receiving*

aid or grant-in-aid from any State or Central Government and includes minority and non-minority professional colleges or institutions;

5. ***'Aided College'*** *means a professional college or an institution receiving recurring financial aid or grant-in-aid from any State or Central Government and includes minority and non-minority professional college or institution, as specified by the Government.*
6. ***'Freeship'*** *means full or partial remission of tuition fee awarded to scheduled caste and Scheduled Tribe and other socially, educationally and economically backward students on merit-cum-means basis by an unaided professional college or institution as may be prescribed;*
7. ***'General Merit Seats'*** *means seats other than specified seats, minority seats and Non- Resident Indian seats and notified as such by Government or any agency authorized by it;*
8. ***'Management'*** *means any person or body by whatever name called, under whose administration any unaided professional college or institution is functioning.*
9. ***'Minority Professional College or Institution'*** *means a professional college or institution established and maintained by a minority that fulfills the non-discriminatory criteria as laid down in this Act and determined as such by the Government;*
10. ***'Minority seats'*** *means seats reserved for students who belong to the community that runs the minority unaided professional college or institution and filled up on the basis of inter se merit in the manner as may be prescribed from the rank list prepared by the Commissioner for Entrance Examinations;*
11. ***'University'*** *means a University established under any law made by the Legislature of the State.*

REFERENCES

Administration Report of the Department of Technical Education for the Year, 1996-97 and 2005-06.

The Kerala Professional Colleges or Institutions (Prohibitions of Capitation Fee, Regulation of Admission, Fixation of Non-Exploitative fee and Other Measures to Ensure and Excellence in Professional Education Act, 2006.

Report of the Hindu daily dated January 5, 2007.

Economic Review, 2004.

The constitutional Law of India (Eighteenth Edition), Dr. J. N. Pandey, Central Law Agency, 1988.

Economics of Education; Odeyer D. Heggade, Himalaya Publishing House, Bombay, 1992.

Office Organization and Management, S. P. Arora, Vilas Publishing House Private Limited

Public administration in Theory and Practice, M. P. Sharma & B. L. Sadana, Kitab Mahal, Allahabad, 1991.

Office Management, R. K. Chopra, Himalaya Publishing House, Bombay, 1994.

Dynamic Personnel Adminitration (Management of Human Resourses), Himalaya Publishing House, Bombay, 1987.

Principles of Management, Gearge R Terry and Stephen G Franklin, AITBS, Publishers and Distributors (Regd.), J-5/6, Krishn Nagar, New Delhi, 110 051, 2000.

Sam Danial

12 Influence of Education on the Life-Long Earnings of Engineers in Kerala

Engineering Education in our country has the crucials has the crucial role of moulding technically skilled human capital for the reconstruction of the nation. "In the past three decades, engineering education in our country has grown to such an extent that we claimed to have the third largest continent of engineers and technologists in the world" (Vijayaraghavan and Purushothaman,1996:397). However, it cannot be claimed that the quality of such engineers is uniform and the standards are at international levels or their efficiency is significantly high. In this fast changing world, engineering education should be viewed as a dynamic process and management of such a process requires formulation of highly progressive objectives, establishment of competitive performance levels, scientific and valid evaluation procedures and appropriate feed-backs and development of self motivating and controlling forces among the students.

As in the case of the country as a whole, engineering education in Kerala too has become very attractive to all categories of people in the society. This has increased its demand in a big way. The reason for this tremendous increase in demand may be two fold. On the one side. It is an item of consumption as it directly satisfies human wants and on the other and the most important side, it is a productive investment on human resources. This has led to a serious misconception that an engineering degree is a gateway to financial success. Engineering education, today, demands heavy investments on the part of the parents as well as the government. But sadly that, there has not been a proportionate increase in the earnings structure of engineers except in the case of a few who are employed in multinational companies especially in the IT field. Patents, students and legislators are highly concerned about the returns to their investment. Saxena (1996:408), in this regard, opines that it will be no good to conceal the truth that many employers, students and educators are highly critical and largely dissatisfied with civil engineering education today. This has become a felt problem related to almost all branches of engineering education. There are considerable disequilibria between the supply of demand for engineering graduates and postgraduates in our country especially in the state of Kerala. This signifies the need for studies relating to the economic aspects of engineering education.

There are several factors affecting the earnings of an individual such as age, education, sex, community, place of residence, nature of management, and so on. But, the most significant among these are age and education. Hence, in order to measure the economic benefits of education, economists make use of age-education-earnings (AEE) profiles. Though there are a good number of studies relating to the economic aspects of general education, studies emphasizing that of engineering education are very limited. This motivated the investigator to have a scientific attempt to study the influence of education on the life-long earnings of engineers in Kerala by estimating and analyzing the AEE profiles.

OBJECTIVES OF THE STUDY

To estimate and interpret age-earning profiles of the different educational categoris of engineers.

To estimate the total life-long earnings, average life-time earnings and peak earnings of engineers in the total sample and in the different Education-sub samples.

To find out whether there exists significant diference in the life-long earnings of different educational categories of engineers.

HYPOTHESIS

There is no significant difference in the life-long earnings of the different educational categories of engineers.

METHODOLOGY

Method used: Cross-sectional survey method was adopted for the present study. The survey was conducted on engineers educated and employed in Kerala, having a minimum of graduation in engineering.

Variables: The dependent variable of the dtudy is earnings (salary earned through the profession) and the independent variables selected are age(ranging from an average age of 23 to 73) and Education (three different levels of engineering education-Graduation (EG group), Postgraduation (EPG group) and Doctorate level (ED group)

Sample: The sample of the study consists of 2010 engineers, drawn up in an objective manner using stratified random sampling method. The sample is distributed among the fourteen districts in Kerala.

Tool: A questionnaire specially prepared to collect data regarding age, education, earnings and other details was the major tool for the study.

FINDINGS OF THE STUDY

Age-Education-Earnings Profiles of Engineers (Objective-1).

The total sample was classified into three educational categories such as EG group, EPG group and ED group. The average annual earnings were condensed into Age-Education-Earnmings(AEE) table as shown below. There are 1203 (59.85) Egs, 525 (26.12%) EPGs and 282 (14.03%) Eds in the total sample.

Table 1 shows that a graduate engineer starts earning at the average of 23 and the other two groups at the average age

Table 1
Age-Education- | Earnings of Engineers

Average Age	*EG*		*EPG*		*ED*	
	Average Annual Earnings (in Rs.)	*No*	*Average Annual Earnings (in Rs.)*	*No*	*Average Annual Earnings (in Rs.)*	*No*
23	52976	138	0	0	0	0
28	79636	169	87799	41	97240	17
33	78742	152	94684	61	103270	30
38	89641	116	106907	92	149280	31
43	96533	135	119813	71	173782	29
48	123859	104	138153	52	1 2640	32
53	135627	153	172675	45	215333	23
58	122925	96	147553	60	200300	36
63	82080	63	109073	38	144020	31
68	70908	36	107658	48	100070	30
73	67180	41	83733	17	98500	23
Total	1000107	1203	1167048	525	1474435	282

Source: Survey data.

of 28. The initial average annual earnings of the EG group is Rs. 52,976.00 and it increases to Rs. 79,636.00 at the age of 28, and after that a slight decline at the age of 33. It is to be noted that a well-behaved AEE profile never has a negative slope. This shows the great under employment prevailed among engineering graduates during their highly productive age. Majority of them are not getting a job suited to their abilities during this period. The earnings of EPG group ranges from Rs. 83,733.00 to Rs. 1,72,675.00, whereas the earnings of EPG group ranges from Rs. 97,240.00 to Rs. 2,15,333.00.

The profiles in the following g figure represent the life-long earnings of engineers in the different educational categories. The ED group has the highest earnings at all ages except at the age of 68. At this age, there is a crossing of the profiles of ED and EPG groups. This is because of the higher earnings of EPG group at this age. After retirement, majority of engineers in the EPG group are found engaged in private employment, for which, the ED group are least interested. During the initial years of earnings, the profile of ED group shows very low progress. This is due to lack of proper placement facilities or other incentives for engineers having doctorate degree during the initial years. It is due to this reason that many of our highly qualified and skilled engineering professionals migrate to other states and foreign countries. But, the rise of the profile of this group after the age of 33, is significantly steep and it lies far above the other two profiles showing considerable difference in the life-long earnings. Besides, when compared with the EG group, the earnings of EPG group also appear considerably higher throughout. This clearly signifies the influence of education on the life-long earnings of engineers in the state of Kerala.

Total Life-long Earnings, Average Life-time Earnings and Peak Earnings of Engineers (Objective-2).

Table 2 shows that a graduate engineer earns Rs.50,00,535 during his/her total earning span of life. The average life-time earnings and peak earnings of the same group are estimated to be Rs.90,919.00 and Rs. 1,35,627.00 respectively. From the table, it is clear that a postgraduate engineer earns Rs. 8,34,705.00 more than a graduate engineer and a doctorate engineer earns Rs.15,36,935.00 more than a postgraduate engineer during the total earning span of life. The average life-time earnings of EPG group is Rs.25,786.00 more than the EG group and that of ED group is Rs.30,739.00 more than the EPG group. This significant influence of higher levels of education acts as a motivating factor for an engineer to acquire higher levels of engineering education.

Table 2

Total Life-long Earnings, Average Life-time Earnings and Peak Earnings of the Different Educational Categories of Engineers in the Total Sample

		Amount (in Rs.)	
Educational Category	*Total Life-long Earnings*	*Average Life-Time Earnings*	*Peak Earnings*
EG	50,00,535	90,919	1,35,627
EPG	58,35,240	1,16,705	1,72,675
ED	73,72,175	1,47,444	2,15,333

Source: Survey data.

Significance of the Difference between Mean Earnings of the different educational categories of Engineers (Objective-3).

Table 3 shows the results of test of significance of the difference between the mean values of earnings of the different educational categories of engineers.

Table 3

Data and Results of Test of Significance of the Difference between Mean Earnings of the Different Educational Categories of Engineers

Sub-sample	*N*	*Mean*	*S.D*	*C.R*	*Remarks*
EG	1203	93,166.62	25,796.38	14.75	Significant at 0.01 level
EPG	525	118,417.10	35,323.12		
EG	1203	93,166.62	25,796.38	13.28	Significant at 0.01 level
ED	282	150,633.68	71,577.21		
EPG	525	118,417.10	35,323.12	7.11	Significant at 0.01 level
ED	282	150,633.68	71,577.21		

From the table, the following inferences are drawn:

1. There is significant difference (0.01 level) between the earnings of EG and EPG groups (CR=14.75;P<0.01). The EPG group earns significantly higher than the EG group.
2. There is significant difference (0.01 level) between the earnings of EG and ED groups (CR=13.28;P<0.01). The ED group earns significantly higher than the EG group.
3. There is significant difference (0.01 level) between the earnings of ED and EPG groups (CR=7.11;P<0.01). The ED group earns significantly higher than the EPG group.

The above inferences reveal that education has significant positive influence on the life-long earnings of engineers. Hence, the hypothesis formulated for the study is rejected.

REFERENCES

AICTE (1976), Manpower Assessment and Analysis in Industry for Education and Training. Culcutta: Eastern Regional Committee.

Anderson, C. A. and Bowman, M. J. (Eds.) (1965), Education and Economic Development, Chiccago: Aldine.

Becker, G. S. (1964), Human Capital: A Theoretical and Empirical Analysis with Special Reference to Education. Princeton: Princeton University Press.

Blaug, M. *et. al.* (1969), Causes of Graduate Unemployment in India. London: Allen Lane, the Penguin Press.

Blaug, M. (1970), An Introduction to Economics of Education, NewYork, Penguin books.

Carnoy, M. (1967), Earnings and Schooling in Mexico, Economic Development and Cultural Change, July.

Chaudhri, D. P. (1979), Education, Innovations and Agricultural Development, London, Croom Helm.

CSES (2000), State Level Workshop Services and National Conference Education in Kerala's Development, Towards a New Agenda, Kochi, Workshop on Professional Education in Kerala, Status Papers, November 05.

Daniel, Sam. V. (2000), A Study on Age, Education and Earnings of Engineers in Kerala, unpublished PH.D Thesis in Education, M.G.University, Kottayam.

Goel, S. C. (1975), Education and Economic Growth in India, New Delhi, the Macmillan Company of India Ltd.

Husen, T. and Postlethwaite, T. N. (Eds), (1994), The International Encyclopaedia of Education, Vol. 5. (2nd Ed.), Oxford, Elsevier Science Ltd.

Maglen, L. and Layard, R. (1970), How Profitable is Engineering Education? Higher Education Review, 11(2).

Nallagoundan, A. M. (1967), Investment in Education in India, *Journal of Human Resources,* 2 (3), (Summer), 347-358.

Nallagoundan, A. M. (1978), Education Employment and Earning, University of Madras.

Pandit, H. N. (1972), Effectiveness and Financing of Investment in Education in India. 1950-1951 to 1965-1966, Unpublished Doctoral Thesis, Delhi University.

Psacharopoulos, G. (1975), Earnings and Education in OECD Countries, Paris, OECD.

Taubman,Paul and Wales, Terene (1974), Higher Education and Earnings, Colleges as an Investment and Screening device, NewYork Me Graw-Hill Book Company.

Saxena, Subash.C(1996), Civil Engineering needs Restructuring in D. Thakur and D. N. Thakur (Eds), Studies in Educational Developmen, Vol. 6 New Delhi, Deep and Deep Publications.

Vijayaraghavan, W.P. and Purushothaman, P. (1996), Systems Approaches to Under graduate Engineering Education in D. Thakur and D. N. Thakur (Eds) Studies in Educational Development Vol. 6. *Op Cit.*

Chacko Jose P & Rosy Thampy

13 Technology and Gender Promoting Technical Education for Women

Attempts for gender mainstreaming have so far seen women merely as consumers and not creators of technology. To get away with such attitudes imparting technical education to women alone will not be enough. Encouraging women to choose and stick on to technical careers is equally important. For this educating the society to neuter its stereotypical perceptions on gender is extremely important.

TECHNOLOGY AND GENDER

Women historically have been under-represented in scientific and technical fields. There are multiple reasons for this, one of the main ones being the cultural stereotypes and definitions of women and men, which, in the Western world, are grounded in the religious and political culture and have been institutionalized through the colonial education and socialization in most of the developing world. Western science and technology have evolved based upon the concepts rationalism and logical positivism inherited from Greek philosophy. (Longino 1990), especially the philosophy of Plato (Arrington, 1989). Thus in Western philosophy, through the language and metaphor, as well as through the history of practice, science and technology have become intertwined and linked to masculinity. Bacon helped to further separate the world into duality, the mind as knower (masculine) and nature (feminine) as the knowable. This implied a division into man as knower and subject and woman as knowable and object, placing man the subject and knower in control of women the object and knowable. (Karen, 1999, Harding, 1986).

However, relying on the argument that technology is masculine, assuming women as mere beneficiaries of technology in shaping this world is an underestimation. Women have always been significant contributors to the making of today's world. Every woman has been a technological being, using and often inventing tools, materials, and processes in order to adapt and modify her world. Their contributions have been either focused on the traditional homemaking roles of females, or they have been diminished in the records of industrial and economic spheres. Researchers propose that many of the anonymous inventions which mark human prehistory were developed by women. "Since women were responsible for gathering food, they probably identified potential food crops. This would qualify them as the inventors of agriculture and agricultural implements such as digging sticks, hoes, cultivators, and early plows. The processing of foods also falls to women in most primitive societies. Grinding roots and grains requires technological development in the form of tools, and storage of perishable food items requires the invention of processes such as drying, jerking, smoking, and pickling. Another field of prehistoric technology which probably fell to women was clothing. The development of preserving, softening, bleaching and dyeing methods for animal skins, the invention of weaving techniques and equipment may all be credited to our unknown fore-mothers. Care for the young, the old, the sick and the injured may also have been the responsibility of women. Along with knowledge of food processing would come knowledge of herbal medicine and various curative remedies. Though none of this prehistory of science and technology can be proven, certainly it is at least probable that following the tradition of 'the worker develops the tools', many of the most important inventions should have been the work of women". (Stanley, 1993).

Hence it is evident that women despite being contributors to science and technology has been confined stereotypes and sidetracked in history. Through the development of modern science and capitalism, intellectual skills (thought to be a male domain) have become more heavily valued over emotional skills (thought to be a female domain). Intellectual skills are to be practised in the 'public' domain of politics, economics and formal employment, while emotional skills are for the 'private' or family domain (Schiebinger 1987).

IT AND GENDER

Perhaps a challenge to the argument that technology is predominately male friendly was raised by Information Technology (IT) where brain was more important and defined a level playing ground for those with equal mental abilities. In its inception IT was suggested to be the first area where men and women would be equally represented. However despite the promising gender balance in the initial stages, IT now has a decreasing proportion of women (Cottrell, 1992). For example, in the USA a nationwide decline in the percentage of women taking bachelor's degrees in computer science has been noted. IT education and the industry continue to be male dominated and less women are entering computing courses at the university level. (Klawe and Levenson, 1995). Research into gender and IT suggests that this is partly due to the failure to overcome the masculine meanings generally ascribed to science and hence computing. Linked to science through the concept of applied science, technology assumes the masculine connotations given to science as an activity of power. Related issues are further discussed in section four.

THE KERALA SCENARIO

As elsewhere in the world, in India also women are under represented in Science and Technology. A study by UNESCO on representation of women in science revels that of the 89 countries with available data, women represent less than 30 percent of researchers. (UNESCO, 2006). In India the share of women researchers is only 10 percent. Table 1 presents the picture in Kerala.

Table 1 revels that at all the three levels of technical education the percentage share of women is less than that of men. Here

Table 1
Enrolment of Women in Technical Educational Institutions in Kerala

Type of institution	*Female students (%)*	*Remarks*
I T I	19.27	Period: 2004-05, *Government ITIs only
Polytechnics	36.00	Period: 2005 *
Engineering colleges	40.16	Period: 2003-04 **

Source: *Economic Review 2005, Govt. of Kerala.
** Selected Educational Statistics, Govt. of India

certain features are worth mentioning. The share of women increases with a movement to higher education. This may be interpreted as an achievement considering the all India average of 23.82 per cent. However it may also be noted that Kerala does not rank first in terms of percentage share of women in higher education. Uttaranchal (49.10 per cent) and Delhi (46.12 per cent), which are placed much, lower than Kerala in terms of Human Development Index share the first two positions. Another factor worth mentioning is that in higher education, though 40.16 percent women study in engineering colleges, the share of women in Arts and Science colleges in Kerala stands at a much higher level of 66.53 percent (2005). The statistics on women faculty members in the higher educational sector also points out to such trend. While 47.63 per cent of teachers are women in Arts and Science colleges (2004-05), the proportion of women teachers in engineering colleges is only 32.80 per cent (2000).

These clearly point to the fact that Kerala despite being ranked high in terms of HDI and GDI, gender biases exist in the perceptions of the society towards imparting technical education to women.

BARRIERS TO WOMEN'S ACCESS TO TECHNICAL CAREERS

As evident from the foregoing discussion, women are under-represented in most areas of science, in most parts of the developing and developed world. Women are not well represented in science, engineering, and technology as students, teachers, professors, researchers or workers. It is possible to argue that the principal reasons for the low numbers of women in science are the social attitudes about the role of women in society, which still strongly define certain careers as male or female, and particularly define traditionally-male careers as not appropriate for women.

Kandaswamy (2003) identifies seven social myths that discourage women from pursuing technical careers and hence education.

1. Women are emotional while technology is strictly logical. As a result, they don't go together
2. Men are good at math and machines while women have no clue about these.
3. Men are the providers while women are nurturers
4. Technical women are unattractive, arrogant, and abnormal.
5. Women can not do it because they are made that way: the divine or the evolution argument
6. Women are not as good at visualizing as men, and hence, don not make good engineers and
7. The social myths perpetuate stereotypes that lead to conditioning. There is pressure on women to look and behave in certain ways, which are deeply ingrained in their psyches.

Further, women tend to be concentrated in end uses, lower skilled IT jobs related to word processing or data entry and make up small percentages of managerial, maintenance, and design personnel in networks, operating systems, or software. Although IT is a new field, gendered division of labour patterns are already emerging. Evidences show that women in the IT sector always end up their upward movement in the hierarchy as they hit the 'glass ceiling'. The decision makers are still men in the IT sector.

Even the Internet which is seen as a 'common' where there are no entry barriers is facing gender inequality. This is basically due to the fact that women are placed mostly in the role of consumers and not creators of the virtual space. A new form of women's movement called Cyberfeminism has emerged to protect the interests of women in the cyber space. Cyberfeminism implies feminism practiced in electronic environments, particularly on the Internet and on the Web. It suggests a fresh ideology, embracing the notions of "cyber" and "feminism" and all they signify. It creates a space for women to invent, dissect and alter the trajectories of the new technological and information era.

BRIDGING THE GENDER GAP

Most of the existing efforts in bridging the gender gap around the world, gender equality is limited to the misconception of equal numbers of women and men benefiting from a programme. This approach over simplifies a much complex problem and does not critically look at the power imbalances gender divide can have through distribution of resources and opportunities. Genuine attempts on bridging the gender divide should examine how discrimination based on masculinity and femininity lead to inequalities in power dynamics, empowerment, distribution of resources and opportunities and suggest measures to solve such satiations. Such attempts undoubtedly demand providing increased opportunities for women to pursue technical education. However educating society to transform its conditioning on gender roles is equally important.

Promoting Technical Education for Women

In developing countries the single most important factor to improve the capability of women to take full advantage of the opportunities offered by technology revolution is education, at all levels from literacy through scientific and technological education. There are several ways to achieve this.

1. Promote a positive image of women in scientific and technological careers
2. Sensitise parents, teachers, educators, school administrative staff, curriculum developers and trainers to counter gender stereotypes with regard to science careers
3. Improve access of girls to scientific and technological education by providing clear ideas of career opportunities
4. Provide teachers with the necessary career guidance tools to meet the needs of female learners seeking careers in science and technology.

5. Integrating technology into a variety of subject areas-for example, music, history, art, and science-can be a stimulus for learning.
6. Designing a curriculum that is attentive and responsive to diverse cultural orientations can also be a motivator when introducing technology. To make technology appealing to people of all cultures, educators must be able to connect technology-related careers to cultural values.
7. Provide Career Information. Unfortunately, many female students are unaware of these projections, especially in the job market for computer engineers, systems analysts, and webmasters. Giving students this information is meaningless, however, if it is not accompanied by real world experiences of observing or talking with people who work in these professions.
8. Preparing for High-Tech Careers: Give adequate exposure to women so that they can take up high tech careers.
9. Change teaching and learning practices. Collaborative and cooperative learning environments are effective teaching strategies for technology learning because they promote learning through social interaction with others. They reflect the constructivist learning theory, which contends that true learning occurs as individuals share their knowledge and interact with each other in the social environment of its application. The purpose of learning must extend beyond the classroom and link to everyday life in order for the acquired knowledge to have real meaning to the learner. Collaborative learning practices encourage interdependence and a sense of shared responsibility, as opposed to individual learning, which rewards leadership through dominance.
10. Provide mentors and role models. Providing role models and mentors for female and minority students is another way to increase their interest in technology careers. In a study of twelve women successfully employed in nontraditional, technology-related professions, many reported being "influenced by either an encouraging male

figure within their personal sphere, and/or by a teacher in the educational sphere.

11. Demonstrate a commitment to equity. Schools can facilitate gender equity and leadership development by employing the following policies
    - Selecting software free of gender and ethnic bias
    - Ensuring that computer laboratories are accessible to each gender, ethnic group, and income level, as well as to students with disabilities
    - Encouraging the incorporation of technology strategies within all sectors of the curriculum
    - Providing staff training in technology
    - Periodically reviewing and revising equity policies as necessary. These strategies provide structured norms that emphasize equity in technology usage and foster relationships that help students achieve their career goals.
12. Develop entrepreneurial skills. The new information economy offers many possibilities for new IT-enabled businesses that could lead to economic and social empowerment of women. To take advantage of the opportunity development of entrepreneurial skills is essential.

EDUCATING THE SOCIETY

Providing technical education to women alone does not warrant emergence of successful women professionals and hence a society with empowered women. Ensuring societal support to women to effectively perform the expected roles in their careers as professionals is extremely essential. In the Indian IT context the number of women who drop out of IT careers after marriage due to family pressure is very high. NSSCOM (2006) reports that the number of women in higher position of Indian IT companies is extremely low. Attempts dedicated exclusively to support women in technical carriers are much needed. Such attempts should begin with educating the society to transform its traditional beliefs on gender roles so that it can get away with the social myths and resultant conditioning (discussed in section four). Social education can effectively be done by media, civil societies, religious movements and government.

CONCLUSION

Policy measures to provide increased educational opportunities to women are undoubtedly needed. Social and cultural beliefs about the role of women in society and the working world have had a powerful influence on determining the social and economic roles played by women in all societies, as well as determining the opportunities that women have access to. Probably the most important measure to ensure increased participation of women in professional education and careers is to educate society to neuter its stereotypical gender perceptions.

Endnote: 1. According to a NIME (National Institute of Multimedia Education, Japan) study, in Asia most families across cultures are willing to invest in technical education for their girl child because it improves marriage prospects but after marriage inevitably, over 50 percent of these women do not pursue a full-time career. 2. The principal of an IT institution in India had reportedly said that those women who pursued a particular professional IT degree course from the institution stood a better chance of finding a good husband with less amount of dowry!

REFERENCES

Longino, H. (1990), Science as Social Knowledge. Princeton, NJ: Princeton University Press

Arrington, R. L. (1989), Rationalism, Realism, and Relativism: Perspectives in Contemporary and Moral Epistemology. Ithaca, NY: Cornell University Press.

Karen F. Zuga (1999), *Journal of Education Technology*, Volume 10, Number 2, Spring 1999, pp. 129-137

Harding, S. (1986), The Science Question in Feminism. Ithaca, NY: Cornell University Press

Stanley, Autumn (1993), Mothers And Daughters of Invention: Notes For A Revised History of Technology. Metuchen, NJ: Scarecrow.

Schiebinger, Londa, (1987), "The History and Philosophy of Women in Science. A Review Essay" in Harding, Sandra and Jean F O'Barr (eds), Sex and Scientific Inquiry, University of Chicago Press: Chicago.

Kandaswamy Deepa, (2003), Talibanism in Technology, Wednesday, February 26, 2003 available online at http://*www.dqindia.com/content/special/103022602.asp*

UNESCO (2006), UIS Bulletin on Science and Technology Statistics, Issue No. 3, November 2006

Klawe, M. and Levenson, N. (1995), Women in Computing: Where Are We Now? Communications of the ACM, January 1995, 38(1): pp. 29-44

Cottrell, J. (1992), I'm a Stranger Here Myself: A Consideration of Women in Computing, Proceedings of ACM SIGUCCS User Services Conference, Cleveland, 8-11 November

NASSCOM (2006), Knowledge Professionals in India, Press Information note.

Austin Linda S. (2001), What's Holding You Back, Perseus Books Group.

Merlin Joseph & Dhanalakshmi T

14 Technology Adoption and Human Resource Development in Tea Plantation Industry of Kerala

Human resource has been recognized as the most important responsible factor for the success of any industrial or business organization. Management of industries today operate in a very different environment than was before. More new knowledge in technology has been developed in the last ten years. In industrial situation, Technology adoption along with HRD is needed by any organization in the changing fields of science, knowledge, technology, communications and economy. Let us analyze the essence of HRD and Technology adoption in tea plantation industry.

Tea Industry has been lagging behind other industries with reforms not taking place to the level expected and the credit flow getting limited. We are in need of restructuring in the country's tea plantation industry. The two pronged restructuring strategy are, the first effort would have to be restructure the regulatory and legal frame work governing the plantation industry. The commodity Act, The Land reforms Act of the state and the minimum wage Act as it applies to plantations are a few of the laws that needs drastic overhaul. The plantation labour Act was enacted when plantation areas were more isolated tropical rain forests than established agro businesses. Some of the social welfare stipulations are not found in any comparable non plantation Labour Act like the Industrial dispute Act. Stipulations like free on-site housing and free medical treatment without any stale participation have a severe effect on our cost of production. Minimum wage Act- In many instance, state government has notified a wage that managements were clearly unable to pay and which the workmen would not have asked for under the collective bargaining system. The second important area that needed reforming is the rationale behind the planning for and development of Industry.

Tea Board plays a vital role in educating the employees and developing the human resources in the organization. The main activities of tea board related to labor welfare measures are as follows:

LABOUR WELFARE ACTIVITIES

During the year, Tea Board had taken a number of labour welfare measures for the benefit of tea plantation workers and their dependents. These include grant of educational stipend to the wards of tea plantation workers for pursuing studies above the primary stage, extension of capital grant/financial assistance to various institutions and organizations towards expansion of school and college buildings, etc.

HUMAN RESOURCE DEVELOPMENT

Human Resource Development Cell of the Tea Board has been arranging various types of training programme, workshop, seminar etc. for the employees/officers of the Board as a part of its activities.

At present the quality of tea produced in India is a major issue of concern. Plucking of coarse leaves and poor manufacturing practices has resulted in deteriorations in quality. A special attention is needed to upgrade the tea plantation industry to meet the global market. For that we stay here for Technology adoption and HRD in Tea plantation industry.

Nowadays, companies are technologically shy and get the possible technology at the least cost and maintain their competitiveness in the international market. The tea plantation industry has been pressing for the upgradation on the ground that there is immense export potential and it could be tapped better if tea technology related education is standardized and brought up to international standards. On paper we produce 200,000 scientist, engineers and technicians every year but the full economic benefit of this is not realized because of the mismatch between the education and the needs of the labor market. According to World Bank report there is a growing gap between their knowledge and real practice in the market place. This calls for immediate reforms in policy and the concerned institutions which can enhance the supply of the right type of knowledge workers. With the above background let us discuss about the technology adoption and human resource development in tea plantation industry in Kerala.

Tea, 'Camellia sinensis,' is believed to have originated from South East Asia. Chinese people were the pioneers in using tea for medicinal purpose. In India tea plant was discovered in North East Assam during the early eighteenth century. Tea plantation industry is a combination of industry and agriculture Production of leaf is an agricultural activity while its processing is an industrial activity. Tea industry is of considerable importance in the national economy of India in terms of income generation, earning foreign exchange, employment generation, particularly for the poor and weaker sections of the population and contribution to the national exchequer. Concentration of women employees is a notable feature in tea plantation industry.

TEA-AN OVERVIEW

Sixty per cent of the total area under tea in the world is located in China and India Asian Countries like India, China, Sri Lanka, Turkey, Indonesia and Japan are the leading producers of tea in the world. Major exporters of tea in the world are Sri Lanka, China, Kenya, India and Indonesia. Commonwealth of Independent States (CIS.), United Kingdom (UK), Pakistan, United States of America (USA), Arab Republic Emirates (ARE) and Japan are the leading importers of tea. India continues to be the largest producer of tea accounting for 27.01 per cent of the global output. India is also the largest consumer of tea. In terms of area, it occupies about 18.79 per cent of the world tea area (Tea Board, 2004). Although India holds a leading position in production and export, the current position of tea trade reveals that its share in the world production and export has been declining steadily over the past three decades.

India's tea plantations can be largely grouped into two regions, North India and South India, occupying 77.90 per cent and 22.10 per cent respectively of the total area under tea in India. In South India, Tamil Nadu, Kerala and Karnataka are the major tea growing states. Tea is one of the traditional plantation crops in Kerala and the State is the fourth largest producer of the crop in the country, with a relative share of 6.96 per cent. Kerala alone accounts 1.88 per cent of the world production. Kerala's tea production is 26.93 per cent of the South Indian production. The tea area of Kerala is 7.12 per cent of area under tea in India and 1.34 per cent of the area under tea in the world and it is 32.21 per cent of the area under tea in South India.

Though tea is grown in all these districts there is considerable spatial concentration in two districts, Idukki and Wayanad. They account for about 87.21 per cent of the total tea area of Kerala. Idukki has 72.47 per cent and Wayanad has 14.83 per cent of tea growing area in the state (Tea Board, 2004).

According to the Tea Board, India, total area under tea in Kerala was 37107 hectares in 2004 and it produced 62146 tonnes of tea. Productivity of tea in Kerala is1675 kg./hectare, South India is 2003 kg./hectare and all India is1713 kg./ hectare.

At the State and central level the tea plantation sector contributes to the exchequer by various types of taxes and duties.

Average daily number of labour in Indian Tea Plantations is 1257610. Of this 597835 are male, 620750 are female and 39025 are adolescents.

The average daily number of employees in tea plantations in Kerala during 2004 was 90358. Besides this, approximately 125000 temporary employees are working in tea plantations in Kerala. In Kerala the percentage of male workers in tea plantations is 39.19 per cent (35407) and female is 60.47 per cent (54639) and adolescents constitutes 0.34 per cent (312) (Tea Board, 2004).

HISTORICAL EVOLUTION OF TEA

Tea was known to the Chinese as early as B.C. 2737. Tea was first used in China, as a medicine, during the fourth century A.D., and by the end of the sixth century onwards it began to be used as a beverage. Tea was not known to the Europeans till the sixteenth century. With the end of the sixteenth century their trades with Eastern countries were flourished and so they became aware about tea. Sri Lanka started its plantation industry in 1825.

Britisher's were the pioneers of tea cultivation in India. The event which marked the birth of the Indian tea industry was the discovery by Major Bruce in 1823, of the indigenous tea plants in Assam. When the trade relations with Britain and China disturbed and East India Company lost its monopoly of tea trade with China by the year 1833, they thought about replacing that trade in some way.

In 1837, the first samples of tea were sent down to Calcutta, which were manufactured from the leaves of indigenous plants growing in tea tracts of Upper Assam. The first historical consignment of Indian tea samples were sent to London in 1838. Until 1886 China had been the largest producer of tea in the world. Since then India has been the largest producer and exporter of tea. Ninety eight per cent of the tea consumed in England in 1905 was exported from India. That was an important period in the development of Indian tea industry. By 1950 tea had become an important agricultural crop of the country. By that year India became the largest producer and exporter of tea in the world.

Tea plantations were introduced in South India on commercial scale around the late 1840s. In the beginning of 1840 coffee plantations were affected by the disease 'Leaf Rust'. That paved way for wide tea cultivation in south India.

Tea cultivation in Kerala started in 1832 and it came on a commercial scale during 1840s. By the year 1875 tea cultivation was started in Peerumedu. A.H. Sharp started tea cultivation in Kannan Devan Hills during 1878. Tea cultivation started at Wayanad in 1889. Later the tea cultivation expanded to a vast area of the State. The unfavourable global market for coffee and devastating coffee leaf disease, 'leaf rust'-caused by

Hemilia vastatrix-gave fillip to the coversion of lands into tea, and as a result, the early decades of this century witnessed phenomenal expansion of tea area.

Historically tea plantation industry played an important role in the colonial activities of the Western Countries. In India tea plantations are concentrated in South India and North East India and these plantations were developed during the British period. After independence, the interest of the British went to African countries and the Indian plantations began to suffer.

According to one of the studies conducted by the author it is clear that, the performance of the Indian tea plantation industry is not impressive with an average annual percentage output growth of 2.43 per annum during the period 1950 to 2000. This is based on the analysis of trends in growth by estimating growth rates of area, production and productivity, employing an exponential model. Estimates are made for Kerala, karnataka and Tamil Nadu, South India, North India and for India, for the period 1950 to 2000. The estimated growth rates for Kerala, Karnataka and Tamil Nadu, were 1.85, 3.48 and 3.41 per cent per annum respectively. Thus among the three states, Kerala stood third in growth performance.

To understand the real conditions and problems prevailing in tea plantation industry and to examine how we can tackle these crisis situations and to analyse the possibility of technology adoption and viability of technical education a study has been conducted in Idukki and Wayanad districts of Kerala in the year 2001. Idukki accounts 72.40 per cent and Wayanad accounts 14.84 per cent of the total tea area of Kerala. There are 89 large tea companies, 163 large estates and 3956 small growers in Kerala (Tea Board, 1998). Acording to Tea Board, India tea companies having estate area above 10.12 hectares are considered as large ones. Major five tea companies having 60.38 per cent of the total tea area of Kerala and other four companies also were selected for the study.

THE CRISIS IN TEA INDUSTRY

Tea plantation industry is an important industry in Kerala. It plays crucial roles in income generation, foreign exchange earning and employment generation both directly and indirectly. However, the overall performance of this industry is found to have been unimpressive.

The tea companies are facing a crisis. The major problem is high cost of production and low price realisation. The cost of production of tea per kg. is Rs. 60/- Sixty five per cent of the total cost of production is accounted for by labour. In Kerala labour unions are very strong and their influence is visible in the case of wage increase. At the same time auction price is decreasing and it is around Rs. 51 to Rs. 52 per kg. Many tea producers highlighted that they do not get the original price for their product.

Tea plantation industry is labour intensive. Plucking or harvesting tea leaves is the most important work. In tea plantations the minimum wage rate is fixed according to the Plantation Labour Act 1951. According to this Act, the present wage rate for field workers (including pluckers) is Rs. 77.26 per day. Standard output for pluckers is 16 kg. per day. In addition to it pluckers get productivity incentives, (for first 10 kg. 44 ps./kg., Second 10 kg., 47 ps./kg. and third 10 kg., 50 ps./kg.). The wage rate for factory workers is Rs. 79.26 per day for eight hours. Factory workers are paid double charge for overtime work. Male and female workers are getting equal wage.

The companies have to provide basic facilities to the employees like housing, water supply, sanitation, health, education, etc. Many companies find it is difficult to provide such facilities in future in the context of declining profitability. The companies highlighted that the higher tax rate is a problem for cost increase.

At the same time the employees are facing the major problem of insufficient wage rate compared to the living expenditure and they are found to be dissatisfied with poor working conditions. With the present working conditions new generation is not willing to work in plantations.

Since the market for tea is of an international one, trade liberalisation is expected to have a substantial impact on this industry. After the removal of quantitative restrictions in April 2001 on of the major threats faced by the tea industry is the increased import of inferior quality of teas into India.

Trade liberalization and free import of inferior quality tea has resulted in slashing of price in the market. Cheaper tea has become available in the market and traders mix low quality tea with high quality ones. Import of cheaper tea for re-export either directly or mixing up with the Indian tea with the Indian brand name reduces the demand and price of Indian tea in domestic and international markets. The disintegration of the former Soviet Union which accounted for more than half of the total exports of India caused serious problems in our tea exports and it has very much affected Kerala tea because Soviet Union used to be the major market for Kerala tea.

As a result of opening up of the market for tea, there exists competition among producers at the international level. Competitiveness has become the key to success. Those units who are having the cost of production above the average international price will find difficult to continue to operate. In the case of Kerala most of the units are in this category. In sum the tea plantation industry is facing a crisis.

Productivity increase through Technology Adoption and Human Resourse Development

Tea factories are found to be reluctant in diversifying their product range and venturing into direct marketing. One of the major reasons for this is absence of professional management. In the case of tea plantation industry in Kerala, efficient factor utilisation is found only in the short run. Inefficiency in long term factor utilisation is evident from the existence of vintage technology, absence of product diversification and non-existence of professional management. For attaining long run growth, capital investments out of short run surplus have to be taken place. But the tea plantations in Kerala seem to have failed to plough back the short run profits for capital investments. It is very important to take proper measures by tea companies to introduce advanced technologies to improve the quality of the manufactured tea. Tea companies could make variety of products through research and development activities.

At the macro level the tea plantation industry has been facing adverse impacts of globalisation and trade liberalisation.

The price has declined sharply and the industry is facing a crisis. If there is any solution to this problem that is to improve the competitiveness of the industry-competitiveness in production of raw leaf and in manufacturing of tea. Productivity in plantations has to be increased by new plantation, replantation, new varieties, scientific harvesting, mechanised pruning etc,. Productivity in manufacturing can be increased by improving quality, product diversification, technological advancement, etc. Companies have to adopt professional management system for making the units competitive. In the liberalised regime of world trade, paramount importance has to be given to the marketing of tea. In this aspect Government has a very important role in developing a system for strict quality control. Of course certain government support in the form of tax concessions, export promotion etc. may be helpful for rejuvenating the tea plantation industry.

Import of low quality tea due to free import of tea has resulted in slashing of price in the market. Cheaper tea has become available in the market and traders mix low quality tea with high quality one. This reduces the price and demand of Indian tea. Here Government can take strict quality control measures. Additional to this through research and development activities and implementation of technology quality of Indian tea can be further increased. This will fetch high price. Tea plantation industry is labour intensive. These industries are situated in remote rural areas and the workers are mainly from the poor and weaker sections of the population. In plantations women workers are more than men. Plantation work is the bread and butter of their family. Other job opportunities are also very limited there. So at any cost these employs must be given employment. Reduction of labour is not possible but productivity increase is necessary. So the adoption of advanced technology for cost reduction and productivity increase must be run by utilizing the existing labour force. The existing employees must be capable to use the adopted new technology. Here comes the relevance of human resource development and technical education in tea plantation industry of Kerala. To understand the capability of the existing employees their education level has been considered for study

LEVEL OF EDUCATION

From the study it is clear that 48 per cent of the workers have 6th to 10th standard education and 23 per cent workers have 11th and above standard education. Table 1 shows the level of education of the employees. The education-wise categorisation is diagrammatically represented in Figure I.

Table 1
Level of education of the employees

Sl. No	*Education*	*Idukki Number*	*Percen-tage*	*Wayanad Number*	*Percen tage*	*Total Number*	*Percen tage*
1	Ist-5th Standard	97	14	51	24	148	16
2	6th-10th Standard	337	49	97	46	434	48
3	11th Standard and above	183	26	22	11	205	23
4	No Education	74	11	39	19	113	13
	Total	691	100	209	100	900	100

Source: Primary survey.

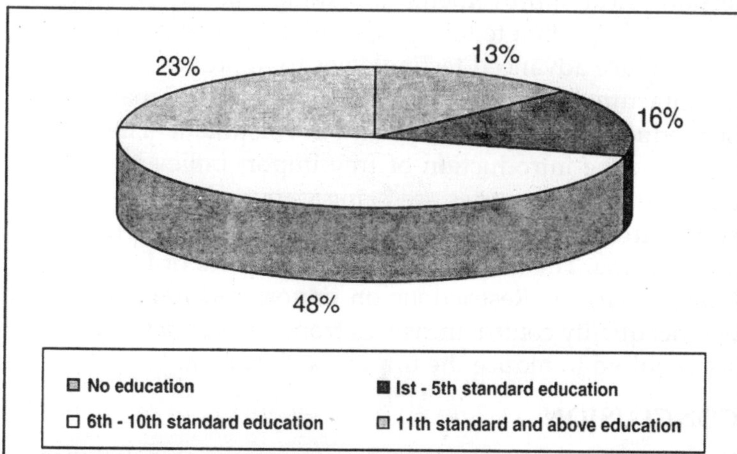

FIGURE 1: EDUCATION WISE CLASSIFICATION OF EMPLOYEES

In plantations only primary education facility is available either by companies or by Government. Most of the schools are Tamil medium because most of the workers are from Tamil Nadu. So the workers from Kerala face problem for educating their children. Higher and technical education facility is not provided by any of the companies. As per the survey 48 per cent of the existing workers have 6th to10th standard education and 23 per cent have 11th and above standard education. Through proper technical education and training they will be able to follow the new technology.

SUGGESTIONS

In plantations higher and technical education facilities are not available. In this regard it is very important to make more education facilities by the companies and Government to improve the quality of life.

Productivity level of tea is affected by the existence of over aged plants. In order to increase the productivity level tea companies could take proper measures for replantation of the over aged plants. Since tea industry is facing crisis and companies are not able to invest for replantation. So Governmental help is required for the same.

Most of the factories are using age old machineries. No technological improvements are taking place in this industry. It is very important to take proper measures by tea companies to introduce advanced technologies to improve quality of the manufactured tea. With this tea companies could make variety of products through research and development activities.

After the introduction of free import policy low quality tea from other countries are being imported and re-exported either directly or mixing up with the Indian tea with the Indian brand name. This reduces demand and price of Indian tea in foreign markets. Restrictions on import and implementation of strict quality control measures from the part of Government are required to reduce the import of cheap tea.

CONCLUSION

For adoption of technology human resource development through technical education is very relevant here for increasing productivity and for solving the crisis. Increasing productivity is required for improving the competitiveness. But huge capital investment is required for replantation and mechanization. Since the companies have been running at a loss quite for some time they are not in a position to make all these huge capital investments Here, if the Government and companies are working in a co operative manner for fund raising, arranging technical education facilities and training in plantations the problems can be solved and productivity and better prosperity of industry can be achieved.

REFERENCES

Asha, K. (1993), Competitiveness of India's Agricultural Exports-A case of Tea Exports, M.Phil. Dissertation, Centre for Development Studies, Trivandrum, (Jawaharlal Nehru University, Delhi.)

Boyce, James K. (1987), Agrarian Impasse in Bengal: Institutional Constraints to Technological Change, Oxford University Press, Oxford.

Chiranjeevi, T. (1994), Tea Economy of India, Rawat Publications, Jaipur.

Dutta, A.C. (1979), Botany for Degree Students, Oxford University Press, Calcutta.

Dwibedi, H.N. (1999), Production of Tea in India, with special reference to Dooars, K.P. Bagchi and Company, Calcutta.

George, Tharian, (1984), 'Historical Roots of the Crisis in the South Indian Tea Industry,' Social Scientist, Issue No. 131, April.

Government of Kerala (1997), Report of the Taskforce on Plantation Crops, Ninth Five Year Plan (1997-2002), State Planning Board, Thiruvananthapuram.

Government of Kerala, (1999,2000,2001,2004), Economic Review, State Planning Board, Thiruvananthapuram.

Hill, Albert, T. (1979), Economic Botany, Tata Mc Graw-Hill Publishing Company Limited, New Delhi.

Hudson, J.B. (1997b), 'Shear Harvesting,' Tata Tea Seithingal, Vol. 4, No.1, July-August.

Hudson, J.B. (1998), 'Enhancing Harvesting Efficiency of Pluckers' Bulletin of UPASI Tea Scientific Department, No. 51, March.

Joseph,Merlin (2002), Problems and Prospects of Tea Plantation Industry in Kerala, Ph.D. Thesis, Department of Applied

Economics, Cochin University of Science and Technology, Cochin-22.

Joseph, Merlin (2005), Economic Reforms and Problems of Tea Plantation Industry in Kerala, Paper presented for the National Seminar on Economic Reforms into the Second Decade February 26& 27, Organised by School of Management Studies, Cochin University of Science and Technology, Cochin-22.

Kirtikar, K.R., Basu, B.D. and An, (1981), Indian Medicinal Plants, Vol. I, Publsihed by Lalit Mohan Basu, 49, Leader Road, Allahabad, India.

Kochhar, S. L. (1981), Economic Botany in the Tropics, Macmillan India Limited, Madras.

Kumar, Sajith, K. (2000), A Study of Indian Tea Exports, with Special Reference to the CIS Countries, Master of International Business (MIB) Project Report, School of Management Studies, Cochin University of Science and Technology, Kochi.

Kumar, N., Khader, Abdul, Rangaswami, P., Irulappan, J. (1997), Introduction to Spices, Plantation Crops, Medicinal and Aromatic Plants, Oxford and IBH Publishing Company Private Limited, New Delhi.

Kurian, Tessy (1999), A study of Women Workers in the Plantation Sector of Kerala, Ph.D. Thesis, Economics Research Centre, Government College, Kottayam (Mahatma Gandhi University, Kottayam.)

Muraleedharan, N. (1998), 'A Review of Recent Attempts on Mechanisation of Field Operations in Tea,' Bulletin of UPASI Tea Scientific Department, No. 51, March.

Nair, P.K.K. (1984), Aspects of Plant Sciences, Vol. 7, Plantation and Agri-Horticultural Resources of Kerala, Today and Tomorrow's Printers and Publishers, New Delhi.

Pandey, B.P. (1988), Economic Botany, S. Chand and Company (Private) Limited, Ram Nagar, New Delhi.

Pillai, K.M. (1985), A Text book of Plantation Crops, Vikas Publishing House Private Limited, New Delhi.

Reddy, V.N. (1991), 'Global Tea Scenario: 2001 AD,' *Economic and Political Weekly*, Vol. XXXVI, No. 8, November 30.

Sabins, S.D. and Daniel, M. (1990), A Phytochemical Approach to Economic Botany, Kalyani Publishers, New Delhi.

Sarkar, Kanchan, and Bhowmik, Sharit, K. (1988) 'Trade Unions and Women Workers in Tea Plantations,' *Economic and Political Weekly*, December 26.

Sen, Chiranjib, and George, Tharian, K. (1992), The Developmental and Financial Problems of the South Indian Tea Industry, Research Report, Centre for Development Studies, Thiruvananthapuram.

Sundaram, Satya, I. (1995). 'Tea Industry: Exports and Quality Hold the Key.' Facts for You, *Market Survey*, Vol. 16, No: 9, March.

Swaminathan, P., Hudson, J.B., Udayakumar, S., Kanthaswami, C. and Anand, S. (1990a), Guidelines on Tea Culture in South India, UPASI Krishi Vignankendra, Coonoor, Tamilnadu.

Swaminathan, P., Hudson, J.B., Udayakumar, S., Kanthaswami, C. and Ramamoorthi, K. (1990b), Dakshinendiayile Theyilakrishi, United Planters Association of Southern India, Coonoor, Nilgiri.

Tea Board (various years: 1969-'70, 1972-'73, 1981-'82, 1983-'84, 1985-'86, 1990-'91, 1993-'94, 1994-'95, 1995-'96, 1996-'97, 1997-'98, 2003-'04) Tea Statistics, Tea Board, India, Calcutta.

Tea Board (1998), Tea Directory, Tea Board, India, Calcutta.

Tea Board (2000), Tea Digest, Tea Board, India, Kolkatta.

Tea Board and UPASI (1999), Souvenir, International Tea Convention, Organised by Tea Board, India and United Planters Association of Southern India, Coonoor, 6th to 7th September, Cochin, India.

Thomas, Tony, K. (1984), Viability of Loose Tea/Semi Branded Tea Operations by Lipton in Calcutta Metro, MBA Project Report, School of Management Studies, Cochin University of Science and Technology, Cochin.

Williams, C. N., Chew, W.Y., Rajaratnam, J.H. (1987), Tree and Field Crops of the Wetter Regions of the Tropics, Longman Group (FE) Limited, England.

Willson and Cifford, M.N. (1992), Tea Cultivation to Consumption, Chapman and Hall, London.

Sukumaran Nair M P

15 Restructuring Technical Education in India

As the country is poised for more than ever before annual growth in GDP during the eleventh plan period econmomic activities in all sectors shall witness epoch making changes in the coming years. The development perspective of future years is very well recognized by Indian agencies like the Planning Commission and the National Manufacturing Competitiveness Council as well as other international policy makers and development planners. The Planning Commission suggests that the national economy can grow between 8 per cent and 9 per cent per year on a sustained basis provided appropriate policies are put in place. The National Manufacturing Competitiveness Council set up by the Ministry of Commerce and Industry estimated that a 12-14per cent growth rate is needed in the manufacturing sector by 2015 so as to raise its contribution to national GDP to 23 per cent. The London Economist has predicted that India will become one of the major developed countries by the year 2020 during which it will compete with Germany to become the second most developed nation. In the developed nation. In the development prospects of any country, there is a major trust on growth in the education sector which has a vital role to play. This is true to education in general and particularly so with regard to technical education.

Technology is visualized to play a key role in socio-economic development. In all the sectors of the economy, whether agriculture, mining, manufacturing, utilities, construction or services, the efficient use of resources-physical, financial and human will be a determining factor in raising the rate of growth. Infrastructure and rural development, social sectors e.g. education, health and social security, and expansion of employment opportunities, which are thrust areas of national planning initiatives, depend upon the application of technology.

The technology induced economic growth shall invariably result in massive employment generation which is essential for a country like ours. Fifty years back if one is fortunate enough to attain general education and is exposed to university education; a life-time employment in the Government was readily available. People in the middle and lower economic strata upon getting an employment in the Government, industry or trade could aspire for reasonably well to do living. Fifty years after independence, we see that the country witness enhanced economic activity in different sectors and thus today general education is not enough for anybody who wants to contribute to national development. They may require multifaceted skills, innovation and a development oriented approach. Contemporary education, therefore, has to take a deviation from hitherto methodologies, practices and approaches being followed in the content and structure of the teaching and learning process.

Thus professional education in general and technical education in particular needs a thorough restructuring so as to enable new generation of professionals to lead massive development missions. There has been an overall awakening in the country in the past ten years with regard to the number of institutions, there quality stipulations and the changes required to be brought about in the curriculum of professional courses. Thus, a number of professional bodies, universities and colleges were instituted along with the Government run institutions. These institutions need good infrastructure and accountable faculty to encourage students to take up projects and research programmes to tackle the many wants of the society. Earlier the private sector was reluctant to make massive investment in education sector and very often it was an activity of the Government as well as a few social institutions, which specifically wanted their communities to be uplifted by expanding the reach and access to education and thus empowering them to contribute to socio-economic development. Today the situation has changed. Education has been identified as a major area of investment and profiteering by a host of private players and thus the cost of professional education has gone up leaps and bounds and rendered inaccessible to the poor people. Several private owned institutions do not have the requisite infrastructure for conducting technical courses and they also indulge in a host of unethical practices in collecting capitation fee, charging exorbitant course fee and flouting established norms for admission, appointment of teachers, conducting examinations etc. The UGC-AICTE combine shall evolve a strict code of conduct and enforce it among those who run technical institutions as business ventures.

Therefore there is an immediate requirement that the structure, content and finances of the technical education be restructured to meet the changing needs of the industry, services, academic, R&D and other sectors and also render it affordable to common people.

Most of these technical institutions yearly churn out number of graduates and most graduates which need a lot of conditioning so as to fit into the frame work of existing institutions. Most of these institutions heavily thrust on their curriculum and related academic subjects and often do not impart any exposure essentially required for the raw graduates to get into the organizational frame work within the least possible time. This situation has to essentially undergo change.

How can professional and technical education be rendered effective is a matter to be discussed among the academicians, industrial leaders and policy planners. One suggestion is that their curriculum shall extend beyond the boundaries of their universities and institutions, At least for a period of one year that too at the fag end of their professional educations students shall undertake an internship with the institutions. This will definitely empower them to easily acclimatize with the environment in which they have to live soon after they leave the university.

In the present economic environment, invention and development play a key role in all spheres of economic environment, invention and development play a key role in all spheres of economic activity. In the developed world for the past so many years centers of higher education, viz., Technology and Management Institutes and Universities interact in close liaison with the Industry world and work together for betterment of existing methodologies as well as seeking new pastures with an innovative outlook. With the huge manpower base having a high order intellectual capital, our country offers an excellent opportunity in this direction. A basic requirement is that the Government shall create avenues and mechanism through which the higher education sector closely interacts with the economic activity sectors. Several attempts have been made in the past for University-Industry interaction, but to a variety of reasons, no tangible result have come out. Similarly several national research institutes belonging the CSIR and other departments have also held a tremendous research projects. Industries may be encouraged to tap viable technologies among these projects so that it may bring economic benefits. This has to be encouraged through a development of a linkage between state level policies operating in industrial development and higher education.

The major challenge being faced globally in the present context is that manby organizations find it difficult to recruit sufficient number of trained people to manage upcoming projects. Consider the construction boom in the Arabian Gulf countries. Most of the companies are in dire need of construction managers and are looking towards countries like India for competent personnel. Taking advantage of this opportunity if some of our engineering colleges redesign their civil engineering curriculum incorporating modules on construction management and providing students with sufficient exposure to operation of well-managed construction companies in the country, a part of the huge demand arising from the gulf countries can be met.

In India, technical graduates undergo a minimum of two years training period before they fit into the industrial organization. It is during this process the raw graduate gets transformed to a capable professional and a contributing team member, later to become a competent manager and an effective leader. These two years by the present industry standards is a very lengthy duration. Industries cannot wait so long to realize the potential of the newcomer. It would be better if this training period has to be shared by the industry and university based on a clear perception.

In recent years several organizations have undergone a major restructuring process so as to adopt in the changes in the new economic environment. One of the major thrust areas of the above restructuring process is on the manpower front. A number of well experienced people from different organizations opted for compensation driven separation plans through voluntary retirement etc, resulting in substantial erosion in the technical expertise of these organizations. It is true that a section of such retirees take up employment to their liking and experienced employees leave the organization in a vaccum, which is not conducive for its growth and development.

Updating the technical education curriculum with the latest information in the respective discipline is important. Formerly universities curriculum runs at least a decade back in their syllabi with regard to most disciplines. Little effort is being made to update the syllabus incorporating new developments in the discipline. The current situation demands that the UGC shall evolve an effective system to update the syllabus of technical education at least once in two years.

Investing in people, sharing skills, knowledge and experience strengthen to build a strong national human resource base is essential for the country to advance further in the path of development and manage the impacts of globalization. The developments in information and communication technologies provide immense scope for delivering the right kind of education to the needy segments. The present practices of teaching-learning process in S&T need to be revitalized through the application of modern tools of communication and transfer of knowledge.

The role of professional bodies is very much relevant in the advancement of technical education. In the developed countries professional bodies are held in high esteem and are often called upon to provide right directions and expertise to the Government in developing the education sector. They also empower their members to continuously learn and update current developments in each discipline through a process of continuing education. In India professional bodies do not enjoy such a prominence and in most cases decisions are taken up on the advice of low caliber bureaucrats. Of late thing are changing in India also. Major industry leaders and IT industry mentors now a days figure on the governing bodies of prestigious technical institutions in the country. If we are able to incorporate the views of learned professional bodies in the policy-making and execution in technical matters, the country will witness an altogether new era of the development.

As the acquisition of knowledge and skill development have to be a continuous phenomenon for engineers in view of the knowledge explosion in science and technology, recognition of engineers on the basis of a degree obtained at one point of time is not enough. Therefore, some kind of a mechanism has to be developed and installed for imparting relevant continuing education to practicing professionals and ensure that they regularly update themselves through a process of certification. It is with this intent that several countries have enacted legislation to make participation in continuing programme mandatory for all registered engineers.

The WTO regulated trade regime has also has a profound impact on the education sector in India. Globalization has its thrust on integration of economies and societies through cross border transactions of trade in goods and services, information, ideas, technologies, manpower, capital and finance. And thus it offers tremendous opportunities to the Indian engineer and at the same time he is challenged by the necessity of maintaining a higher order of professional competence and strict adherence to the ethics of the profession.

According to National Association of Software and Service\ companies (Nasscom) outsourced engineering services with market potential of $7-12 billion could be the next big opportunity for India. At preset, the value of work undertaken by the India-based vendors was around $500 million only, which suggests that a great deal of opportunities remains to be tapped. The engineering services currently offered from India are around product design, process engineering, plant operation, enterprise asset management; IT services (R&D) and ITES-BPO (engineering BPO) services. The target verticals for Indian firms in engineering services are identified as automotive, aerospace, pharmaceuticals, construction, manufacturing and embedded software and chip design.

The above opportunities are challenged by the requirements of the WTO led General Agreement on Trade and Services (GATS) which besides call for opening up these services to international competition and free movement of professionals also necessitate international recognition on equivalence of profession across the world to ensure an acceptable level of professional competence for engineers. The global market also demands that the engineering professionals must uphold the dignity of profession through adherence to an internationally acceptable code of ethics and being transparent. Even though scores of engineering professional are working with major international companies in the developed world in lead roles, presently the Indian engineer is recognized mostly based on individual merits and talents rather than as a branded Indian professional. Non-recognition of qualifications by developed countries often acts as a serious barrier to market entry and movement of natural persons.

This need to be changed to facilitate the cross border mobility of experienced professional engineers by establishing a system of mutual recognition which is based on confidence in the integrity of national assessment systems, secured through continuing mutual inspection and evaluation of those systems. In short a branded Indian engineering professional is to emerge following an international accreditation taking care of the entire requirements of the services under the globalized economic environment.

A lot of Government efforts are needed in this area to facilitate such Mutual Recognition Agreements (MRAs) among the different countries. To start with we need to devise a

National Register of Professional Engineers and than seek lateral recognition with other similar bodies and groups such a s the Washington Accord signatory countries or with the Engineers' Mobility Forum. Regulation of a profession normally entails two aspects. They are regulation of education so as to ensure that the professionals will get the right contents and quality of knowledge and skills in the educational programme and regulation of practice so as to ensure that professional activities are carried out only by competent persons with due accountability for their technical decisions.

It is indeed a sad state of affairs that even under pressing needs there are no concerted efforts to address issues of national and international level of accrdiation for Indian engineering professionals. In the past two attempts were held to enact a national legislation say, Engineers' Bill and institute a statutory body to undertake responsibility of registration and accreditation of engineers. One such attempt was by the Engineering Council of India, a body constituted with participation of several professional bodies in the different engineering disciplines and the other was by the All India Council for Technical Education (AICTE), a statutory body which has been overseeing institution and governance of engineering colleges. Both did not bear fruit and thus even today after ten years of the GATS agreements coming to effect we do not have a statutory body and a system for regulating the engineering profession and imparting national accreditation of professional engineers. It is the Commerce Ministry of the Government of India along with a host of other issues relating WTO in different areas that is taking up the GATS related issues also at the various international forums. Thus there is an urgent need that the Government shall undertake the above legislation with out any loss of time.

Though the WTO stipulate that it does not dictate policies and all the agreements arise out of negotiations among member governments decisions made by consensus fact remains that they are not agreements among members equal in all respects. The interest of the developed countries always has an edge over others and hitherto experience tells us that there has been increasing restriction on market access to products from developing countries through tariff as well as non-tariff barriers. Similarly lack of international accreditation can be cited as one of the barriers of entry for Indian professionals to the expanding global trade in services where India holds a major strength and several countries in the west including US is fearful of massive shedding of jobs of own nationals against replacement of cheap and talented technical manpower from India and China and also through technical business process outsourcing.

Business Week reported, "No wonder India is at the center of a brewing storm in America, where politicians are starting to view offshore outsourcing as the root of the jobless recovery in tech and services. An outcry in Indiana recently prompted the state to cancel a $15 million IT contract with India's Tata Consulting. The telecom workers' union was up in arms and Congress was probing whether the security of financial and medical records was at risk. As hiring explodes in India, the jobless rate is 6.7 per cent for electrical engineers has more than doubled, to 4.6 per cent, in three years. The rate is 6.7 per cent for electrical engineers and 7.7 per cent for network administrators. In all, the US Bureau of Labor Statistics reports that 234,000 IT professionals are unemployed".

This all the more necessitate the Government and professional bodies of repute to act immediately with regard to a national level accreditation of Indian professionals so that their qualifications are mutually recognized by nations where there is a growing potential for export of engineering and technical services and expertise.

Industries world over are undergoing extensive shift in organizational structure of management. Mergers and acquisitions taking place in the industrial world with a view to consolidate activities draw the synergy of associations and steadily maintain core competence. This new situation demand new traits from the professionals. They have to work along with people who are in different culture, value tradition and move around continents. In short they have to be highly flexible and at the same time adapting them with operating social economic conditions.

The agenda for such a restructuring process shall include curriculum innovation and examination reforms, systematic framework for closer interaction with application areas such as industry and commerce, development of facultuy, national and global networking and a system for performance audit for teaching profession and there shall be a scheme for continuing education to update their knowledge in the field. The compensation packages available to the teachers remain very low compared to their counterparts in the industry or services sector and need to be adequately brought up. International accreditation of our professional courses shall be obtained through acquisition of relevant training and experience, assessment of competence, and professional conduct so that there will be mobility of such trained manpower across the globe.

The goal of improving the social and economic well being of people is a pre requisite for creating a stable and sustainable world. It can be achieved only through the application of technology and the dedicated effort of committed professionals from all fields including the social sciences, engineering and medicine. It will also require collaboration for development, acceptance and dissemination of innovative solutions and better use of existing technologies. Engineers will be required to deliver solutions that are technically viable, commercially feasible and, environmentally and socially sustainable. The structure and content of technical education shall empower engineering community to meet societal needs through capacity building, improved education, training, information development and dissemination.

REFERENCES

Duttaguptha, Ishani (2006), 'Go Euro', *The Economic Times*, Chennai, 30 Oct.

Ministry of Human Resources Development, Annual Reports (2003, 2004 and 2005) , Government of India, New Delhi.

Ministry of Human Resources Development, Analysis of Budgeted Expenditure on Education (2004 and 2005), Government of India, New Delhi.

Stewart, F. (1996), ' Globalisation and Education', *International Journal of Educational Development*, 16 (4).

PART-2

Zakkariya K A & Jagathy Raj V P

16 An Introspection to the Problems and Issues of Engineering Education in Kerala

The state of affairs of Kerala's Engineering education sector is an issue of grave concern for everyone in the state for the last few years due to several reasons. Kerala is a state with cent per cent literacy and has attained an enviable track record in the case of Primary education. The State has been criticised for not providing the quality education in the higher education sector. Though the percentage of people go for higher education is high in the state, the performance of the students after their education has not been up to the mark. Not only that, the technical education sector of the state had been neglected by the government for so many decades. The number of institutions imparting technical education was a few in number till the recent past. But recently there has been drastic change in the technical education sector of the state and there has been a commendable improvement in the number of institutions providing the professional education among which engineering education is the most prominent. There have been initiatives to enhance quality also. Still, our Engineering education sector remains as a sector with a lot of problems and potential for creating further issues.

The higher education sector in Kerala has undergone a real revolution with the introduction of the Self finance sector. The concept of self financed education sector flooded everywhere in the state and both the technical and the non-technical education sectors had utilised this opportunity for growth and development. Engineering and Medical education sectors are the two important sections of higher education which found their rapid growth under the self finance scheme. Kerala, which was a trend setter in the primary education sector, never happened to be a trend setter in the field of technical education, it always happened to be a trend follower.

The government was never capable of providing adequate number of institutions for professional education as per the requirements of the state. Students of the state had been depending on our neighbouring states such as Karnataka and Tamilnadu for their engineering and medical education. The financial constraints to mobilise resources for the development of professional education had made the governments to think about initiating the self financing sector in higher education. The beginning of the self financing sector was with controversy and the same is still continuing to cripple the qualitative growth of the higher education. To some extend the problems and issues existing in the self financed technical education sector is a certificate for the "Management skills" and vision of the government.

This paper is a humble effort of the authors, who were members of the inspection teams to various engineering colleges in the state in the capacity as members of the Syndicate of two different Universities in the state, to analyse and organize various problems and issues faced by the engineering education in the state based of their firsthand experience. While examining the problems and issues of the engineering education in the paper the authors had taken only the education imparted by the engineering colleges into their discussion.

A BRIEF HISTORY OF EVOLUTION OF ENGINEERING EDUCATION IN THE STATE

The first engineering college in the state-College of Engineering, Trivandrum-was established in the year 1940. The level of initiative taken by the state government to promote the technical education is evident from the fact that the state had to wait nearly two decades from the inception of the first college to set up a second one. The number of the engineering colleges remained less than 10 till 1991.

Table 1
Growth of Engineering Colleges in the State

Sl. No.	*Year*	*Number of college sexisting*	*Sl.No.*	*Year*	*Number of colleges existing*
1.	1946	1	14	1993	12
2.	1951	1	15	1994	13
3.	1956	1	16	1995	16
4.	1961	6	17	1996	17
5.	1966	6	18	1997	17
6.	1971	6	19	1998	17
7.	1976	6	20	1999	24
8.	1981	6	21	2000	33
9.	1986	8	22	2001	45
10.	1989	9	23	2002	74
11.	1990	9	24	2003	81
12.	1991	10	25	2004	87
13.	1992	10	26	2005	87

**Source:* Annual Technical Manpower Review (Engineering) Kerala-2006

By 1996 it became 17 in number and in 1999 seven more colleges were started. There after a steady and rapid development had been taking place in the engineering education sector of Kerala. The total number of engineering colleges became 87 by the year 2005. These 87 colleges comprise of 31 Government Colleges, three Private Aided Colleges and 53 Private self financing Colleges.

Table 2
Increase in Number of Engineering Colleges by Type and Level

Sl. No.	*Type*	*Year* 1993	1998	2003	2005
1.	Govt. Institutions	9	13	31	31
2.	Aided Institutions	3	3	3	3
3.	Private Institutions	0	1	47	53
	Total	12	17	81	87

Source: Annual Technical Manpower Review (Engineering) Kerala-2006

The corresponding increase in the total sanctioned intake and actual intake was also recorded a phenomenal increase

(Tale 3), the total sanctioned intake of 2,810 in 1991 for various engineering degree courses has been increased up to 24,526 in 2005. That is, the increase in the total sanctioned intake was nine fold within 14 years of time.

Table 3
Sanctioned Intake, Actual Intake and Outturn of Engineering Degree Courses

Sl. No.	Year	Sanctioned Intake	Actual Intake	Outturn
1.	1991	2810	2795	2280
2.	1995	3930	4441	2507
3.	1996	4699	4657	2404
4.	1997	4871	4792	2753
5.	1998	4979	5122	2959
6.	1999	6668	6126	3531
7.	2000	8820	8739	3836
8.	2001	11293	11147	4089
9.	2002	18280	16143	3724
10.	2003	19889	16563	3944
11.	2004	23613	16810	6639
12.	2005	24526	21814	8781

Source: Annual Technical Manpower Review (Engineering) Kerala-2006

PROBLEMS IN THE CURRENT ENGINEERING EDUCATION SCENARIO OF KERALA

The present engineering education scenario of Kerala has been facing with many severe problems which are to be addressed effectively for strengthening the quality of education.

If we make an introspection with respect to the growth and development we had with the engineering education sector, we would be forced to conclude that the growth and development which had taken place in the engineering education sector is a quantitative phenomenon without ensuring a qualitative development. It is easy to understand that our present system of education makes our engineering colleges as mere production units that produce engineering graduates than of a training institute that refines the skills and developing efficient engineers. After all, it is the inherent weakness of Kerala that, it cannot become a trend setter in higher education as in the case of primary education and it always happened to be a trend follower.

The basic problems identified by the authors with the present education provided by the engineering colleges in the state are listed below:

- Dearth of competent and qualified teachers
- High Teacher turnover
- Incompetent institution Heads
- Low employability rate
- Lack of entrepreneurial orientation
- Absence of a need based study while sanctioning Colleges and courses
- Curriculum revision is not timely
- Lack of interdisciplinary approach

DEARTH OF QUALIFIED AND COMPETENT TEACHERS

The availability of Qualified and competent teachers is the most crucial problem that storms the engineering education in the state. This is the most important problem that affects the quality of the training imparted to the students during their course. It is learned that 22 to 25 per cent of the sanctioned teaching posts are remaining vacant. It is revealed during the survey conducted by the National Technical Manpower Information System (NTMIS) through its nodal centre located at Cochin University of Science and Technology (CUSAT) that the engineering colleges in Kerala are facing severe shortage of qualified teachers. The finding is based on the data collected from 87 engineering institutions in the state during the academic year 2005-06. Out of the 4911 teachers who were working during the academic year, about 50 per cent has only graduation as their qualification. The survey also showed that share of the teachers with post graduate degrees are about 43 percent and just 7.9 per cent teachers held doctorate degrees. The detailed break up of the qualifications of the teachers in engineering colleges of the state including the branch wise information are shown in Table 4.

The authors directly experienced this problem while making inspections to various engineering colleges in the state under the Cochin University of Science and Technology and University of Kerala. The number of junior teachers at Lecturer level seemed to be satisfactory with most of the colleges, but there is absolute scarcity of qualified teachers at senior level as Associate Professors and Professors. The available junior teachers are not competent to compensate the deficiency of the highly experienced senior teachers.

The major problem comes not with the conventional branches of engineering such as Civil Engineering and Mechanical Engineering, but with today's prestigious Computer Science and Information Technology related Engineering branches and also with Electronics Engineering. As per the statistics shown in the Table 4, the percentage of teachers in Computer Science Engineering with post graduate degree is less than 18 per cent, while the same is 62 per cent and 51 per cent in the case of Civil engineering and Mechanical engineering respectively.

Table 4
Discipline wise and Qualification wise Teachers in Engineering Colleges of Kerala in 2005-06

Sl.No	*Discipline*	*Graduates*	*Post-Graduates*	*Doctorates*	*Total*
1.	Civil Engineering	78 (21.4%)	227 (62.2%)	60 (16.4%)	365
2.	Computer Engineering	799 (79.7%)	178 (17.8%)	25 (2.5%)	1002
3.	Electrical and Electronics Engineering	304 (49.0%)	275 (44.4%)	41 (6.6%)	620
4.	Electronics Engineering	770 (71.0%)	282 (26.0%)	32 (3.0%)	1084
5.	Mechanical Engineering	245 (37.2%)	336 (51.0%)	78 (11.8%)	659
6.	Others	214 (18.1%)	816 (69.1%)	151 (12.8%)	1181
	Total	2410 (49.1%)	2114 (43.0%)	387 (7.9%)	4911

Source: Annual Technical Manpower Review (Engineering) Kerala-2006

One other important aspect is that most of the teachers in the Computer Science related and Electronics branches are industry rejected candidates who find their means of earnings through teaching. These teachers are not possessing any teaching skills and unable to either impart knowledge and experience to the students or to motivate the students professionally. Such teachers may be trained rigorously to improve their teaching effectiveness. Teachers certainly have the technical knowledge needed to instruct tomorrow's engineers. Teachers should have the skills and mind to effectively accomplish many of the changes suggested by industry and the accreditation boards.

HIGH TEACHER TURNOVER

High teacher turnover is also an important issue to be addressed in the technical education sector. There are occasions in many institutions where the same paper had been handled by more than two teachers in the same semester. How can we guarantee quality education in such an environment? There are two important reasons for this high teacher turnover.

Firstly, it is due to the incompetency of the teacher, that is teachers without the teaching aptitude and requisite skills finds it difficult to survive with the institutions and quits the jobs. In other words the teachers who were originally rejected by the industry are forced to quit the teaching job also as they getting convinced that they are rejected by the students too. Secondly, the remuneration given to the teachers are not adequate in many institutions and the dissatisfied teachers quits their job and finds a better employer. Though the AICTE scale is insisted by the AICTE and the government most of the employers giving only the basic pay of the AICTE scale, benefits like D.A. and other allowances are not provided. Most of the institutions are not providing any opportunity such as QIP or FIP to teachers for upgrading their qualifications.

INCOMPETENT INSTITUTION HEADS

One of the most important problems with large number of engineering colleges in the state is lack of effective academic and administrative leadership. As in the case of the teachers, there is severe shortage for getting qualified principals also. Individuals satisfying the qualifications as per the AICTE requirements are not easily available. Consequently, managements of most of the self financing institutions, both in the private sector and public sector started employing retired teachers as the principal. There is nothing wrong in utilizing the service of the retired teachers as teachers and also as principals in cases where competent people are available.

But unfortunately what happened is, the retired teachers who are good teachers but poor administrators were appointed as principals in many engineering colleges. These principals are attracted only by the remuneration which they get after the retirement and neither interested nor capable to make effective academic management in the respective institutions. The philosophy which guides them is "somehow management". The minds of these institution heads are too narrow and myopic and not prepared to move with the demands of the environment. The authors had unforgettable experiences with such institutional heads while making institution inspections as members of the syndicate for granting recognition from the university. We do not ignore the capabilities and vision manifested by a few number of aged and experienced principals, which can be numbered in fingers and they constitute only negligible percentage of the population.

LOW EMPLOYABILITY RATE

It is learnt from the report of the National Association of Software and Service Companies (NASSCOM) that only a small percentage of the large number of available engineering graduates in the country is employable. A study by Mckinsey Global Institute on the labour market has pointed out that the multinational companies in India find only 35 per cent of the engineering students who graduate every year are in the employable category. With the increase in number of engineering colleges, Kerala is emerging out as one of the potential sources for qualified manpower for large number of corporate houses. But the major problem faced by these companies while recruiting our graduates is their lack of employability. Though the problem of lack of employability is a phenomenon with all most all the states in the country, the problem is a little bit severe in our state.

This gives the message that our engineering graduates are not industry ready finished products and they need to be further processed or refined in order to sharpen their finishing skills. The term employability refers to the presence of certain competencies among the candidates required by the employers which often grouped and termed as "Soft Skills". The concept of 'Finishing Schools' has come up in the context of these extreme demands for the development of soft skills among our graduates. The concept of 'unemployability' addresses the problems of lack of technical and presentation skills, English fluency, career orientation, domain expertise, leadership qualities and team skills.

The problem of 'unemployability' occurs not as the result of deficiency in the course contents or syllabus of our engineering programmes but because of the deficiencies in the pedagogy of our engineering education. Some of the most important deficiencies with our existing pedagogy can be summarized as follows:

(i) It is not encouraging training on soft skills development

(ii) Opportunity is limited for personal grooming

(iii) Emphasis on team skills and communication skills development are not adequate

(iv) Existing pedagogy is not learner centric but teacher centric

(v) Present teaching is text book oriented teaching and not industry oriented

(vi) Emphasis given only to enhancement of conceptual knowledge and not to Problem-solving skills.

(vii) Training limited to examination view point and no scope for kindling the professionalism in the young minds

LACK OF ENTREPRENEURIAL ORIENTATION

One other important aspect which needs to be taken along with low employability rate is the lack or entrepreneurial orientation among young Graduates. Our present system of engineering education has been a failure in building effective entrepreneurship among the budding engineers. We are moving under the shadow of Globalisation and living in a fast moving technological world. Both of this gives immense opportunities for the young professionals with entrepreneurial skills and a number of examples in front of us. But our Curriculum and pedagogy has not been equipped properly to develop the entrepreneurial skills of the students. Our present system is producing a number of job seekers in bulk but not the job creators as desired by the nation.

ABSENCE OF A NEED BASED STUDY WHILE SANCTIONING COLLEGES AND COURSES

It is obvious from the Table 3 that the phenomenal increase which had taken place in the total sanctioned intake is not the reflection of the actual requirement of the state. In other words it is to be learned from the table that the demand for the engineering courses is not shown any increase in proportion to the increase in the number of seats offered by the engineering colleges. This is why, there is a huge gap between sanctioned intake and actual intake exists from the year 2002 onwards. For example, during the year 2005, out of the 24,526 seats made available for 23 engineering courses, only 21,814 seats were taken last year leaving 2,712 seats vacant. This is a better situation compared to the previous year as there were 6,800 seats were vacant in 2004.

This gap is a true reflection of the sad state of affairs of technical education in the state. Education sector in Kerala had undergone drastic changes and providing education is no more a service or charity but a true commercialised activity. The so called phenomenal increase in the number of professional education institutions are the result of this transformation. But even in any commercial activity, an appropriate marketing research and planning precedes the actual release of the product. But in Kerala's technical education sector, it did not work due to one or other reasons. The State Government who gave sanctions for establishing new institutions never made a scientific study or systematic evaluation regarding what are the actual requirements and deficiencies with respect to the colleges and courses in the state, but they were quite liberal in sanctioning colleges and courses every here and there. The distribution of the engineering colleges in various districts and sanctioned intake for various branches of study are not as a result of a scientific study about the requirements. What happened is, those who wanted to start engineering colleges at places where they had interest, they were permitted to do the same.

ISSUES TO BE ADDRESSED TO STRENGTHEN ENGINEERING EDUCATION SECTOR IN KERALA

With the globalization Indian market is thrown open to the whole world and competition has become intensive in all respects. It is in this context that the need for maintaining quality has become a great concern to everyone. After analyzing various problems existing in the current engineering education scenario, it is felt that there are a few number of issues which are to be addressed at the earliest in order to enhance the quality and ensure stability in our engineering education sector. The most important issues with regard to our present engineering education sector are as follows:

(i) Regulating the Self financed sector
(ii) Need for training teachers
(iii) Need for State level Accreditation
(iv) Need for compulsory training for soft skills development
(v) Need for implementing the concept of finishing schools
(vi) Need for timely curriculum revision and Inter-disciplinary approach
(vii) Need for industry collaboration for teaching, training and placement

DOMINANCE OF PRIVATE SELF FINANCE SECTOR IN ENGINEERING EDUCATION

It is the self financing sector that led the rapid development in the higher education sector of Kerala including the technical education sector during the last decade. The number of engineering colleges went up from 12 in 1993 to 87 in 2005 just because of the presence, effort and investment of the Self financing sector. Out of the 87 colleges 53 are in the self finance sector, which indicates the prominent role played by the self-financing colleges under the private management in providing engineering education. That is the responsibility of providing technical education seems to have shifted from the government to the private sector. This shift made education become a costly afire in the state and the burden falls on the households.

This situation is going to create a lot of socio-economic issues in the state in the near future. The efforts in the form of legislation taken by the government so far not found any effective means for regulating the self financing sector. Any way, regulating the functioning of self financing sector with out damaging the quality of education and developing a concept of social responsibility among the various managements of self financing institutions are issues of great concern to everyone in the state.

NEED FOR STATE LEVEL ACCREDITATION FOR QUALITY MANAGEMENT

After analysing various problems mentioned above it became imperative to think about developing a system that ensure certain level of quality with respect to all aspects of engineering education. It is undoubted to say that a right step to develop an overall quality is possible only by addressing the severe issues independently. We are evaluating the quality and status of engineering education at a time when companies are forced to adapt and adjust to a changing marketplace. Engineering educators have an obligation and responsibility to do the same if they are truly to serve both industry and our students. Technical education must define and assure quality in terms of instructional resources, its institutional identity and the demands of its environment.

In short, it can be concluded that the quality technical education must be defined in terms of its outcomes and contexts. Since the engineering education sector in the state is largely in the private sector, that too in the self finance sector, government has to evolve a mechanism for ensuring a minimum quality with respect to all the three factors mentioned above with every engineering colleges in the state. What we suggest is, formation of a state level Technical

Education Accreditation Board which certifies the standard of facilities and performance of each engineering college in the state and would grade the institutions to group them into various categories. If the certification from the said board is made compulsory then the managements of the institution would become more alert in maintaining overall quality of the institutions.

NEED FOR TRAINING PROGRAMMES FOR TEACHERS

The Improvement of teaching quality and training quality are issues of great concern to everyone involved in the engineering education. When we talk about improving quality of teachers, it is a multidimensional issue. It includes not only expanding the depth and breadth of their knowledge but also expanding the range of skills and qualities they have as trainers. We have already seen in our discussion earlier that the quality of instructional resources is one of the most important components in the total quality management of our engineering education.

We feel that their must be special efforts from the sides of both the government and the universities to evolve a training package for the teachers. Specially designed teacher training programmes, summer training schools etc. may be initiated by the universities to make the teachers competent to impart the teaching and training to the students as desired by both the students and the industry. The government has to bring out an effective plan to enhance the education level of the teachers also by instituting special Quality Improvement Programmes (QIP) to increase the percentage of teachers with Masters Degree and Doctoral Degree in all branches of engineering studies.

FINISHING SCHOOLS AND SOFT SKILLS DEVELOPMENT

The teaching quality and training quality with respect to the development of finishing skills of the students are issues of immediate concern as the state can not miss the employment opportunities which are at the door step of our budding engineering professionals. The National Association of Software and Service Companies (NASSCOM) in its recent report on employment trends in the country has indicated that total IT, software and service employment figure will touch 1.6 million in the financial year 2007-08 and the country and, the government and other stakeholders need to take several initiatives to enhance the availability and access to suitable talent for the IT and ITES sectors.

In this context the issue of employability of engineering and other graduates has become a severe concern of everyone. As mentioned earlier the employability rate of engineering graduates in the country is only 35 per cent and the same in Kerala is much lower than the national rate. This means that the rest of the students need to upgrade their technical as well as soft skills suggesting that the education system could be overhauled significantly to cater the requirement of the industry. Our engineering curriculum need to be restructured for including inputs that would definitely make our students employable. In order to materialize this objective our engineering curriculum must be broadened to include training modules with respect to the following:

(i) Team skills development and Communication skills development

(ii) Leadership skills development

(iii) Behavioural etiquettes, professional ethics and Holistic thinking

(iv) A system perspective with multidisciplinary dimension

(v) An understanding and Appreciation of diversity

(vi) An appreciation of different cultures and business practices

(vii) A commitment to quality, timeliness and continuous improvement and

(viii) An understanding of the societal, economic and environmental impacts of engineering decisions

The soft skills development among our engineering graduates is not possible with mere inclusion of the above into the syllabus. There must be appropriate initiatives to effect the same in the pedagogy of the programmes. Setting up of 'Finishing Schools' at college level or university level to train the students on their soft skills along with their regular curriculum would be a right beginning for enhancing the employability rate of our engineering graduates.

CURRICULUM REVISION AND INTERDISCIPLINARY APPROACH

One thing that is common among the universities in Kerala is their inability to revise the engineering curriculum on a yearly basis by incorporating the changes taking place both in the industry and academia. The concept of interdisciplinary approach is also not encouraged very much by the universities in Kerala. Since the Globalisation has made the job market highly competitive and the fast changing technology had created the concept of knowledge worker, the interdisciplinary approach is inevitable. For example, the developments taking place in the areas of Biotechnology, Bioinformatics, etc. are to be adequately reflected in our curriculum and similar developments taking place in other areas may also be duly identified and incorporated in our syllabi in order to develop an interdisciplinary approach as desired by the present "knowledge economy'. Universities may think in multidisciplinary line and their academic bodies are to be reconstituted accordingly to encourage timely revision of curriculum to respond to the demands of the corporate world positively.

NEED FOR INDUSTRY COLLABORATION FOR TEACHING, TRAINING AND PLACEMENT

Industry professionals can easily imbibe the changing needs of the corporate world and they can effectively support the faculty and academia in planning and implementing effective measures to cope up with the demands of the industry. In order to ensure such a healthy and productive support from the industrial sector to the academic sector, an effective industry institute interaction should take place on regular basis. But our existing academic environment is not conducive for encouraging effective industry institute interaction. The scope of industry institute interaction is very wide. An effective interface between the industry and institute can bring fruitful results in building infrastructures, ensuring professionally qualified and experienced faculty resources, developing joint research and projects of mutual interests, patents and ultimately it guarantee better placements to the students.

While educational institutions are the centers of learning, industries can apply what is learned after modifying the suitability, to meet the specific requirements. Many industrial organisations in the country such as L&T, TATA and many others make a giant leap as they maintain continual relations with academic institutions. Large numbers of projects in various institutes in the country are funded by the industries and they often help institutes in building their infrastructure. Typical examples are Xerox, Boeing, IBM etc. Hence, there must be planned efforts from the side of the government and the educational institutions to develop healthy and effective Industry-Institute collaboration with an objective of strengthening the infrastructure, developing quality instructional resources, and providing excellent learning environment.

CONCLUSION

The present world has been witnessing unprecedented changes and development due to rapid technological revolution over the last 20 years. Our economy has undergone drastic changes and the concept of 'global village' accepted everywhere. We are gradually moving to the era of 'knowledge economy', where knowledge is the order of the day. The 'knowledge economy' deserves a new category of technical manpower, now-a-days often termed as 'knowledge workers' in popular parlance. The concept of 'knowledge worker' was first discussed by Peter F. Drucker in the year 1959. That has evolved as a reality today. In this context, our engineering education system has to undergo a drastic change to accommodate the needs of the emerging 'knowledge economy' by providing quality 'knowledge workers'.

To conclude, it is to be categorically stated that Kerala's engineering education sector need to be innovated effectively to ensure a high quality education to produce entrepreneurial oriented, industry ready, employable professionals meeting the global employer's requirements.

REFERENCES

Annual Technical Manpower Review, Kerala-2006 (Engineering), National Technical Manpower Information System, Nodal Centre, Cochin University of Science And Technology, Kochi-22.

Drucker F. P. (1959), Landmarks of Tomorrow, Transaction Publishers.

Everett, J.; Gershwin, M.; Hayes, H.; Jacobs, J. and Mundhenk, R. (2001), How should "Quality" Technical Education and Training be Defined? Concept Paper prepared for US Department of Education.

Manas Bhuniya and Bhattacharya A. (2004), 'The Knowledge Economy and its Requirements: The type of Technical Manpower We Need' in Technical Manpower Planning, Sudhir Reddy, Murali Krishna P., Ramkrishna Reddy. K. and Lal Kishor, (eds), Discovery Publishing, New Delhi, Vol. II, p. 1-7.

Pande, R. S., (2004), 'Globalisation and Technical Education: Promises and Compromises in Technical Manpower Planning' in Globalisation and Manpower Planning, Sudhir Reddy, Murali Krishna P., Ramkrishna Reddy.K. and Lal Kishor, eds, Discovery Publishing, New Delhi, Vol. I, P. 151-160.

Russell, J.S., Pfatteicher, S. K. A. and Meier, J.R. (1997), What you can do to improve engineering education. Journal of Management in Engineering, 1997 December issue, p. 37-41.

Sunitha, S. and Duraisamy, M. (2004), 'Technical Education in Kerala: Issues and Concerns, Technical Manpower Planning' in Technical Manpower Planning, Sudhir Reddy, Murali Krishna P., Ramkrishna Reddy.K. and Lal Kishor, eds., Discovery Publishing, New Delhi. Vol. II, p. 157-171.

Devasia M D

17 Technical Higher Education Expansion Bane or Boon for Kerala?

The technical education system in the State covers courses in engineering, technology, architecture, etc. at diploma, degree, postgraduate and research levels. Industrial Training Institutes, Technical High Schools, Fine Arts Colleges, etc also come under Technical Education system. NIT Kozhikkode having the Deemed University status offers graduate and postgraduate course. Cochin University of Science and Technology, functions in line with the status of a technical university in the State.

The total number of approved engineering colleges in India is 1358 with annual sanctioned intake of 4,50,954. Though one million students are being admitted to technical courses (including private sector) every year in India, it still meets only 15 to 20 per cent in the appropriate age group. This wide gap has to be bridged. Therefore, enrolments in technical education need to be at least doubled in the next five to seven years. Also, there is a serious regional imbalance in the growth of technical institutions and capacity. TN, AP, Maharashtra, Karnataka account for 70 per cent of the capacity in technical courses. Kerala hold only 6.2 per cent of institutions and 5.1 per cent of approved sanctioned seats (AICTE Report 2005). Progress of enrollments in Professional Education in Kerala for 1990-2003 is shown in Table 1. The enrollment in professional education in the State has gone

Table 1
Annual Enrollments in Higher Education in Kerala

Year	*General Education**	*Professional Education***	*Total Enrollment*	*% of Professional Enrollment*
1990	41628	4052	45680	8.9
1991	44731	4207	48938	8.6
1992	44858	4273	49131	8.7
1993	49394	4344	53738	8.1
1994	45888	4206	50094	8.4
1995	47120	4221	51341	8.2
1996	35148	4063	39211	10.4
1997	41276	6334	47610	13.3
1998	49187	6434	55621	11.6
1999	54422	7240	61662	11.7
2000	45363	9985	55348	18.0
2001	49096	11539	60635	19.0
2002	51517	18603	70120	26.5
2003	50895	21083	71978	29.3

* I Year B.A, B.Sc, B.COM

** I Year Engineering, Medicine (allopathic, ayurveda & homeo)

Source: Economic Review, State Planning Board, Trivandrum 1992 PP. 99-101, 250; 1994 PP. 142, 2000 PP 156, 161-62; 2002 PP 243, 254-56, S216, S222; 2003 PP 3,S209-10,278-9.

up from less 10 per cent in 1990 to nearly 30 per cent in 2003 and the pace still continues.

CURRENT STATUS

In recent years there has been a remarkable increase in the number of engineering colleges especially in the number of private self-financing colleges. By the end of IX Five Year Plan, the number of engineering colleges was 44. At present there are 84 engineering colleges with a sanctioned annual intake of 23,196 seats. Out of 84, only 9 are government, 3 are private aided and 72 are Self-financing. Out of 23,196 sanctioned seats 11.14 per cent (2583) are in government sector, 6.21 per cent (1440) in private aided and 82.65 per cent are in the self-financing streams.

Despite these, it is argued that the available number of seats is not adequate to meet the growing demand for engineering courses. Table 3 shows that out of the total batches in Plus 2 courses in the State 58 per cent and 45 per cent (146570

Table 2
University -wise Distribution of Engineering Colleges in Kerala (2005)

Name of University	*No. of colleges*
Kerala University	19
Mahatma Gandhi University	22
Calicut University	18
Kannur University	5
Cochin University of Science and Technology	18
Agricutural University	2
Total	84

Source: Economic Review 2005, State Planning Board, Trivandrum.

students) of intake are in Science subject. An equivalent or more than that is enrolled in CBSE streams in science. All through these years, it is revealed that the first priority of parents and their pupils who undergo a pre-university course in science subject is to get either in Medicine or in Engineering. So they try their best in entrance examination. Obviously, out of more than 2 lakh students who demand technical courses, only less than 24 thousand (12 per cent) are getting accommodation in engineering courses. In other words, there is severe supply demand mismatch in the provision of higher technical education in the State.

Table 3
Batch-wise Annual Intake of Students in Plus + 2 (2004-05)

Name of course	*No. of Batch*	*Govt*	*Aided*	*Unaided*	*Total*	*% to grand Total*
Science	3164 (58)	57640	68680	20250	146570	45
Humanities	1005 (18)	33655	37670	2650	73975	23
Commerce	1324 (24)	51280	44020	7600	102900	32
Grand Total	5493 (100)	142575	150370	30500	323445	100

Source: Economic Review 2005, State Planning Board, Trivandrum.

Besides, the dropout in primary stage is another important impediment in the entry to the higher education stages. Although the dropout rate is shown to be declining, the actual dropout rate still is nearly 50 per cent, as shown in Table 4. Yes, if the dropouts in primary classes are brought to the minimum, and if the percentage score in their finals were

Table 4
Rate in Primary Stage of Education Kerala

Enrolled in Year	*STD 1 No.*	*Registered Year*	*For SSLC No.*	*Dropout SSLC (in %)*	*SSLC Result (in %)*	*Actual Dropout (Fail + Dropout)*
1981	631479	1991	394848	37.5	51.02	(430028) 68.10
1985	617681	1995	439617	28.8	50.55	(395455) 64.02
1986	630639	1996	446466	29.2	48.92	412228) 65.37
1990	594548	2000	454525	23.6	55.03	(344423) 57.93
1991	601030	2001	461884	23.2	54.94	(347271) 57.78
1992	575909	2002	422483	26.6	59.3	(285377) 49.55

Source: Economic Review, SPB, TVM (2001) PP S 167-170: (2003) PP 271, S 202; & Statistics for Planning, Govt. of Kerala (2001) PP 378.

raised, there will definitely be a sizeable increase in the demand for technical education in the near future. The analysis also reveals that, other thing remain the same enrollment rate is highly determined by dropout rate.

Regression

Variables Entered/Removed[b]

Model	*Variables Entered*	*Variables Removed*	*Method*
1	D. RATE[a]	.	Enter

a. All requested variales entered.
b. Dependent Variable: E. Rate

Model Summary[b]

Model	*R*	*R Square*	*Adjusted R Square*	*Std. Error of the Estimate*	*Durbin-Watson*
1	.911[a]	.830	.813	3.1409	2.214

a. Predictors: (Constant), D. Rate
b. Dependent Variable: E. Rate

RISING DROPOUTS IN ENGINEERING

Yet, the vitality of a higher education system is not only measured in terms of the number of students enrolled, or institutions established, but by the quality of the people it brings out. According to the "Open Doors 2006 International Students in the USA" reports, India sent 80,466 youth to the USA to study in 2004-05 and 76,503 in 2005-06, occupying the top place of origin of International Students. It is in the light of which the Chairman of AICTE has said steps are being taken to regulate the quality of engineering education, especially by making it mandatory for colleges to disclose their performance/infrastructure record while seeking affiliation. But, reports show that the dropouts from engineering colleges have spiralled to 24 per cent in 2000 from 9.7 per cent in 1991 (Table 5).

Similarly, there is acute shortage of manpower in civil and mechanical engineering branches due to the imbalance in the increased preference for IT oriented courses. Against this backdrop, IIT Madras plans to establish a centre of excellence in engineering design with a Science-meets-Aesthetic curriculum, first of its kind in India, aims to produce engineers with multi-disciplinary background with aesthetic approach.

Table 5
Dropout in Technical Education in Kerala (1991-2000)

Year	*Intake*	*Out-turn*	*Missing*	*% Loss*
1991	2795	2547	248	9.74
1995	4441	3571	870	19.59
1996	4657	3877	780	16.75
1997	4792	4126	666	13.90
1998	4913	3764	1149	23.19
1999	6126	3944	2182	35.39
2000	8739	6639	2100	24.03

Source: AICTE Report 2005

Source of Funding

It is pointed out that, public expenditure on education in the State is hardly 3 per cent of the GDP. Out of which Higher Education received the least priority with 15 per cent on an average and Technical Education together receives only 4-5 per cent. But the actual spending is far greater. So where does the money come from? This brings forth three basic issues: (A) academic, (B) social and (C) economic.

Table 5

Public Expenditure on Education in Kerala (Stage-wise) Rs. In Crores

Stage	*2002-2003*	*% to total*	*2003-2004*	*% to total*	*2004-2005*	*% to total*
Uty & HE	552.14	18.9	503.05	16.6	524.61	14.7
Techn Edn	132.21	4.5	138.81	4.6	192.36	5.4
SubTot HE	684.35	23.4	641.86	21.2	716.97	20.1
Others	2243.9	76.6	2392.53	78.8	2852.22	79.9
Total	2928.25	100.0	3034.39	100.0	3569.19	100.0

Source: Economic Review 2005, State Planning Board, Trivandrum.

(A) On academic front, the question is (a) how to increase quantity without compromising quality-Global competition put pressure on enhanced quality; (b) how to link education to productive sectors-Employment Market directs the content; (c) how to assure employment as higher education is no longer an elitist idea or purely intellectual pursuit, but has become closely linked to 'bread and butter'. Market requirements get the upper hand. Therefore, flexibility and fast changes are required.

Studies have shown that, 'malayalee' migrants were able to enter into the formal labour market due to their better educational status, vocational training.... The share of Keralites to total Indian migrants in Middle East is almost 50 per cent and that the remittances to Kerala as per cent of NSDP was 10.7 in 1990 and that increased to 21.5 in 1995 (Prakash 1999). Nearly 20 lakh NRI's sending 29 thousand crores to Kerala every year, which is more than 40 per cent of the total bank deposit. History of Keralites migration dates back to the formation of Kerala State. Migration at the later half of 70s and 80s to South Asia, especially to Arab- Persia, in search of employment and better earnings has even shaped Kerala to this present fashion. Now education is the prominent migration factor. In the globalization scenario the source of demand for labour is worldwide (Todaro 1985; Zacharia 1999 & 2000; Lakshmi & Renuka 2003). In the present job competition scenario wage rate is not the prime factor in determining the demand for labour, because wage rate (salary scale) is fixed a priori for almost all occupations and even pays that 'matches the best' in the industry. 'Higher Salary Scales will be offered on soaring performance, which is highly linked to ones educational qualification, skill and experience (Lloyed Byars & Leslie 1997; Leinert 1995). 5500 job aspirants flocked with technical training to a job fair held recently at Chennai were given offer letters with Rs. 2.5 lakhs per annum on an average. But to the dismay the campus recruitment is 3-4 per cent in Kerala.

Since education is the fundamental requirement for migration and acquisition of jobs abroad, foreign exchange flow to the country through manpower exports need to be stressed. One need not hesitate to export the precious manpower in the present technology age in which information can be collected from any corner of the world and exported manpower can be immediately substituted or replaced (except in very few cases).

(B) On social scene, access, equity and pricing are the important crises. According to World Education Report 2000, only 6.9 per cent of youth (17-23) are enrolled for higher education in India. While it is 80.9 per cent in US, 52.3 per cent in UK, 79.8 per cent in Australia and 62.6 per cent in New Zealand (UNESCO). The world is now capturing to become a Knowledge Driven Society. Unprecedented knowledge explosion is taking place across the world through the integration of disciplines. Knowledge monopoly ended instead democratization of education is taking place.

Education and training are now considered valued commodities. But, how to price it when (a) majority are so poor (b) Government is in resource crunch (c) colleges are not like firms although operated by private sector. Especially in Kerala, technical higher education investments in private sector are mainly done by religious or charitable institutions. In fact, the funds are mobilized from public or through donations or charitable contributions.

Earlier studies have shown that, higher education in India is mostly availed by the top 30 per cent income groups. They receive free elementary education and occupy 70 per cent seats in secondary education and 80 per cent higher education (Balachander 1989). But a recent field survey conducted in a few engineering colleges of the State reveals that there are only very few students at the lowest ebb of income ladder both in self-financing colleges as well as government colleges. Besides, education brings forth innumerable private and social benefits. Generally the benefits of education are measured in terms of the extra lifetime incomes or earnings enjoyed by the educated (Hipple 2001). Again, positive contributions to cognitive or affective attributes, externalities/spillovers: on consumption (Lazear 1977; Gustafson 1978), on health & living (Grossman 1976; Lando 1975), on mother's education and child's IQ (Leibowitz 1974; Benson 1982), on educated women & unplanned babies (Michael 1982), wife's schooling raises her husband's earnings (Benham 1974; Welch 1974; Mc Mahon 1987), effective democracy (Thomas Jefferson), efficient market & technical change (Schultz 1975), lower crimes & penal system expense (Spiegleman 1968; Webb 1977; Ehrlich 1975; Phillips *et. al*, 1972), lower welfare Medicaid, unemployment compensation & public health costs (Garfinkle and Haveman 1977), lower accident rate, leadership (Weisbrod 1962)....to mention a few.

Table 6
Total Intake and Their Family Income Status

Year	*Tly*	*Knr*	*Vdk*	*Total*	*No. below Rs.1 lakh p/a*	*% to total*
2000-01	176	300	235	711	9	1.27
2001-02	147	300	215	662	3	0.45
2002-03	130	330	210	670	6	0.90
2003-04	155	330	220	705	2	0.28
2004-05	225	330	165	720	11	1.53
2005-06	325	330	236	891	5	0.56
2006-07	359	330	235	924	6	0.65

Source: College of Engineering Thalassery, Govt. College of Engineering, Kannur, Co-operative Institute of Technology, Vadakara.

Taking note of these, the price burden must be shared between students, managements and govt., at par with cost &

benefit (private & social), source of funding (donation, charities or else) and the financial capabilities of students. At par with the social benefit, government has to provide a general subsidy applicable to all the students. That is 'sticker price' or the price that 'full-pay student' has to bear must be estimated after deducting the general subsidy.

Sticker Price = Price-General Subsidy

The difference between sticker price and the price that a 'financially weaker student' (FWS) can afford to pay must be paid out from public exchequer. If all the students admitted could meet this, then the government need not pay anything. The 'differential fee' or "individual subsidy" has to be estimated on the basis of students' financial capabilities.

1. If a student can afford to pay the sticker price, then he gets zero govt. subsidies.
2. If he/she can study only with full concession, then the subsidy will be equal to sticker price (i.e., 100 per cent subsidy).
3. If a student can meet the expenses only partially, then the subsidy will be less than sticker price and that may be divided into convenient slabs, say 25 or 50 or 75 per cent of sticker price.

Looking from this angle, there is no need of bifurcating student admission into 50-50 or 25-75. All students get admission on merit basis and they may be free to choose the institution (either aided/govt. or self-financing) or course.

Scholarship is an incentive for education and the purpose of which is to encourage meritorious students. It is a grant/award to all (full-pay or partial-pay or no-pay student) those students depending on their educational merit.

In short, it is observed that, there exists unequal treatment in the area of pricing after the initiation of private self-financing institutions. But, it is the responsibility of the government to encounter the difficulties faced by the poor students and their parents by way of subsidies to meet the differences in sticker price that are not affordable by the poor sections (Devasia 2005), bearing the innumerable social benefits that higher education brings to the State.

(C) On economic aspect, cost, return and source of funding are important issues. Since every government operates under budget constraints, cost scrutinization and analysis are of primordial importance in educational planning. But one should be extremely careful in distinguishing them as Cost-Benefit Analyze in education is complex due to: (1) Asymmetric information; (2) Time span of cost and benefit; (3) Nature of cost and benefit; (4) Individual differences; (5) Level and type of education; (6) Heterogeneity of institutions; (7) Motives of both educationalist and learners.

Government of Kerala has spent Rs. 2928 crores for education in 2002-03 and that increased to Rs. 3569 crores in 2004-05. Out of which technical education received only less than 5 per cent. But the actual spending in this area is far greater. This has produced a spectacular overall growth in the economy, as educational investment generated various externalities. This includes increased employment, capital mobility, market performance and above all the speed of velocity of circulation of money.

CONCLUSION

Physical resources and Human resources determine the progress of any nation. Some countries are abundant in physical resource while others are blessed with population. Unless a country transforms its population into human resource, it will be hog-tied to develop anything else. Education creates assets in the form of knowledge and skills, which are valuable for the market as it leads to better earnings, enhanced employability and compensate skill shortage.

Almost two centuries have elapsed since Macaulay devised a system of education. Nearly 60 years after independence we continue to blame him that it creates only clerks overlooking the fact that what independent India and its government have done in the past six decades.

India wants to take the cue from countries that make massive investments to fuel the growth of Knowledge Driven Economies. XI Plan document of Planning Commission seek to invest Rs. 7300 crores in this line. There must be Industry-Institution partnership or interface. Hon' President A P J Abdul

Kalam highlight areas which require Industry-Education interface like (a) Bio-Fuel Generation; (b) Interlinking rivers; (c) Bamboo Mission; (d) Textile industry; (e) knowledge (IT) products; (f) Muncipal waste; (g) Power sector; (h) water; (i) desalination technology; (j) Nano Technology; (k) Nano science; (l) Nano engineering; etc. India's largest Butterfly Conservatory opened in Nov' 2006 at the Bannerghatta National Park 25 KM South of Bangalore is a magnificent example of multi-institutional sharing of expertise to achieve the best in a cost-effective manner. Nearly 30000 butterflies flutter around it.

Kerala's hopes too flutter around the Globe as it is turning to be a hub of intellectual capital and labour force. In the world of top executives a stint in India is now the ultimate status symbol. According to National Association of Software and Service Companies, over 30000 expiates are working in the IT, aviation and offshore industries in India. The world is now converted as a work place with new and most glaring philosophy "taking work to the workers". In other words, employment growth within India is also a promising one.

The New Year must be an year of regeneration and renewal radiant with inspiration of new ideas. SENSEX is gyrating above 14,000. Economy grows at 9.1 per cent per annum. A whopping Rs. 14,50,000 crores is what the XI Plan estimated should go into infrastructure to keep Indian growth story around double digit. There was a big spurt by attracting a total of $ 20.2 billion (FII+FDI) investment to India in 2005-06 and the momentum is expected to continue. Most ambitious companies of India are planning to launch over three dozen boutique hotels in India in 2007. TATA's are going to invest Rs. 1,10,000 crores across business segments: steel plant, telecom, auto and retail, in 2007. Mukesh Abani to invest Rs.1,00,000 crores in new refinery, oil and gas exploration, telecom, retail and special economic zones. Sunil Mittal expects that revenue of the group will cross Rs. 67,000 crore by 2010 with 50 crore subscribers in telecom. Mahindra & Mahindra hopes that its revenues will double to over Rs. 17500 crores by March 2007 and it has acquired nine companies in China, US and Europe (India Today, January 2007). Definitely, Technical Higher Education Expansion is a boon to the State of Kerala. Within no time we have to realize the potentiality of such an investment and set our mind to harvest the best.

REFERENCES

Prakash B. A. (1999), Kerala's Economic Development: Issues and Problems, Sage Publications, New Delhi.

Todaro Michael, P. (1985), Economics for a Developing World, 2nd ed. Longman, New York.

Zacharia K. C. *et, al.* (1999), Impact of Migration on Kerala's Economy and Society, CDS Working Paper 297, Trivandrum.

———(2000), Socio-Economic and Demographic Consequences of Migration in Kerala, CDS Working Paper 303, Trivandrum.

Lakshmi Devi K. R. & P. Renuka (2003), Asian Indian Women Immigrants in US: A Socio-Economic Profile, *Indian Journal of Economics and Business*, Vol. 2 No.1, pp. 101-109

Lloyed L. Byars & Leslie W. Rue (1997), Human Resource Management, Mc Graw Hill, pp. 338-354

Balachander, K. K. (1989), Financing of Higher Education; A Public Finance Perspective, Mainstream, March 25.

Hipple F. Steb (February 2001), A Cost-Benefit Analysis of Higher Education in Tennessee, College of Business, East Tennessee State University, February, Presented before the College of Business Advisory Board, Adelphia Center, Johnson City, Tennessee, e-mail: H*ipples@ETSU.edu*, website: h*ttp://faculty.estu.edu/hipples Hipple 2001*

Lazear, E. P. (1977), Education: Consumption or Production? *Journal of Political Economy*, No. 85, pp. 569-97.

Gustafson, S. (1978), Cost Benefit Analysis of Early Childhood, Care and Education, Working Paper, Industrial Institute for Economic and Social Research, Stockholm.

Grossman, M. (1976), The Correlation Between Health and Schooling, ed. in: Terleckyj, N (1976), Household Production and Consumption, Columbia University Press, New York, pp. 147-211

Lando, M (1975), The Interaction Between Health and Education, Social Securities Bulletin, No. 38, Vol. 12, pp. 16-22

Leibovitz, A (1974), Home Investment in Children, ed. in: Schultz, T. W. (1974), Economics of the Family, Marriage, Children and Human Capital, University of Chicago Press, Chicago, Illinois, pp. 432-52.

Benson, C. S. (1982), Household Production of Human Capital, ed. in: Mc Mahon, W. W., Geske, T. (1982), Financing Education: Overcoming Inefficiency and Inequity, University of Illinois Press

Michael, R. T. (1982), Measuring Non-monetary Benefits of Education, ed. in Mc Mahon, W. W., Geske, T. (1982), Financing Education. Overcoming Inefficiency and Inequity, University of Illinois Press

Benham, L. (1974), Benefits of Women's Education Within Marriage, ed. in: Schultz, T. W. (1974), Economics of the Family, Marriage, Children and Human Capital, University of Chicago Press, Chicago, Illinois.

Welch (1974), in T. W. Schultz, Economics of the Family: Marriage, Children and Human Capital, University of Chicago Press, Illionois.

Mc Mahon, W. W. (1987), Consumption and Other Benefits of Education, ed. in: Psacharopauos, G. (1987), Economics of Education: Research of Studies, Pergamon Press, New York, pp. 129-133

Schultz (1975), The Value of the Ability to Deal with Disequilibria, *Journal of Economic Literature,* No. p. 843

Spiegleman (1968), in Bosworth D. *et, al* (1996), The Economics of the Labour Market, Addison Wesley Longman Ltd, U.K.

Webb (1977), in Bosworth D. *et, al* (1996), The Economics of the Labour Market, Addison Wesley Longman Ltd, U K

Ehrlich (1975) in Bosworth D. *et, al* (1996), The Economics of the Labour Market, Addison Wesley Longman Ltd, U.K.

Phillips (1972), in Bosworth D. *et, al* (1996), The Economics of the Labour Market, Addison Wesley Longman Ltd, U.K.

Garfinkle & Haveman (1977), in Bosworth D. *et, al* (1996), The Economics of the Labour Market, Addison Wesley Longman Ltd, U. K.

Weisbrod, B. A. (1962), External Benefits of Education: An Economic Analysis, Research Report 105, Dept. of Economics, Princeton University, New Jersey.

Devasia, M. D (2005), Economics of Human Resource Planning With Special Reference to Higher Education in Kerala, Ph. D Thesis, Dept. of Applied Economics, Cochin University of Science and Technology, Kochi.

Manoj P K & Meera Bai M

18 Technical Education in India The Way Ahead

Education is one of the most important inputs that influences the all round development of any economy-economic, physical, social, cultural, ethical and spiritual. Jean Dreze and Amartya Sen (1995) have observed that education enables people to 'build up their capabilities', thereby 'broadening their entitlements' and 'facilitating expansion of freedom' which in turn is the primary end and principal means of development. In the emerging deregulated economic environment, education has got added significance because production of knowledge has attained the status of the most decisive economic activity. Knowledge has become the most important raw material in the 'knowledge economy' of the 21st century. Gnanam (2004) observes that 'the ability of a society to generate, select, adapt, commercialize and use knowledge has now become critical for sustained economic growth and for improving the quality of life for all.' The existing 'market economy' of India characterized by Liberalization, Privatization and Globalization (LPG), has influenced all aspects of human life, the case of education system being one of utmost significance in this regard. Of late, with General Agreement on Trade in Services (GATS) becoming fully operational under the World Trade Organization (WTO) regime, it will be difficult for India to survive as a nation without developing its 'intellectual knowledge' through diligent monitoring, expansion, strengthening and re-orientation of its education system as per the ever-increasing demands of the market.

Because of the onslaught of economic deregulation, the last decade of twentieth century has seen many significant changes in the global environment that are having a bearing on the role, function, shape and mode of operation of higher education systems across the world. As far as the technical education in particular is concerned the implications of these developments are much more significant, most notable among these developments being the transition towards societies which are highly knowledge-based and more technology-intensive. The impact of globalisation on higher (and technical) education in respect of the newly deregulated economies, mostly developing nations, has been really significant. In India too there have been a few very prominent changes in the higher (and technical) education system since the initiation of the economic deregulation in the early nineties. Firstly there has been a trend towards privatization and commercialization of education and secondly there has been growing competition from increasing presence of foreign educational institutions. Both the central and state governments have been encouraging the establishment of universities and colleges in their respective areas of jurisdiction. Tilak (2001) [23] has observed that one of the consequences of the above policy of 'laissez faireism' of the governments has been the erratic and unregulated growth of private higher education. Patel (2004) has observed that the new developments have resulted in numerous problems, the most important among these being the significant decrease in budget outlay per student from Rs. 7676 in 1993-'94 to Rs. 5873 in 2001-'02. Further, as already noted, there are clear indications of international competition with the foreign universities setting up their campuses in India resulting in high level of student mobility and fast commercialization and privatization of education.

In the above context, this paper attempts to look into the higher education system in India (with special reference to technical education system) in the LPG regime that is undergoing a paradigm transformation, primarily manifested as pressures of internationalization. It makes a SWOT (Strengths, Weaknesses, Opportunities and Threats) analysis of the Indian technical education system with a view to identify the most appropriate skills to be imparted to the technical students, the desired orientation of the technical graduates and practitioners in the emerging scenario, the need for internationalization of the technical education system and after all the necessary policy initiatives to bring about these changes.

In today's 'knowledge economy', the scope and significance of higher education in general and technical education in particular need not be overemphasized. Because of the economic globalization measures sweeping across the globe, resulting in fierce international competition in every walks of life, survival of any nation depends on a sound system of higher education that can effectively address the ever-changing needs of the open economy. Here, the role that can be played by the technical education system is of utmost importance as it has a direct bearing on the technological competitiveness of the nation in the days to come..' It appears that a systematic study as to the relevance, adequacy and market-friendliness of the Indian technical education system in view of the growing internationalization pressures of today's globalized economy is quite relevant. Such a study made with a global perspective i.e. after taking into account the relevant global developments and emerging practices, can help formulate the necessary strategies to be adopted for re-orienting the technical education system in the country, in such a way that it can keep itself abreast of the global developments and also boldly face the challenges posed by growing pressures of privatization and internationalization.

The present paper throws light to the current status in respect of higher education system in general and technical education in particular and the preparedness of the technical education system in India to address the growing demands of the globalized economic environment by making a SWOT analysis of the system .The paper also tries to identify strategies for making the technical education system in India more dynamic, market friendly, internationally competitive and nationally relevant.

The data used for this study are essentially secondary data. The major sources of data include, inter alia, official statistics published by various Government departments, papers in the relevant topics published in reputed research journals, publications as well as the official web-sites of the AICTE, ISTE, UGC, UNESCO and World bank, and books in the relevant topics written by well-known experts in the field. The methodology is basically analytical in nature. It is analytical to the extent that it critically evaluates the present scenario in respect of Indian technical education system and also tries to develop appropriate strategies for reforming the system so that it can withstand the growing pressures of privatisation and internationalisation.

The paper is organized into four major parts. Part-I gives an overall picture of the Indian higher education system and its strengths and weaknesses vis-à-vis other major economies of the world, along with a brief discussion of the impact of GATS on the higher education system. Part-II gives an overview of the technical education scenario in India and discusses the major developments till date. Part-III makes a SWOT analysis of the Indian technical education system. Finally, Part-IV enumerates a few strategies for effecting certain meaningful reforms in the Indian technical education system to make it internationally competitive as well as nationally relevant.

PART I
HIGHER EDUCATION IN INDIA-AN OVERALL PICTURE

The higher education in modern India commenced with the establishment of Hindu College at Calcutta in 1781 by Raja Ram Mohan Roy with his friend David Hare. East India Company did not take any interest in educating the masses. However, the British started Sanskrit College in Calcutta in 1824, Elphinstone College at Bombay in 1834 and Madras Christian College at Madras in 1837. The British encouraged the English system of education which was introduced in 1835 by Lord Macauly. Higher education in India was largely reckoned by the British to be an instrument for effective development of a 'colonial state' during the pre-independence period, and was tailored for promoting and strengthening colonialism; its access, teaching and research being oriented to suit the requirements of the colonial state policy. Concepts such as liberal education, education with societal concerns and the like received little policy support.

The Woods Education Dispatch (1854) is known as Magna Carta of English Education in India. It prescribed for the first time, a detailed educational policy for India. Based on one of its recommendations, the first three modern Universities were set up in India in 1857; one each in Bombay, Madras and Calcutta. These were constituted based on the erstwhile model of the London University. At the end of 1900, there were five universities in India, the fourth and fifth universities viz. Lahore and Allahabad Universities being founded in 1882 and 1887 respectively. In 1901-'02, there were 191 Colleges and 23009 students in India. At the time of independence we had 18 universities. In order to facilitate co-ordination among the Universities in their activities, an Inter-University Board was established in 1925. [Later on, in 1973, this Board was converted into the present set up-Association of Indian Universities (AIU)]. Soon after the independence priority was given to basic education as advocated by Mahatma Gandhi. In respect of higher education, the first action taken by the Government of India was the appointment of the University Education Commission in 1948 under the Chairmanship of Dr. S Radhakrishnan-a well-known teacher by himself. The Commission stressed on restructuring of higher education and it recommended for reorganization of the University Grants Commission (UGC) so as to enjoy the powers to allocate the grants within the total limits set up by the Government. An interim UGC was set up in 1953. It was given autonomous statutory status by an Act of the Parliament in 1956.

CURRENT STATUS OF HIGHER EDUCATION IN INDIA

There has been quite remarkable growth in the higher education system in our country over the years. India has got the one of the largest higher education systems in the world, and is second only to that of USA.

The significant quantitative growth in Indian higher education is evident from the statistics given in Table 1. Of the 343 Universities in all, comprising of 19 Central Universities (including newly established Allahabad University which was

Table 1
Growth in the Number of Higher Education Institutions in India

S. No.	*Particulars*	*1947*	*2005*
1.	No. of Universities/University-level institutions	18	343
2.	Enrolment of students	2,28,804	99,53,506
3.	No. of University Colleges and Affiliated Colleges	591	17625

Source: (i) Official Website of UGC, www.ugc.ac.in
(ii) Sharma, J P & Jain Tanusree, University News, Association of Indian Universities, Vol. 44, No.30. July 24-30, 2006, pp.1.

incorporated as a Central University in 2005), 204 State Universities, 95 Deemed Universities, 5 Institutions established under State Legislation Acts, 13 Institutes of National Importance and 7 Private Universities. Besides, there are 10 Open Universities. The overall growth in higher education institutions in India over the years is depicted in Table 2.

Table 2
Overall Growth in the Number of Higher Education Institutions in India (Universities or University-Level Institutions) 1950 to 2005

Year	*Central Universities*	*State Universities*	*Deemed Universities*	*Institutes of National Importance**	*Private Universities*	*Total*
1950-51	3	24	–	–	–	27
1960-61	4	41	2	2	–	49
1970-71	5	79	9	9	–	102
1980-81	7	105	11	9	–	132
1990-91	10	137	29	9	–	185
2005	19	204	95	18	7	343

(*Includes five Institutes established through Legislature Acts).
Source: Sharma, J. P. & Jain Tanusree, University News, Association of Indian Universities, Vol. 44, No. 30. July 24-30, 2006, pp. 2.

Higher Education in India-Some Disappointing Facts

In spite of the remarkable quantitative growth in higher education in India over the years as suggested by the substantial growth in student enrolments and the number of higher education institutions, it has to be stated that in respect of Enrolment Ratio (i.e. the ratio of students in the relevant age group attending higher education institutions) the situation in India still remains to be very poor.

Table 3
Gross Enrolment in Higher Education in Selected Countries.

Particulars: Name of the Country/Group (Year)	*Enrol. Ratio*	*Particulars: Name of the Country/Group. (Year)*	*Enrol. Ratio*
World total (1997)	17	Developing Countries (1997)	10
Developed Countries (1997)	52	Asia (1997)	11
USA (1995)	92	Korea (1997)	68
Canada (1995)	88	China (1997)	6
UK (1996)	52	India (1997)	7
Australia (1997)	80	Less Developed Countries (1997)	3
Japan (2002)	45*	Africa (1997)	7

Source: UNESCO (1999)
Sharma, J P & Jain, Tanusree., University News, Association of Indian Universities, Vol. 44, No.30, July 24-30, 2006, pp.1; *Altbach and Ogawa (2002)

Table 3 depicts the comparative statistics in respect of Enrolment ratio of various nations. It is worth noting that in India the Enrolment ratio is just 7 per cent in India, though it has improved from the level of 1.5 per cent in 1960. Obviously, the position of India is far behind that of the developed countries and also that of some of the developing countries.

Table 4
Share of Public Expenditure on Higher Education in terms of GDP and (Total) Government Expenditure on Education.

Year	*Expenditure on Education as a Percentage of GDP*	*Expenditure on Higher Education as a % of Expenditure on Education*	*Expenditure on Higher Education as a % of GDP*
1981-82	2.49	15.25	0.38
1985-86	3.00	14.04	0.42
1990-91	3.59	10.16	0.34
1992-93	3.78	10.79	0.40
1994-95	3.61	10.81	0.37
1996-97	3.57	9.77	0.35
1998-99	3.85	9.93	0.46
2000-01(B)*	3.91	12.14	0.60

Source: (i) Analysis of Budgeted Expenditure on Education, Ministry of Human Resource Development, New Delhi; (ii) Indian Economic Survey (2000-'01).
Based on the new series of GDP with base 93-94 = 100 [*Quick Estimates of GDP].

Apart from the low enrolment ratio, another serious issue concerning the Indian higher education system has been low share of public expenditure on education in general and higher education in particular. Table 4 depicts the relevant details and it may be noted that the expenditure on higher education continues to be quite low over the years; whether it is in terms of the total GDP or the total expenditure on education. Quite similar is the case if we consider the expenditure on higher education as a percentage of GNP or Total Government Expenditure. (Table 5). Likewise, if we consider the outlay on higher education during the different Plans (viz. Plan I to Plan X), a similar disappointing trend can be observed (Table 6)

The trend in respect of expenditure on higher education per student over the years may be noted to be quite disappointing. Table 1.7 below depicts this dismal situation as we observe that the public expenditure which was as high as Rs. 7676 in 1990-91 (at 1993-94 price level) has declined rather constantly over the years to reach a level of just Rs. 5873 in 2001-02-a decline by nearly 24 percentage.

Table 5
Share of Public Expenditure on Higher Education in terms of GNP and (Total)Government Expenditure.

Years	*Government Expenditure on HE as a Percentage of GNP*	*Government Expenditure on HE as a Percentage of Government Expenditure*
1990-91	0.46	1.57
1991-92	0.42	1.43
1992-93	0.41	1.42
1993-94	0.40	1.42
1994-95	0.39	1.40
1995-96	0.37	1.35
1996-97	0.35	1.30
1997-98	0.35	1.31
1998-99	0.43	1.39
1999-00	0.47	1.61
2000-01	0.54	1.76
2001-02	0.41	1.33

Source: (i) Analysis of Budgeted Expenditure on Education, Ministry of Human Resource Development, New Delhi-various issues.

Latest Statistics (World Development Indicators 2005)

The recent statistics released by the Worıd Bank (2005) reveals that though there has been appreciable improvement in respect of higher education in India over the years, it is still lagging behind not only the developed economies but many of the developing nations as well. Table 8 shows the comparative statistics in respect of Gross Enrolment Ratio in higher education (tertiary education) of a few selected economies.

Table 6
Plan Outlay on Higher Education.

Name of the Five Year Plan	*Percentage of Plan Outlay on Higher Education to Total Plan Outlay*
I Plan	09
II Plan	18
III Plan	15
IV Plan	25
V Plan	22
VI Plan	26
VII Plan	16
VIII Plan	08
IX Plan	12
X Plan	09

Source: (i) Powar, K.B, Indian Higher Education, Concept Publishing Company, New Delhi; (ii) RBI Bulletin-various issues.

Table 7
Expenditure on Higher Education per Student.

Years	*In Current Prices (Rs.)*	*In 1993-94 Prices*	*Index*
1990-91	5652	7676	100.00
1991-92	5632	6727	87.64
1992-93	6111	6710	87.42
1993-94	6738	6738	87.78
1994-95	7329	6687	87.12
1995-96	6944	5812	75.72
1996-97	7207	5610	73.20
1997-98	7793	5692	74.15
1998-99	9536	6448	84.00
1999-00	10683	6954	90.59
2000-01	11989	7484	97.50
2001-02	9723	5873	76.51

Source: Compiled from Budgeted Expenditure on Education (Various years).

Table 8
Gross Enrolment Ratio for Higher Education-Comparative Statistics

Name of the Country	*Gross Enrolment Ratio* 1990-91	*(Tertiary Education)* 2002-03
Australia	36	74
Canada	93	58
Russian Federation	53	70
United Kingdom	30	64
United States	72	81
Brazil	11	18
China	3	13
India	6	11
Indonesia	9	15
Israel	36	58
Korea	39	85
Malaysia	07	27
Philippines	28	31
South Africa	12	15
Thailand	NA	37
Low Income Countries	5	10
Middle Income Countries	13	22
Middle Income (Lower)	12	21
Middle Income (Upper)	17	36
High Income Countries	47	66
Europe EMU	35	56
World	16	24

Source: Compiled from World Development Indicators 2005, The World Bank, March 2005.

Indian Higher Education in the LPG Regime-the Impact of General Agreement on Trade in Services (GATS) on Indian Higher Education System

As already pointed out, the ongoing process of economic deregulation in India, characterized by Liberalization, Privatization, and Globalization ("LPG", in short), has resulted in paradigm changes in every field of Indian economy. A plethora of factors-fast vanishing trade barriers, increasing technological progress particularly the rapid advances in the field of Information and Communication Technology (ICT), declining costs on communication and transportation etc. have resulted in a situation named World Economic Integration-an irreversible process with lots of implications. Within such an integrated system, knowledge and technological progress are of vital importance; and in respect of the higher educational system of an economy, especially the technical and scientific education, the implications are multifarious.

Many an international report has underlined the utmost significance of the role of higher education in enabling economic development of nations as well as in transforming them as vibrant knowledge economies of the world. For instance, the International Commission on Education for 21st Century states, "Higher education is at one and at the same time one of the driving forces of economic development and the focal point of learning in a society. It is both repository and creator of knowledge. Moreover, it is the principal instrument for passing on the accumulated experience, cultural and scientific, of humanity" (Delors, 1996. p.130) [5]. Further, the recent UNESCO Report, "Towards Knowledge Societies" states, "Institutions of higher education are destined to play a fundamental role in knowledge societies, based on radical changes in the traditional patterns of knowledge production, diffusion and application." (UNESCO-2005, p.87) [31]. This report has pointed out that there has been a growing flow of foreign students in search of quality higher education. The percentage of foreign students in various foreign countries as reported by the above report is as shown in Table 9.

Table 9
Percentage of Foreign Students in Higher Education in various countries.

Name of the Country	*% of foreign students*	*Name of the Country*	*% of foreign students*
USA	25% (Highest)	Japan	04 %
UK	11%	Russia	03 %
Germany	10%	Belgium, Canada, Italy, Spain	02 %
France	09%	Austria, Malaysia, Sweden and	01 %
Australia	08%	Switzerland	

Source: Compiled from Towards Knowledge Societies, UNESCO-2005, Paris

The General Agreement on Trade in Services (GATS) and Higher Education:

One of the most prominent developments in this era of world economic integration which is having a bearing on

Indian higher education system has been the adoption of GATS (General Agreement on Trade in Services). GATS is a comprehensive legal framework of rules and disciplines covering 161 service activities across 12 classified sectors; comprising of a wide range of activities such as education, health, finance, environment etc. GATS define services trade as occurring through four possible modes of supply. [Exhibit (1) below].

Mode (1): Cross border supply i.e. supply of a service from one country to another country, e.g. provision of research work via Internet.

Mode (2): Consumption abroad, i.e. the supply of a service in one country to the service consumer of any other member, e.g. through movement of students.

Mode (3): Commercial presence, e.g. supply of service by a service supplier of one country through commercial presence in another country, e.g. establishment or investment in educational institutes; and

Mode (4): Movement of natural persons, i.e. temporary cross-border movement of service providers, e.g. teachers.

EXHIBIT 1.1: THE FOUR MODES SERVICES TRADE CONTEMPLATED IN GATS.

Considering the specific case of India, it may be noted that India has got a comparative advantage in a number of services falling under Mode (4) discussed above [Exhibit (1)]. Mode (4) services which could be provided very meaningfully by India include, inter alia, health care services, software services, construction and integrated engineering services. But India's exports of the above types of specialised services is constrained by various restrictions imposed by the advanced nations. These include immigration and labour market regulations, regulations concerning recognition of work experience, discrimination between domestic and foreign service personnel etc. The developed nations are not inclined to liberalise these restrictions, primarily because of the adverse impact it will have on their domestic employment (like, downsizing and outsourcing). On the other hand, developing nations are often forced to liberalise many of their mode (3) services, in which they are primarily importers. In short, the impact of the implications of GATS, in general, is skewed less favourably towards the developing nations, unlike in the case of developed nations. Higher education being a tradable commodity under GATS, the educational systems of its member countries including India has virtually been internationalized today. Because of the adverse impact of GATS on developing as noted above, there is an urgent need for India to tread very cautiously in this regard.

On the one hand, internationalization has made the competitiveness of education extremely important, hence posing a threat to many of the domestic educational institutions. On the other hand, it is bringing in tremendous financial benefits, as well as so many academic, political and social advantages through the presence of foreign students. In this regard, the observation by Albach (1989) [1] is quite relevant, 'Foreign students and scholars are one of the most important elements of the international knowledge system. They are the carriers of knowledge across borders. They are the embodiment of the cosmopolitan culture and they are one of the most visible and important parts of the world wide exchange of ideas.

Another development which is likely to have revolutionary influence on the education systems the world over is that of the advances in ICT. The traditional boundaries indicating geographical jurisdiction of universities are fast vanishing and distance and other informal modes (like, e.g. virtual campuses) of education are spreading throughout the world. GATS and ICT revolution have resulted in many an advanced country setting up their campuses, both physical and virtual, in developing nations.

In short, as far as higher education institutions in developing nations like India are concerned, the need of the hour is to bring in very high level of competitiveness for their educational programmes and hence to make it market-friendly. Competitiveness pressures arising mainly out of internationalization in the field of education has enormously enhanced the need for more and more amounts of latest knowledge.

The observation by Kulandai Swamy (2003) [13] is worth mentioning in this regard: "Students from developing countries were moving to Universities in the advanced countries for higher studies; but today the universities in advanced countries are setting up their campuses in developing countries. It is now possible through satellite communication for a university in the USA to offer its programmes with the same lectures, assignments and discussions in China or Russia. Academics in India must prepare themselves for international competition right on our soil in the field of higher and continuing education."

PART II

TECHNICAL EDUCATION IN INDIA-AN OVERVIEW

Technical Education in India-a Historical Perspective

The beginning of formal technical education in India can be dated back to the mid nineteenth century. The British rulers of those days felt the need for starting technical training centers out of the necessity for training overseers for construction and maintenance of public buildings, roads, canals, and ports. Accordingly, the first engineering college was established in 1847 at Roorkee, Uttar Pradesh. [Roorkee Engineering College was later converted into an Indian Institute of Technology (IIT) in 2001.] This engineering college was started for training civil engineers. Afterwards, three more engineering colleges were started by 1856, one each in Sibpur, Poona and Guindy. Though the demand for mechanical and electrical engineering was felt by 1880s, the above three engineering colleges started only apprenticeship classes in these disciplines. But, the Victoria Jubilee Technical Institute which was started in 1887, has as its objective the training of licentiates in mechanical and electrical engineering. The 1990s has witnessed the birth of several new branches of engineering and technology, apart from the classical branches of civil, mechanical and electrical.

Since 1970s, there has been quite radical and rapid changes in the industrial and educational fields, which resulted in the growing need for skilled manpower in different technical disciplines. Besides, the rapid advances in the field of information and communication technologies (ICT) necessitated the need for trained manpower in these fields as well. As a consequence of such a growing need for skilled manpower, a large number of technical institutions were set up through out the country offering technical courses in a variety of disciplines. It is worth pointing out that in terms of the magnitude of human resources, expertise available and of physical facilities created over the last three decades, the system of technical education in India has emerged as a formidable reservoir of technical expertise for the entire globe.

Apart from the significant quantitative growth in respect of technical education in India as noted above, it is worth pointing out that there are a few elite technical institutions in the country which offer technical education of international quality. These institutions, called Indian Institutes of Technology (IITs), are currently seven in number and two more IITs are about to be set up in the near future. The details of the existing IITs are as follows: (i) Kharagpur (1951), (ii) Bombay (Mumbai) (1958), (iii) Madras (Chennai) (1959), (iv) Kanpur (1959), (v) Delhi (1961), (vi) Guwahati (1994), and (vii) Roorke (2001; originally Roorkee Engineering College, which was converted into an IIT as already noted). Over the years, the IITs have carved out a unique status in respect of quality in technical education, consultancy and research; and have attained international reputation. Indian Institute of Science (IISc) at Bangalore in 1909 was another landmark achievement. IISc has also emerged as an elite scientific institution in the country having international standards in advanced instructions and research in frontier areas of science and technology.

REGULATION OF TECHNICAL EDUCATION INDIA AND ITS CURRENT STATUS

Technical education in India is imparted at various levels such as craftsmanship, diploma, degree, post-graduate and research in various specialized fields. The major policy initiatives in the pre-independence period included appointment of the

Indian Universities Commission in 1902, issue of Indian Education policy resolution in 1904 and the Governor General's policy statement of 1913 stressing the importance of technical education. Other major developments in the pre-independence era include, (i) Constitution of the Technical Education Committee of the Central Advisory Board of Education (CABE) of 1943, (ii) Preparation of the Sergeant Report of 1944, and (iii) Formation of the All India Council for Technical Education (AICTE) in 1945.

AICTE was set-up in November 1945 as a national level Apex Advisory Body to conduct survey on the facilities on technical education and to promote development in the country in a coordinated and integrated manner. And to ensure the same, as stipulated in, the National Policy of Education (1986), AICTE be vested with statutory authority for planning, formulation and maintenance of norms and standards, quality assurance through accreditation, funding in priority areas, monitoring and evaluation, maintaining parity of certification and awards and ensuring coordinated and integrated development and management of technical education in the country. The AICTE Act of 1987 which came into force with effect from March 28, 1988, pursuant to the recommendations of a National Working Group constituted by the Government of India, Ministry of Human Resource Development. The statutory All India Council for Technical Education was established on May 12, 1988 with a view to proper planning and coordinated development of technical education system throughout the country, the promotion of qualitative improvement of such education in relation to planned quantitative growth and the regulation and proper maintenance of norms and standards in the technical education system and for matters connected therewith.

AICTE regulates the functioning of institutions offering engineering courses (at diploma, degree and post-graduate levels). Further, it regulates institutions offering courses in pharmacy, architecture & applied arts, and hotel management & catering technology; and also those offering post-graduate level courses in computer applications (MCA) and business administration (MBA). The current statistics regarding the number of technical institutions approved by AICTE (along with the total intake allotted) as of 2004-'05 are given in Table 10.

Table 10
Current Statistics Relating to the Technical Institutions Approved by AICTE (as of 2004-'05)

Type of the Institution	*Number of Institutions Approved*	*Total Intake Allotted*
Engineering (Degree level)	1346	439689
Engineering (Diploma level)	1244	265416
Pharmacy (Degree level)	445	24672
Pharmacy (Diploma level)	415	24029
Hotel Management (Degree level)	60	3685
Hotel Management (Diploma level)	63	4020
Architecture (Degree level)	228	3560
Architecture (Diploma level)	25	905
Master of Computer Applications (MCA)	1012	54167

Source: Compiled from the official website of AICTE, *www.aicte.ernet*.in
Note: Regarding approved post graduate level management courses (MBA or equivalent) the latest statistics are not completely available and is left out.

PART III

STRENGTHS, WEAKNESSES, OPPORTUNITIES AND THREATS (SWOT) ANALYSIS OF TECHNICAL EDUCATION SYSTEM IN INDIA

In this section, an attempt is made to identify the major strengths, weaknesses, opportunities and threats of the technical education system in India. These are discussed below one by one.

Strengths of Indian Technical Education System: These Include Mainly The Following:

(i) There has been quite appreciable quantitative growth in the number of technical institutions as well as in the umber of students for these courses. During the last two decades the increase in the number of institutions could be observed to be quite significant. (Table 11 and Figure 1).

Table 11
Growth in Undergraduate Engineering Colleges in India

Period	*Upto 1980*	*1981-1990*	*1991-1995*	*1996-2000*	*2001-2004*
No. of Govt.-aided Colleges	90	117	150	204	220
No. of Self-financing Colleges	44	149	222	602	1047
Total no. of Engg. Colleges	134	266	372	806	1247

Source: Compiled from publications of AICTE for various years.

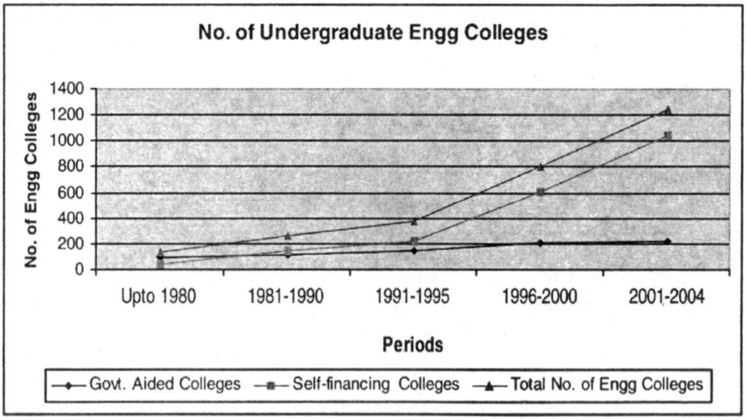

FIGURE 1: GROWTH IN UNDERGRADUATE ENGINEERING COLLEGES IN INDIA
Source: Compiled from publications of AICTE for various years.

(ii) India has got the unique advantage of having a large pool of English speaking technical manpower, in contrast with many of the developing nations like China, and even with some of the developed nations.

(iii) India could be proud of some of the world class institutes in Technology and Management, like the IITs, IIMs, IISc etc. These institutions are well reputed and are producing graduates of international quality.

(iv) Favourable demographics may help India more than any other nation, ie. India is expected to have majority of people under the age of 40 years and if they are properly trained India could end up as the supplier of skilled workforce to the entire globe.

Weaknesses of Indian Technical Education System: These are Mainly the Following:

(i) The quality of the technical education in India is comparatively poor, except, of course, that of a few elite institutions like the IITs, IIMs and IISc. The following statistics (Table 3.2) reported based on a recent survey (2006) relating to quality of Indian higher education is self-explanatory in this regard. It may be noted that India lags not just on global but also on Asian benchmarks.

Table 12
World University Rankings

Name of the country	*Top 20*	*Top 50*	*Top 100*	*Top 200*
China	1	2	2	6
Hong Kong	0	2	3	4
India	0	0	2	3
Japan	1	2	3	11
Other Asia	1	1	3	9
Sub-Total	3	7	13	33
Australia	1	6	7	13
Canada	0	3	3	7
New Zealand	0	1	2	2
UK	4	8	16	30
US	11	22	33	55

Source: The Times Higher Education Supplement, cited in Thakur, Ramesh (2006), "The quality of India's higher education, The Hindu, Kochi Edition, 09 Dec. 2006.

Note: In the above survey, even IITs were ranked just 57, IIMs 68 and just one Indian University viz. Jawaharlal Nehru University, New Delhi as 183rd.

(ii) Because of the paucity of funds, the number of government aided institutions are very less. As is evident from the statistics given in Table 3.1 and also line graph depicted in Figure 3.1 above, the share of government or government-aided institutions are fast becoming quite ignorable over the years. As of 2004, out of 1247 engineering colleges, only 220 belong to the government-aided category.

(iii) Self-financing colleges form the majority among the engineering colleges. But, in respect of the quality of education of these colleges they are lagging far behind the government institutions, particularly in respect of the quality of the faculty.

(iv) Huge level of educated unemployment; technically educated are often not employable because of lack of adequate quality and/or relevance.

(v) Too much of political interference in every sphere of higher education in general, including technical education.

(vi) Very poor interaction between technical institutions and the industry.

(vii) There exists high level of inflexibility in the academic structure. This in turn inhibits innovation and promotes mediocrity.

(viii) Wide variations among universities and institutions in respect of quality of education, and curriculum content.

(ix) Unnecessary centralization of decision-making powers with the universities. For instance, in respect of the affiliating system which is followed by most of the universities the decisions are centralized and accountability is discouraged.

(x) Low infrastructure for postgraduate and doctoral studies. Further, generally there is lack of interest to take up such advanced studies also.

(xi) Methods of recruitment and promotion of teachers are not properly standardized and are grossly unscientific. In most of the technical institutions, the faculty members are less qualified and have virtually no industry exposure. In majority of the undergraduate engineering colleges, particularly those in self-financing category, graduates are taking classes.

Opportunities of Indian Technical Education System

These include mainly the following:

(i) Because of the growing trend in respect of internationalization of higher education, increase in the quality of higher education arising from ever increasing competitive pressures can naturally be expected. That is, in order to survive the domestic higher education institutions have to improvise themselves by revising and updating their curriculum and providing better infrastructural facilities including enhanced use of ICT.

(ii) In general, for developing nations like India which are finding it difficult to raise adequate resources for providing higher and technical education. Internationalization will provide easier access to facilities for higher education available elsewhere, particularly in the developed nations.

(iii) Because of the relatively superior position in respect of the ICT infrastructure in India, the country may be in a better position to leverage its position in order to deliver quality education through the ICT route.

(iv) A large number of educational institutions, both at home and abroad, will provide better opportunities for the students. The emerging market is going to be a 'Buyer's Market' which would provide the students greater access and wider range in their educational pursuit. Further, this will facilitate the reduction of knowledge gap between developed and developing nations.

(v) High growth in the enrolment of women for higher education with the changing attitudes in favour of gender equity and the setting up of special institutions (including universities) for women.

(vi) Constant rise in the learning through Distance and Open University system. The courses offered by Indira Gandhi National Open University (IGNOU)-the apex body in respect of distance and open learning-is well reputed the world over and is the second largest university of its kind in the entire world. Further, recently all the seven IITs together with IISc, Bangalore have gone for a Joint venture named "National Programme on Technology Enhanced Learning" (NPTEL). This portal has been formally launched on September 03, 2006. The information resources available on this website is offered free to all and are updated every week.

(vii) Availability of bank finance for higher and technical education is on the rise, as the banks are in the process of easing their relevant credit norms.

(viii) Easier migration to other countries in search of technical education can be expected in the future because of the agreements like WTO and GATS. For instance, the number of Indian students who has migrated to Germany during the period 1990-2004 is given below, which shows steady increase over the years; the number as of 2004 being almost 7 times as that of 1990.

Table 13
Number of Indian Students who Migrated to Germany for Higher Education

Year	*1990*	*1995*	*1998*	*1999*	*2000*	*2001*	*2002*	*2003*	*2004*
No. of Students	609	675	846	1117	1412	2100	3303	4112	4249

Source: Duttagupta, Ishani., "Go Euro", The Economic Times, Chennai Ed., 30 Oct. 2006.

(ix) Rapid rise in the number of private/corporate universities as a result of the Government's policy of privatization and liberalization of higher education. Similar is the case of self-financing and autonomous colleges.

Threats of Indian Technical Education System

These include mainly the following:

(i) In the twentieth century, higher education was almost entirely by the Government and the same was as high as 90 percent in 1990, Today, however, there is an increasing trend in respect of the Governments, both at the Centre and States, withdrawing from the field of higher education in general, particularly the technical and professional.

(ii) There is the big threat of international competition with the foreign universities entering the Indian soil to set up their campuses over here. This trend is on the rise. Because of the better quality facilities available to the foreign institutions, the Indian counterparts may be losing their share.

(iii) Replacement of the permanent system of employment of teachers by the contract system. Further, there is the move to provide performance (results)-linked salary to teachers. These measures may result in reduced sincerity and commitment of the teachers, resulting in gradual dilution in the quality of education.

(iv) Higher level of expectation of the public from the educational institutions and hence only those having the higher grades from NBA (under AICTE) or other similar regulatory bodies will be surviving.

PART IV
TECHNICAL EDUCATION IN INDIA: THE FUTURE STRATEGIES

In view of the foregoing, the following strategies appear to be quite meaningful and appropriate to make the Indian technical education system more effective and responsive to the demands of the market.

(i) The most important need is that of formulating a national pattern of technical education that specifically addresses our economic, social and cultural requirements. This is because of the fact that we still follow an education system that follows, by and large, the one left behind by the British.

(ii) Need for flexible and pragmatic education policies: In view of the rapidity of the developments in the field of education these days, what is really required is education policies which are flexible enough and pragmatic to address to the ever growing needs of the globalized world. The traditional rigidities associated with the Indian university system should definitely change. The latest experiments in respect autonomous colleges, self-financing institutions, private universities etc. appear to be a welcome initiative in this direction, in an economy that is becoming increasingly global, wherein "survival of the fittest" is the natural rule.

(iii) In order to ensure a quality of the highest order, there should be a permanent and rigorous mechanism for quality assurance of all higher education institutions on an ongoing basis. Accreditation be made mandatory for all such institutions. Some commendable efforts already made in this direction by NBA (under AICTE) should be further streamlined and systematized.

(iv) Higher education institutions in general and technical institutions in particular should be 'Learning Organizations'. The basic purpose of higher education to shape up the inherent process of cultural reproduction. Besides, they not only train academic professionals, but also nurture the scientific temper of questioning facts and norms and accordingly they raise critical consciousness about the process of general socialization. Further, apart from providing subject expertise in specific disciplines, these institutions have to contribute substantially to intellectual enlightenment with the help of duly researched and diagnostic interpretations. In short, the institutions of higher education, technical as well as academic, themselves have to be learning organizations i.e. those which can sense the changes in the environment fast and also respond proactively to such changes.

(v) Because of the tremendous benefits that ICT can provide in any field, particularly in respect of an ever-dynamic and strategic field like higher education; and also because of the already available ICT infrastructure of India as being the best outsourcing destination of the globe, it is imperative that any policy initiative in this field should also be one that embraces ICT to the extent possible.

(vi) Lastly, but not the least, special emphasis on studies relating to Intellectual Property Rights (IPR) has become an imminent need. In today's knowledge economy, technical courses should necessarily include compulsory courses on IPR, preferably with additional (elective/optional) courses. This will stimulate innovation and creation of intellectual rights among the graduates and also equip them to effectively protect the same.

CONCLUSION

India has got a higher education system that is second largest in the world, with about 350 universities and 17000 colleges, and there has been commendable growth in institutions over the years. Simialrly, in respect of technical education also, the position of India in quantitative terms appear to be quite appreciable. However, in respect of quality of education our higher education in general and technical education in particular are lagging behind. Except for a few elite institutions like the IITs, IIMs and IISc, not a single university or higher education institution is figuring in international rankings. This should be an eye opener for us. Thus, the imminent need is to improve the quality of education and also to improve the network still further. In such a case, because of the peculiar demographic position as well as other favourable factors like the command of our graduates in English language, expertise in ICT and such other services, India can very well become global supplier for skilled manpower and may go for a 'global takeover' of offices the world over.

REFERENCES

Altbach G. Philip and Y. Ogawa (2002), "Introduction", Higher Education, 43(1), Special Issue, 'Japan: Reform and Change in the Twenty First Century', pp. 01-06.

AICTE (1994), Report of the High Power Committee for Mobilization of Additional Resources for Technical Education, All India Council for Technical Education, New Delhi.

Bidanda, Bopaya, Arisoy, Ozlem, and Shuman, Larry J. (2006), "Offshoring manufacturing: Implications for engineering jobs and education: A survey and case study", Robotics and Computer-Integrated Manufacturing, Vol. 22, 2006, pp. 576-587. (Available online at *www.sciencedirect.com*).

Bowles, S. (2001), 'Globalization versus Redistribution: Egalitarian Policies in a Competitive World Economy', *Indian Economic Review*, 36(2), pp. 315-339.

Carnoy, M. (1999), Globalization and Educational Reforms: What Planners Need to Know, Report No. 63, International Institute of Educational Planning, Paris.

Delors, J. (Chairman) (1996), Learning: The Treasure Within, Report of UNESCO, International Commission on Education for the Twenty-First Century, UNESCO, Paris.

Duttagupta, Ishani (2006), "Go Euro", *The Economic Times*, Chennai, 30 Oct.

Dre'ze, Jean, and Sen, Amartya, India: Economic Development and Social Opportunities, Oxford.

Gnanam, A. (2004), "Challenges of Higher Education in the New Millennia: Lessons from International Experiences" in Higher Education in India: EmergingChallenges, Proceedings of UGC-Sponsored National Seminar, 20-21 Nov., KLE Society's Lingaraj College, Belgaum, pp. 01-08.

Goswami, Urmi A. (2006), "From the Youth Mart", *The Economic Times*, Chennai (Kochi) Edition, 11th December, p. 11.

Government of India (1997-2002), Ninth Five Year Plan: 1997-2002, Planning Commission, New Delhi.

Government of India (2001), Approach Paper to Tenth Five Year Plan: 2002-2007, Planning Commission, New Delhi.

Ilon, L. (1994), 'Structural Adjustment and Education: Adapting to a Growing Global Market', *International Journal of Educational Development*, 14 (2), pp. 95-108.

Kulandai Swamy, V. C. (2003), Higher Education in India: Crisis in Management, Viva Book Private Limited (New Delhi, Mumbai, Chennai and Kolkata).

Manoj, P. K. (2006), "Higher Education in India: Retrospect and Prospects", Proceedings of the XXX th Annual Conference, Indian Academy of Social Sciences, Allahabad, Alagappa University, Karaikudi, Tamil Nadu, Dec. 27-31.

Maske Pradip (2004), Globalization and its Impact on Higher Education', University News, May, 17-23.

Ministry of Human Resources Development, Annual Reports (for 2003, 2004 and 2005), Government of India, New Delhi.

Ministry of Human Resources Development, Analysis of Budgeted Expenditure on Education (2004, 2005), Govt. of India, New Delhi.

Ministry of Finance, *Indian Economic Survey* (for 2005 and 2006), Department of Economic Affairs, Government of India, New Delhi.

Powar, K. B. (2002), The Changing Role and Functions of Universities, Concept Publishing Company, New Delhi.

Ramachandran, K. (2006), "The Task of Assessment", *The Hindu*, Education Plus, 31 Oct.

Salmi, J. (1999), 'Perspectives on the Financing of Higher Education', Higher Education Policy, 5 (2), pp. 13-19.

Sen, Amartya (2000), Development as Freedom, University Press, New Delhi.

Stewart, F. (1996), 'Globalization and Education', *International Journal of Educational Development*, 16 (4), pp. 327-333.

Thakur, Ramesh (2006), "The Quality of Indian Higher Education", *The Hindu*, Kochi Edition, 09 December 2006.

Tilak, J. B. G. (2001), 'Education and Globalization: The Changing Concerns in Economics of Indian Education', (Editorial), Perspectives in Education, 17, Special Issue, pp. 05-08.

Tilak, J. B. G. and Geetha Rani, P. (2000), University Finances in India: A Profile, National Institute of Educational Planning and Administration, Mimeo, New Delhi.

Tilak, J. B. G. and Varghese, N. V. (1985), Discriminatory Pricing in Education, Occasional Paper: No. 8, National Institute of Educational Planning and Administration, Mimeo, New Delhi.

UGC (2004 & 2005), Annual Reports, 2003-04 and 2004-05; University Grants Commission, Government of India.

UGC (2004 & 2005), University Hand Book 2004 and 2005; University Grants Commission, New Delhi.

UNESCO (1998), Higher Education in the Twenty-first Century: Vision and Action, Final Report, World Conference on Higher Education, UNESCO, Paris, October 1998.

UNESCO (1999), Statistical Year Book, UNESCO, Paris.

UNESCO (2000), World Education Report:2000, UNESCO, Paris.

UNESCO (2005), Towards Knowledge Societies, UNESCO, Paris.

Viswanadhan, K.G., Rao, N. J. and Mukhopadhyay, C (2005), "Impact of Privatization on Engineering Education-a Study through the Analysis of Performance of Self-financing Engineering programmes in India", *Journal of Services Research*, Special Issue, December 2005, Institute of International Management and Technology, Noida, New Delhi., pp. 109-129.

World Development Indicators 2005, The World Bank, 1818 H Street N. W., Washington. D. C., 20433 USA., March 2005.

World Bank (2002), Constructing Knowledge Societies: New Challenges for Tertiary Education, Washington, D.C.

Ziderman, A. and D., Albrecht (1995), Financing Universities in Developing Countries, The Stanford

Series on Education and Public Policy, The Falmer Press, Washington, D.C.

Manoj P K & Arunachalam P

19 Saving Management Education in India from Irrelevance Some Strategic Imperatives

As part of the ongoing privatization and globalization process in India, as in the case of any business or industry, there have been many changes in the field of management education also. While the demand for management graduates has been on the rise over the years, there has also been unprecedented growth in the number of institutes offering management programmes, like, MBA or it variants. On the one hand, mushrooming of management training institutes has resulted in erosion of quality; primarily because of the lack of adequate infrastructure facilities including qualified and skilled faculty. On the other hand, trained managerial talents are not available in certain vital sectors of Indian economy. While the IIMs and a few other premier institutes could maintain very high quality of education right from their inception, and their graduates are of great demand world over, there are widespread apprehensions regarding the competitiveness of the management graduates from majority of the other business schools particularly the new entrants to this field.

Many economies of the world have been opened up during the last two decades and in India also the process is going on since the early nineties. This has resulted in tremendous opportunities to the business management graduates. However, in order to exploit this immense potential to the fullest extent, there exists the need to fine-tune and orient Indian management education system as per national priorities and also in tune with the international developments. Only then, we can bring out high caliber management graduates who are equipped to face the ever-growing challenges arising from globalization and are also capable of responding effectively to the specific problems of this nation. These management graduates have to be driven by sound ethical values and should also be capable of appreciating the cultural contexts of their society while making their business decisions. In this context, it is relevant to systematically study the existing management education system in India, to identify the weaknesses and problems of the system as well as the prospects and also to make constructive suggestions for improving the system. This article is an earnest attempt in the above direction and is organized under four main parts. Part-I deals with the Evolution of management education in India (including the present status), Part-II the Weaknesses of management education in India and Part-III the Prospects of management education in India and finally Part-IV the Suggestions for making Indian management education more relevant to the national realities.

PART I
EVOLUTION OF MANAGEMENT EDUCATION IN INDIA

The pioneers in management education in India were not the Indian Institutes of Management. Rather, the beginning was with the setting up of departments of business administration in the 1950s, in the four metropolitan universities of Mumbai, Delhi, Kolkata and Chennai. Among these the best-known university departments were the Faculty of Management Studies under Delhi University and Jamnalal Bajaj Institute of Management under Mumbai University. However, the real impetus for quality in management education was with the emergence of Indian Institutes of Management (IIMs) in the early sixties. IIM-Calcutta (IIMC)was established as the first national institute for Post-Graduate studies and Research in Management by the Central Government in November 1961 in collaboration with Alfred P. Sloan School of Management

(MIT), the Government of West Bengal, the Ford Foundation and the industry. Immediately afterwards, IIM-Ahmedabad (IIMA) was set up in the same year 1961 as an autonomous body with the active collaboration of the Government of India, Government of Gujarat, and the industry. IIM-Bangalore (IIMB) was set up in 1973 and IIM-Lucknow (IIML) was established in 1984, by the Government of India, as a national level school of excellence in management science. IIM-Kozhikode (IIMK) and IIM-Indore (IIMI) the youngsters among IIMs were started in the late nineties (1998). The IIMs continued to maintain superb quality in management education and naturally their reputed brands assured excellent job placement to their students. In spite of their heavy dependence on the government for finance, the IIMs have been enjoying right from their inception unfettered freedom in the formulation of syllabi, recruitment of teachers, international collaborations and faculty development.

Later, Indian Institutes of Technologies (IITs) and many leading engineering colleges including Regional Engineering Colleges (ie. RECs; presently these are renamed as National Institutes of Technology, NITs) felt the need to be in management education and started their own departments for imparting management education. Afterwards, many leading autonomous colleges and reputed affiliated colleges all over India also followed the suit. Still, till late eighties the total number of management institutes (ie. Business Schools, or in short, B-Schools as they are commonly called) was less than fifty.

In India, management education is regulated by All India Council for Technical Education (AICTE). AICTE was established in 1945 to regulate the technical education in the country. At that time its jurisdiction was only engineering and technology education. The growth of industries in the country during post-independence era, necessitated professionals in other fields also, like, Business Management, Architecture, Hotel Management, Pharmacy etc. Although the diverse elements of management such as commerce, economics, finance, psychology, industrial psychology etc. were being taught for quite a long time, the need for a formal management education was felt only in the fifties. Accordingly, the Government of India decided in 1954 to set up a Board of Management Studies under AICTE to formulate standards and promote management education. Other major initiatives by the Government in the area of promotion of management education include setting up of the Administrative Staff College of India at Hyderabad in the late fifties, National Productivity Council and Indian Institutes of Management in the early sixties.

Nineties saw a substantial increase in the number of management institutes and by late nineties there was an unprecedented growth in the number of business schools in India. Over the last few years, All India Council of Technical Education (AICTE) has been following a lenient policy towards recognition of business schools. Even in colleges running conventional courses (like, Arts, Science, Commerce etc.) MBA and allied courses (like MFT, MIB etc.) were started and in most of such colleges, the student intake has been as low as 30-60 students. Many such institutes lack the adequate infrastructure like spacious class rooms, computer facilities, library facilities, qualified and permanent faculty etc. and also the much required industry-interaction facilities. Courses have been run just like any other conventional course.

At present, there are 958 AICTE recognized business schools in India and more than 70,000 students are graduating every year from these business schools. Among these there are stand-alone institutes as well as departments of management associated with some leading Engineering colleges /Arts & Science Colleges. Regarding the number of management graduates produced every year, presently India is second only to US and regarding the number of business schools India is number one. Apart from AICTE recognized business schools as above, there are quite a large number of autonomous institutes offering their own management courses. Of these, some are very reputed, like, the Symbiosis management institutes based at Pune. Further, there are many private universities offering their management programmes and further many universities are offering management courses under distance learning mode.

Among the management institutes in India, the Indian Institutes of Management (IIMs) adorn a place of pride and these institutes are offering world class management education. Likewise, there are a few other very reputed management institutes like, Xaviers Labour Relations Institute (XLRI), Jamshedpur; Jamnalal Bajaj Institute of Management, Mumbai; Symbiosis institutes based at Pune, SP Jain's Institute of Management and Research, Mubai; Bharatidasan Institute of Management (BIM), Trichy etc. which are also offering management education of very high standard.

PART-II
WEAKNESSES OF INDIAN MANAGEMENT EDUCATION SYSTEM

QUALITY CONCERNS

As pointed out earlier, though there has been very high increase in the number of management institutes as well as the number of management graduates coming out every year, the quality in general is far below the expectations. The IIMs and a few top-notch institutes are exceptions to the above rule, where the quality is comparable to international standards of management education. However, in respect of the vast majority of the business schools, the picture is miserably poor.

The government has, over the years, performed its duties as regulator of management schools very poorly. Out of 958 AICTE recognized business schools only 45 got accreditation from National Board of Accreditation (NBA). Thus, majority of the institutes are lagging far behind in ensuring the requisite facilities to obtain NBA Accreditation. More than 70,000 students are passing out every year from these management institutes and this figure is second only to the US.

AICTE-the Regulatory Authority of Mana-gement Education in India

Though AICTE is the regulatory authority in respect of management education, it does not have the resources to ensure that all business management schools meet the stipulated norms. Further, it is believed that political and other interests are influencing many decisions of AICTE. The monitoring by AICTE of the quality of management education needs improvement. Often there is the criticism that the AICTE has succumbed to pressures from well-connected promoters of educational agencies and accordingly been induced to grant recognitions to such a very large number courses and institutes over the years. There is no facility to inspect the business schools regularly and to ensure that they meet the stipulations regarding various infrastructure facilities like qualified faculty, computer facilities, library facilities, industry-linkages, spacious buildings, conference rooms etc. Many management institutes recognized by AICTE continue to have non-existent libraries, poor computer availability, faculty that is quite unsuited for the work, high fees and poor industry linkages. But, AICTE has rarely de-recognised any such institutions.

Whether Management Education be Regulated by AICTE itself?

Whether management education in India should be regulated by AICTE itself ?. As pointed out earlier, AICTE was set up to regulate education in engineering and technology. Management as a discipline was added within its purview afterwards (in 1954 with the setting up of Board of Management studies). As per AICTE Act, 1987 also, Management is just one among the different disciplines coming under the purview of AICTE; the major disciplines being engineering and technology, architecture, town planning, management, pharmacy, applied arts and crafts. Considering the fact that management education is such an important discipline which has got a direct bearing on the sustainable growth of an economy, it is high time that it is de-linked from AICTE and a separate full-fledged regulatory body is set up at the national level with adequate powers to constantly monitor and regulate the system.

Outdated Curriculum

Another challenge faced by management education system in India is regarding the outdated curriculum. Business management being a very dynamic discipline, the curriculum needs revision very frequently, probably every six months.

But, majority of the institutes being either university departments or institutes affiliated to different universities, often revision of syllabus takes time. As such, most of the institutes are imparting courses based on outdated syllabus. Many of the autonomous institutes, including the IIMs, are better off in this regard since they have more flexibility in refining their curriculum. This fact further points to the fact that autonomous colleges should be encouraged in the place of affiliated colleges, as recommended by many educational reforms commissions.

Lack of Skilled and Trained Management Teachers

Yet another handicap of the management education in India is the lack of adequate trained manpower. Though India can boast of such a large number of business schools which are producing more than 70000 graduates every year, it is an unfortunate fact that there is very little original conceptual or applied research work that is produced by the over 5,000 management teachers in India. This fact points to the urgent need for focusing on business management research. The number of Ph.D holders in Management discipline to handle these classes is far less than the actual requirement. One reason for this state of affairs may be the less stringent norms applicable to management teachers in India. In India, it is easier to become a management teacher or to get promoted as a professor. Because, here, norms are so flexible that large number of research publications are not essential. Lack of adequate funding from the government may be another impediment which limits the research initiatives of faculty in the field of business management. On the other hand, in US and other advanced countries where such research publications are very much required and naturally management teachers there are gaining more reputation than their Indian counterparts. Further, because of the above reasons Indian management teachers working outside are gaining more reputation than those working here itself. In India, many faculty members do not have domain knowledge in business management nor do they have teaching experience in business management at post graduate leve!. Rather, their background may be in other disciplines like Commerce or Engineering (like,

Mechanical or Industrial Engineering). Often, because of easier and faster promotion prospects such people take up teaching assignments in management discipline.

Management Education under Distance Mode: Wide-spread Quality Concerns

There has been a huge increase in the number of University departments running management programmes on distance learning mode. Except a few universities like Indira Gandhi National Open University (IGNOU) or ICFAI University which are maintaining good quality in course materials, curriculum development as well as in course delivery and examinations, there are wide-spread apprehensions regarding the quality of management education offered by distance education departments of various universities.

Paucity of Funds with the Government-a Serious Problem

There is shortage funds for the Government to administer B-schools in such a way that they are meeting international standards. Two years back, there was lots of hues and cries regarding the government's decision to change the fee-structure of IIMs by reducing the fees, to reduce the government's grant to the IIMs, increasing the student to faculty ratio and also to increase the work load of the faculty members. Such measures may have an adverse impact on the quality of IIM education, particularly because it is a well-known fact that increase in student to teacher ratio may reduce the quality of education, especially for a professional course at post-graduate level. It is really essential that in order to maintain high quality for post-graduate level professional courses like MBA, there should be constant interaction between students and faculty. But, this not at all the case with the vast majority of business schools. Many business schools are run with four to five permanent faculty, the balance being contract or visiting faculty.

Though privatization of the education system is one way to get out of the problem of funds shortage. Many educational reforms commissions had warned that privatization may also lead to commercialization; as such we should be careful. Now that privatization has already become a reality and we see that many business schools in the private sector are oriented towards profits alone. This points to the fact that private sector institutes must be strictly regulated in order to maintain the quality of education.

Pro-Urban and Pro-Rich Orientation of Management Education

The management education system in India is very much pro-urban and pro-rich in its orientation. Many bright young people from socially and/or economically backward classes have poor confidence in their ability to compete in English with their rich counterparts from the cities. They may also lack the social skills to compete with those from more developed social and economic classes. Another most important factor in this regard is that management education cannot at all be divorced from the ground realities, culture and people of a country. Most of the big businessmen do not have such a formal training in management. Rather, what distinguishes them is that all of them have empathy to the common man of the country, knowledge of the power structures and relationship equations of the country. While working knowledge of English is required for any profession especially business management, extra-ordinary proficiency in English may not be required. On the other hand, proficiency in local language would definitely help a professional manager to understand the various stakeholders of business better. It is pertinent notice here that, quite often management graduates end up as efficient tools for running business for their white masters or as management consultants; and not as effective businessmen or entrepreneurs.

Management education is too costly for a common man to afford. Management students need hefty amounts to pay tuition, boarding and lodging to go through the courses. There is no government mechanism to ensure that the needy students are getting the financial assistance. Though educational loans are given by banks the procedural requirements are very lengthy and cumbersome for an ordinary student that quite often the same is not availed by many needy students.

Multiplicity of Tests Conducted by Different Business Schools

Too many tests used to be conducted by different business schools and universities in order to select students for their courses. While such tests ensure enormous profits to the private institutes and governmental agencies which administer them, they impose very heavy financial burden as well as mental strain on the part of young students. They have to apply for different tests, to prepare for these tests several times and to attend the same on different dates and that too at different locations. These innumerable number of admission tests should be stopped to give way to just a few national level tests, so that the individual institutes can select the candidates from the score of the students in such tests. (We have already made some progress in this respect and as per the latest guidelines of AICTE, only five tests at All India level is permissible, using the score of which individual institutes have to select their students).

Lack of Impartial Ratings of Business Schools

Lack of impartial ratings of different business schools is another weakness of our management education system. Currently, many business magazines are going for their ratings of business schools and often there may not be much uniformity between different ratings so given to various business schools. These ratings are often aimed at raising funds for their publication in the magazine rather than helping the students. This is evident from the numerous advertisements coming in such issues of business magazines.

Lack of Value Orientation or Ethical Considerations in The Curriculum

Generally, a typical management curriculum provides no significance in imparting values to the students. Moreover, the considerations made in judging the worth of a management institute are often the placement track record of the institute, starting salary of the placements; number of job offers etc. rather than the contents of the course, its value orientation or the ultimate contribution to the society at large.

Apart from the above, there is also the drawback of ignoring the cultural contexts of Indian society; often the management concepts are borrowed as such from westerners.

Need for Management Graduates Suited to the Indian

Socio-Economic Scenario. India may not require many more management graduates since the market is already flooded with them. But, we really need quite a large number of management graduates who are trained as per the needs of the socio-economic conditions in India. That is those who are specialized in certain specific sectors of relevance to Indian economy, like non-governmental organizations, co-operative sector, tourism, micro-finance, arts & culture etc. where there is paucity of trained manpower. Probably, the institutes and students are not interested in these sectors because these sectors normally cannot offer such high salaries as the corporates can afford.

PART-III

PROSPECTS OF MANAGEMENT EDUCATION IN INDIA

In spite of the different handicaps of our management education system, there exists excellent scope for the development of the same for the benefit of the economy as a whole. The graduates from IIMs as well as a few top notch management institutes in India are of very high demand internationally. India has contributed some of the most reputed and world-famous management gurus like C K Prahlad, Sumantra Ghoshal, Krishna Paleppu, Nitin Nohria, Jagdish Seth and so on. The business community, in general, is willing to pay huge salaries to management graduates and especially those from IIMs and similar reputed business schools. This attraction lures many parents to provide management education to their offspring. With the privatization and globalization of Indian economy and also those of many other countries world over, the scope of management education has increased manifold.

IIMs: The Hallmark of Quality in Management Education

The IIMs (and of course, a few very reputed institutes) have been maintaining their superiority in management education throughout their history. There has been huge rush to the admissions to these institutes and their business graduates have been rated very high internationally. Government ownership enables IIMs to source enormous amounts of funds for their functioning. Apart from that, they have access to other sources of income like, fees for application forms and for CAT (Common Admission Test). Abundance of funds enabled all the IIMs to arrange excellent physical infrastructure, like, spacious buildings, vast libraries, sylvan campuses, excellent computer facilities etc. The government used to provide substantial annual grants to cover the deficits. Apart from the excellent physical infrastructure as above, IIMs have large number of teachers and a low student to teacher ratio. IIMs attracted the best and the brightest students from the country from a variety of disciplines (dominated by engineering). All the above factors made the IIMs the most attractive recruiting ground for the companies for new managers. Further, IIMs have increasingly been utilized by many employers as the preferred location for training their executives. The brand advantage in turn, enabled IIMs to command premium fees for their training courses, like, management development programmes.

Economic Deregulation: Huge Job Opportunities for Management Graduates

Economic reforms have opened the floodgates of competition among businesses and industries of all sorts. For survival and growth in such an environment of cut-throat competition, the services of manpower with specialized management qualifications have become somewhat indispensable. More and more companies are hiring MBAs for such specialized assignments. Similar jobs are increasingly available in other countries as well. Only problem is that unlike in the past very large number of MBA graduates are available in the market. Then, the final test lies on one's competence to keep ahead of others; or in short, the principle of 'survival of the fittest' is applicable here also.

Economic Deregulation: Need for Internationalisation of Management Education

As per studies conducted by Association of Indian Universities (AIU), there is growing need for internationalization of higher education in India. It may be seen that this is particularly applicable in the case of management education. In this 'knowledge era' development of any organizations depends on the extent to which it has got access to information or knowledge sources. Naturally, it has to interact constantly with other organizations, universities etc. all over the world. Further, such partnerships and networkings among various institutions have the dual benefits of enriching teaching-learning process and improving the quality of research. Moreover, such initiatives will improve the standards of higher education, promote Indian culture abroad, generate goodwill and understanding, provide better chances for career enhancement and after all yield financial benefits. Here also, as mentioned earlier, our final success depends on the quality of education that is imparted

PART-IV

SUGGESTIONS FOR MAKING INDIAN MANAGEMENT EDUCATION NATIONALLY RELEVANT

A few realistic and pragmatic suggestions are made in this section for making a more effective system for management education and training in India:

Change in the Structure and Functions of AICTE-the Regulatory Body

The government should make AICTE an independent regulatory body whose functions need to be transparent. The members of this body should be selected from among the reputed industrialists as well as well-known academicians. Further, these members should be those who have the courage to ensure that educational standards are strictly maintained. Efficient functioning of the AICTE will need far more funding than the present limited budgets that the HRD ministry provides to it. The government should take immediate steps to adequately finance this regulatory authority considering the pivotal role it has to play in the development of the nation. Board of Management Studies, the advisory board functioning under AICTE should be provided adequate powers for taking decisions as well as to effectively implement the same, including imposing penalties in applicable cases. This Board should ideally have a mix of reputed academicians and industrialists, all of whom should have full-time responsibility and independent powers in specified areas. (However, as already pointed earlier, it is always better to have a separate, full-fledged regulatory body for the management discipline rather than the present system wherein it is a only a part of technical education. But, let constitution of such a separate body be our medium-term objective and restructuring and reorienting AICTE viz. Board of Management Studies, as the immediate objective.)

Management Education Suited to Meet the Requirements of Various Sectors

There are many sectors in the economy which really require trained managers such as arts & culture, non-governmental organizations, SHGs & micro-financing, co-operatives etc. Urgent measures have to be taken to promote management education catering to the specific needs of these sectors of the economy. Government should provide the necessary financial and administrative support in the above direction.

Focus on Graduates from Rural Populace; Remedial Training for Rural Graduates

Government has to earmark funds to provide remedial training to improve the confidence of bright young graduates in rural areas who cannot effectively compete with their more fortunate brethren hailing from the socially advanced sections, mostly from urban areas. They should be equipped well for the written test, interview and group-discussion. Thus, a balanced growth of all sections of the society can be ensured.

Model Curriculum and Broad Norms

There should be broad norms at the national level regarding the curriculum of post-graduate level management courses (ie.

Model Curriculum) and these should be revised very frequently. It must be ensured that syllabi of various management courses offered by universities and institutes (including those offering distance learning courses) are by and large within this framework. An expert committee at the national level having representatives from both academic and industrial fields should be entrusted with the above responsibility of closely monitoring and modifying the curriculum. (Presently, model curriculums of a few selected undergraduate technical courses alone are published by AICTE.)

Multiplicity of Admission Tests to be Curtailed

Multiplicity of admission tests being administered by different management institutes and universities should be curtailed and a few admission tests in the all India level should be conducted. This may be conducted following the pattern of CAT (Common Admission Test) administered by the different IIMs jointly for selecting students for post graduate and research programmes.

Complete Information about Business Schools to the Students

To provide the students with the relevant academic information about the quality of the different business schools, the government has to initiate necessary steps. Apart from the placement track record that is usually the sole parameter that is made available to the students on request, other relevant factors like the infrastructure facilities like permanent faculty, library facilities, industry linkages, profile of the existing students, elective subjects offered etc. should also be made available to the students, by AICTE by maintaining and updating the necessary database on a regular basis. In such a case, students can make a rational choice regarding the business school where he should join.

Impartial Rating of Business Schools on an Annual Basis

Government should ideally commission some independent governmental body to do such a rating exercise in an impartial manner on an annual basis, wherein all recognized management institutes should participate compulsorily. Such a rating should form an authentic record to facilitate the students to make rational decisions regarding their admissions to business schools.

Due Emphasis on Ethical Values:

The government should initiate measures to ensure that ethical values are given due emphasis in management curriculum. Such a move will ensure that the best and brightest students in the country are brought up on sound ethical values and that they have concern to their society rather than to their pay packets alone. Further, there is also the need to impart management education which bases itself on cultural contexts of our society. Further, the learners should also know the realities surmounting Indian markets so that they can consider the poor as a major chunk of their customer base.

Enhanced Thrust on Business Management Research

There is urgent need for promoting research in business management in India. Further, there should be constant efforts for continuously upgrading the skills of faculty through regular training, testing, funding for research and case writing. Management faculty must themselves be subjected to regular, objective and rigorous testing and further, they must be placed under the strict discipline of work norms, research and publications, preparation of cases etc. Original research publications should be made a compulsory requirement for internal promotions. Further, case studies relating to Indian business should be given more significance in management training, rather than those of other countries. Developing such cases should also form a part and parcel of the work of management teachers, apart from research publications.

Internationalisation of Management Education in India-a Vital Need:

In this LPG era, wherein the world is fast transforming into a knowledge economy, internationalisation of management education is in fact an imperative rather than an option. Internationalisation has to be done in a well thought-out manner and should touch upon all relevant variables. The following strategies towards internationalization appear to be quite logical. (Exhihit: (1), below)

Relevant Variables		*Recommended Strategies for Bringing about International Competitiveness in Management Education and Training.*
Faculty	(i)	Periodical Faculty Development Programmes must be conducted on a regular basis; separately for different functional areas.
	(ii)	Faculty Exchange Programmes with good foreign universities and business schools. Further, encourage foreign visits of the faculty members for the purpose of study and research. Joint research projects with foreign faculty must also encouraged to the extent possible.
	(iii)	Collaborative case-writings with foreign faculty must be encouraged to enable the students to get an international outlook and awareness regarding management practices prevalent in other countries.
	(iv)	Encourage academic collaboration with reputed institutes and universities abroad. Twinning programmes, sandwhich courses etc, with facility for mutual credit transfers may be encouraged maximum.
Students	(i)	Student Exchange programmes with reputed foreign universities and management institutes. Twinning programmes/Sandwhich programmes etc. should be offered in order to facilitate their international exposure.
	(ii)	Students should be encouraged to undertake case-studies, projects etc. abroad and also projects sponsored by foreign companies.
	(iii)	Foreign tours, visits to companies and key business destinations abroad etc. must be facilitated/ encouraged.
Curriculum design, Course-content etc.	(i)	Maximum emphasis on international case-studies and also on the study of international management practices/philosophies.
	(ii)	International context to be in-built into whatever theories, approaches and perspectives included in the curriculum.
	(iii)	Special focus on international comparative studies in all subjects.

Contd...

Relevant Variables	*Recommended Strategies for Bringing about International Competitiveness in Management Education and Training.*
	(iv) Encourage various group projects, exercises etc. jointly with foreign counterparts, say with the help of ICT tools facilities.
	(v) Provide maximum interaction of students and faculty with their foreign counterparts with the use of all modern ICT tools, like, internet, video conferencing, electronic mail etc.
	(vi) Courses with an international/multi-national character be included more (like, international trade and finance, international marketing, international banking, management of multi-national companies etc.)
Research on management.	(i) Management research has to be promoted on a continuous basis.
	(ii) Faculty members shall be evaluated giving due weightage to their research output. Further, their work load on teaching shall be reduced depending on their performance in research. Moreover, deserving faculty members should be rewarded for their notable research contributions.
	(iii) Adequate opportunities for faculty members to undertake research on a full-time basis. Sabbatical leave, Leave for research purpose etc. should be provided to deserving teachers.
	(iv) Specified number of research publications in approved research journals must be prescribed for teachers under each level.
General Facilities, Accreditation from various Agencies etc.	(i) Excellent infrastructure facilities have to be ensured in the business schools to enable them to be internationally competitive. These include, inter alia, Computer lab with 24 hours internet connectivity, wired campus, excellent library facilities with large number of national and international journals including good online journals etc. Providing laptop computer to every business student.
	(ii) Accreditation from regulatory agencies should essentially be ensured; in Indian context NBA (of AICTE). More importantly, accreditations from international bodies/agencies are equally important.

Contd...

Relevant Variables	*Recommended Strategies for Bringing about International Competitiveness in Management Education and Training.*
	For instance, those of AACSB (Goal of Advance Collegiate Schools of Business), EQUIS (European Quality Improvement System), Association of MBAs (AMBA) etc. are quite necessary. These accreditations provide such benefits for the business school as legitimacy, quality standards, global recognition, continuous improvement, international branding etc.

EXHIBIT (1): STRATEGIES FOR INTERNATIONALISATION OF MANAGEMENT EDUCATION-AN OVERVIEW

Rural Specific Management Education-a Meaningful Proposition

Lastly, but not the least. considering the typical socio-economic environment of India, rural specific MBA courses appear to be quite meaningful. Accordingly, such an Indian paradigm of management education, considering the local social and cultural attributes, can really transform the rural areas-the heart of Indian economy; and hence can ensure rapid economic development. While going for such rural specific management courses, care should be taken not to adopt a "helicopter" of taking modern management practices to rural India. Rather, B-Schools should work closely with sociologists and anthropologists to arrive at more pragmatic ways of reaching them.

CONCLUSION

In spite of the various handicaps as discussed earlier, management education has developed well in India, thanks to the vision of past governments that set up IIMs as role models. However, the kind of quality that is enjoyed by the premier institutes needs to be gradually injected into the very large number of other less reputed institutes as well. Accordingly, our policy makers have the urgent responsibility to start consolidating our position in management education by upgrading the standards of the large number of business schools that have already been set up; so that students get substantial value-addition from their management education, apart from their own inherent caliber. Further, Government needs to invest more of its funds in imparting management education in hitherto neglected and specific areas like non-governmental organizations, arts & culture, co-operative sector etc. where there is ample scope for using such trained manpower in country. Business schools have the responsibility to ensure that apart from the sole objective of finding high-paid jobs for the students, there should be equal emphasis for inculcating in them, an ethical approach to business situations as well as an orientation specific to our socio-cultural setting. Moreover, business management research should be given maximum thrust at all levels of management education, in tune with international practices. Let's hope that India will come up as one of the most sought-after destinations for world-class management education, in the near future.

REFERENCES

Anand, R. (2004), "Have MBAs Lost their Fire", *Indian Management, AIMA*, New Delhi, Sept., pp. 82-84.

Anand, Adkoli (2006), "An Agenda for ICT-enabled Education", *Indian Management, AIMA*, New Delhi, Jan., pp. 44-50.

Bennis, Warren G., and O'Toole, James (2005), "How Business Schools Lost their Way", *Indian Management, AIMA*, New Delhi, Sept., pp. 84-98.

Internationalisation of Indian Higher Education, Association of Indian Universities, New Delhi, 2001.

Justin Paul (2001), "Rank and the B-School File", *The Economic Times*, 03 Jan.

Kulandai Swamy, V.C. (2003), Higher Education in India-Crisis in Management, Viva Books Private Limited, New Delhi.

Kumar, Manoj, and Kodwani, Amitabh (2004), "How to Rejig Facutly Time", *Indian Management, AIMA*, New Delhi, Dec., pp. 64-70.

Mannivannan, D. G. (2006), "A New Model for B-School Grading", *Indian Management, AIMA*, New Delhi, Feb., pp. 74-80.

Narayan, Tarun (2005), "Giving IIMs a Wide Berth", *Indian Management, AIMA,* New Delhi, Sept., pp. 100-101.

Narayan, Tarun (2006), "Rebooting on-line MBAs", *Indian Management, AIMA,* New Delhi, Jan., pp. 44-50.

Prasad, V. V. Durga (2007), "Management Education in India: SWOT Analysis", University News, Vol. 45, No. 06. February 05-11, pp. 15-17.

Rao, K. Raghavendra (2004), "But Where are the Faculty", *Indian Management, AIMA,* New Delhi, Dec., pp. 56-60

Rao, S. L. (2006), "Reinventing Management Education", *Indian Management, AIMA,* New Delhi, Sept., pp. 36-38.

Ramachander, S. (2005), "Making Global Managers", *The Hindu.* Magazine, 15 May, p. 1.

Reforms and Innovations in Higher Education, Association of Indian Universities, New Delhi, 2001.

Sangameshwaran, Prasad (2004), "What We Got from B-School", *Indian Management, AIMA,* New Delhi, Sept., pp. 88-90.

Sharma, Arti. (2003), "The Corporate View of MBAs", *Indian Management, AIMA,* New Delhi, Dec., pp. 48-54.

Shukla, Gouri, and Giriprakash, K. (2003), "Battle for the B-Schools Market", *Indian Management, AIMA,* New Delhi, Feb., pp.12-13.

Swamy, K. (2006), "Patterns of Management Education in India", *University News,* Volume 44, No. 22, June 19-25, pp. 7-16.

Srinivasan, N. S. (2005), "Is B-School Really all that Bad?", *Indian Management, AIMA,* New Delhi, Feb., pp. 58-64

Thomas T. T. (2001), "World Class Management Education is a Must", *The Economic Times,* Chennai, January 19.

Sangeetha K Pratap, Sajitha P P & Bindu George

20 Quality Assurance & Excellence in Technical Education An Assessment of Service Quality Perception

Quality assurance in education is a multifaceted term. Present competitive environment requires the student to have not only adequate knowledge and understanding of their specific area of study but also interpersonal and communication skills to survive competition .The way which education is provided to the student's fraternity, their way of their assimilation requires an urgent of academicians. Everyone doing his or her best is not answering knowledge of what to do? In words of Aristotle quality is a habit, an attitude. But the demand of the time is to implement, institutionalize and internalize it.

The new age is caught in the webs GOLIT where globalization, open market economy, liberalization and information technology are directing the future course of the world. Teachers have not only their minds or the books but also their vast repertoire stored in thousands of services the world over. Another striking feature is that of emerging society shall be the shift from directed learning to self initiated learning. (Yojana, 2006).

Numerous educational institutions educational institutions are promising five star qualities have sprung and mushrooming rapidly. Hordes of students are taking admissions for taking degrees. There are different stakeholders when quality of education is the talk. These are the students, parents, teachers, institutions etc .the means of education being imparted needs to be diagnosed keeping in view of the players concerned. This paper is one such attempt in this direction with due importance to students fraternity.

ALTERNATIVE PERSPECTIVES OF QUALITY IN EDUCATION

The concepts and practices of quality in education are of recent origin and debates and discussions are continuing in a variety of forums regarding development of models and alternative perspectives of existing ones. There is no consensus worldwide on models in higher education. Mostly adopted and efficient is the TQM methodology essentially having industrial origin. A model can be rated as effective when it proves the capacity and sustenance of operations of the educational institution (Sreekantan and Dairymple., 2003). This is reiterated by the view that quality assurance in educational sector draws heavily from industrial quality management systems which seeks to build flexible systems in dealing with a large customer base, in an uncertain environment (Seymour et al., 1996 cited in Sreekantan and Dairymple., 2003)

Quality assurance is the achievement of desired standards through application of agreed procedures (Colder, 1994 cited in Negi and Bhalla, 1999). Green and Harvey (1993) have identified five different approaches of viewing of quality in the field of higher education. Quality may be viewed.

- In terms of exceptional (highest standards)
- In terms of consistency (without defects and getting it right the first time)
- As fitness for purpose
- As value for money
- As a transformative (transformation of participants)

A diverse argument amongst these is that stakeholders interests are often neglected in the historical transect of educational service quality assessments (Birnbanm, 2000). This holds good on the grounds that a model would be accepted community wide, which is sensitive to different groups of people involved (Schulman and Houser, in Seymour et. Al., 1996)

It may however be argued that quality of education cannot be student oriented alone since it is the society that pays for operation of educational system (Henderix.,1992). In the field of education, the focus groups may be students (for the facilities), teachers (about the teaching/learning process), management, parents and prospective employers (Powar, in Negi and Bhalla., 1999). International educational fraternities have already started research into student feedback particularly in North America and UK with emphasis on customer satisfaction. Students are important stakeholders in the quality monitoring and assessment process. It is thus imperative that the universities providing higher education lay due emphasis on customer satisfaction and quality assurance (Popli, 2002). Most of the research on course evaluations and performance use the criteria of satisfaction or dissatisfaction resulting from reaching or not reaching the expectations (Anderson, 1973; Ortinau and Anderson, 1986 cited by Popli 2002). The theoretical underpinnings of the expectations-performance paradigm imply that levels of student satisfaction are a direct function of the extent to which expectations are realised (Ortinau et al., 1987 in Palihawadana and Holmes, 1999 cited by Popli, 2002).

Opening of economy has induced growing concerns about quality in every sector for which education is no exception. This has also instigated 'consumerism' of higher and technical education and there has been a significant growth in collection of views from students. This may include perceptions about the learning and teaching, the learning support facilities, the learning environment, other support facilities and external aspects of being a student (Harvey, 2001cited in Popli 2002). These can also be considered as the variables of customer satisfaction. On this ground an attempt has been made to assess the edúcational service quality from the viewpoint of stakeholders-students of the university, regarding physical facilities available, learning process and learning outcome. Educational service quality may be defined as an attitude resulting from student perceptions of school performance regarding both functional and technical quality (Holdford and Reiders., 2001). SERVQUAL, originally deigned for assessing service quality in marketing literature have some criticisms that led to the instrument called SERVPERF that measures the perceptions. Methodology used in this study measures the student perceptions hence draws from SERVPERF instrument. While the current scenario presents a highly competitive picture with large number of options available to students, it is imperative on the part of the institution to uphold conformity to quality assurance and excellence standards. Apart from this, stakeholders' perspective help to identify the potential problems from the grass roots and formulate tailor made solutions.

ACCREDITATION: UPHOLDING EXCELLENCE OF INSTITUTIONS

Accreditation is a tag of quality assurance for a technical institution. How does it work? And why should it make a difference to students, employers and the institution itself? Quality is not an act; it is a habit (Abdul Latheef Naha, 2005). The All India Council for Technical Education (AICTE), the country's statutory body for technical education, has reposed strong faith in this Aristotelian maxim. The National Board of Accreditation (NBA), an autonomous body set up by AICTE in 1987, has been a result. This has ensured importance to quality and not quantity. Several measures adopted to bring home quality assurance. One such is the NBA accreditation. Today it is viewed as a true stamp of quality maintained by the country's technical institutions. The fact that hardly 15 per cent of the courses offered by engineering colleges and polytechnics have NBA accreditation indicates its exclusivity.

The University Grants Commission (UGC) is a statutory organization established by an Act of Parliament in 1956 for the coordination, determination and maintenance of standards of university education apart from providing grants to universities and colleges. The UGC has established the National Assessment & Accreditation Council (NAAC), a model of assessment and accreditation, in 1994. The objectives are to grade institutions of higher education, to help institutes realize their academic objectives, to promote necessary changes to achieve the above and to encourage innovations. The modus operandi is different in the case of NAAC and NBA, as the former goes for macro assessment and the latter does the micro evaluation of the individual teaching departments.

To promote sustainable human development, the Tenth Plan states in its general objectives that education should become an effective promoter of sustainable human development by achieving quality in teaching, research and business and community extension functions, including lifelong learning. This is further stressed in the specific objectives of the Plan in providing importance to evaluation and accreditation and R&D. In conformity with the above stated objectives Rs. 757.98 crore has been earmarked under general development assistance to universities.

An institution and its programs are required to be accredited to uphold excellence in technical education. Such practice brings the development of a quality conscious system of technical education where excellence, relevance to market needs and participation by all stakeholders are major determinants. There should be periodical evaluation of technical institutions and their programs on the basis of specified guidelines and standards, and recommend to their recognition.

Quality assurance through Accreditation could be given to courses on the basis of factors such as

- Availability of potential for sustaining and improving upon assessment criteria;
- Recognition by all stakeholders including the industry and the community at large;
- Demonstrated capability of the institution and
- Program to adhere to quality standards;
- Assessment by peer groups of experts.

Quality assurance means different things to different stakeholders. For the institution, it means identification of strengths, weaknesses and opportunities for future growth. For students, it means that they have entered the portals of an institution offering quality professional education. For parents, it means that their child goes through a teaching-learning environment as per accepted good practices. For employers, it signifies that the students passing out have competence based on well-grounded technical inputs. Giving importance to the former; students point of view we bring out the present paper to highlight the quality of technical education.

CRITERIA FOR QUALITY ASSURANCE

The first criterion applies to institutional management, organization and governance. Various factors such as definition of mission and goals, scholarships, research, public service, leadership, motivation, delegation of powers and general efficiency are considered. The second criterion assures that the financial resources should be adequate to sustain not only the achievement of current educational objectives, but also provide for improvements in the foreseeable future, says NBA. The third criterion ensures physical resources, including building laboratories, equipment, material, library and other ancillary facilities. There should be provisions for safety, security and hygiene.

The next criterion deals with human resources, particularly faculty and staff. There should be self-appraisal and in-house performance appraisal mechanisms to monitor and ensure their continued effectiveness. Student strengths of the program seeking accreditation is another criteria, of which number of qualified candidates in national and state level tests, number admitted and dropouts, their ranking in the overall merit list of candidates seeking admission, etc. are some of the factors that reflect the institutional effectiveness.

Teaching and learning processes are the next criterion. A diploma program should be comprehensive to provide the student sufficient inputs in basic sciences, technical subjects, different technologies and training in relevant technical skills. An undergraduate degree program should embody general and specialized professional content of adequate depth and breadth, and should include appropriate humanities and science components. A PG degree program should be designed to give students mastery in their specialized field of study. Various factors such as academic calendar, number of instructional days, contact hours per week, delivery of syllabus, student evaluation and feedback are also considered. Another criterion looks at whether the institution provides and fosters an environment for intellectual and personality development of its students. Students should have access to facilities for career development, counseling and health education. And lastly, it looks at research and development and interaction efforts. In the case of diploma and undergraduate degree programs, teachers should participate in projects and quality improvement programs in research institutions and university departments. In the case of postgraduate programs, the aim should be to attain the stature of a center of excellence.

These criteria are transformed into parameters, giving weightage to each differently for diploma, undergraduate and postgraduate programs. Other than these those parameters that cannot be quantified through figures, such as institutional morale and academic ambience and capability of staff are also taken as parameters of quality of technical education. The variables of quality assurance includes the name of the program, approved intake, fees charged per annum, pass percentage in the last five years, teacher-student ratio, faculty members number and list, faculty's experience, details of individual members (including names, photograph, qualification, professional experience, research interests), industrial consultancy and R and D work by the department staff in terms of amount earned through consultancy, the number of sponsored research projects on hand, publications, patents earned, papers published in international journals, or presented in conferences, placement record, including companies that visited the campus, budget allocation for the program, new initiatives and future vision of the department/ program. However, most of institutions, which claim high standards by their educational officers, hardly observe this, as depicted by a survey.

In the realm to technical education too, developments in the last one-decade have turned the demand-supply position upside down. With over 90,000 seats lying vacant in engineering colleges in the country, it is evident that the student is going to choose from among several education providers. It would be the survival of the fittest! Accreditation by the Board must really be a true stamp of quality parameters, processes;

people need to be first-rate, capable of commanding respect and recognition.

THE TECHNICAL EDUCATION SYSTEM IN THE STATE

The Technical Education System in the State functions directly under the Higher Education Department of Government of Kerala. The policy decisions of the Government in the Technical Education sector are carried out with the supervision of the Minister for Education. The Principal Secretary Higher Education, through necessary executive orders implements the scheme in the sector. The Directorate of Technical Education is the Administrative Department facilitating the Government orders. Engineering Colleges, Polytechnics, College of Fine Arts, technical High School, Commercial Institute, Food Craft Institutes etc is the functional units coming under the purview of the Technical Education System in the State. In addition to these, there are also other collaborating units like Industry Institute Interaction Cell, Supervisory Development Centre, State Board of Technical Education and Centre for Curriculum Development. In Kerala there is a great demand for technical courses, for it ensures a secure profession. Currently there are 32 engineering colleges, 9 are government colleges, 5 private aided colleges, including one each under Cochin University and M.G. University, 16 Self-financing colleges and one Regional Engineering College at Ernakulam. Of the 54 Polytechnics, 41 were in government Sector including 7 Women's polytechnics, 6 in Private aided Sector and 7 Self Financing Polytechnics.

EVALUATION OF STAKEHOLDERS' PERSPECTIVE: A CASE STUDY

An Overview of the Programme

The Faculty of Engineering of CUSAT carries out academic programmes leading to B. Tech , M Tech. and Research in various disciplines. There are two campuses for CUSAT namely Kuttanad and Thrikkakkara where specialisation streams offered include B. Tech in Civil Engineering, Computer Science

& Engg, Electrical & Electronics Engg, Electronics and Communication Engg, Information Technology, Mechanical Engineering, Marine Engineering, Fire and Safety Engineering and M Tech in civil, chemical and mechanical engineering and research programmes. School of Engineering, Trikkakkara was established in 1979 for offering part time M.Tech programmes in the major disciplines of engineering. CUSAT Kuttanad Campus was established in 1999 under the aegis of the University at Pulincunnoo, Kuttanad. It comprises Cochin Universty College of Engineering, Kuttanad (CUCEK) offering various B.Tech. programmes and Cochin University College of Computer Applications, Kuttanad (CUCCAK) offering M.C.A. programme.

The duration of the programme is B. Tech programme is 4 semesters. The intake capacity is total 90 students per academic year. Selection process (Entrance examination) ensures that a student entering the programme have the minimum requirements along with desirable skill sets in This serves as a criterion in ensuring quality of the programme. The selection test is conducted with all India coverage ensuring effective participation to ensure selection of best of the cream. The entrance test comprises two papers, namely Mathematics, Physics and Chemistry. Each of these papers consists of 125 objective type questions, which maintain a ratio of 5:3:2 among the three subjects.

Well-maintained and equipped classroom facilities are available in addition to laboratory facilities. There is a rich library with an array of engineering and related books and journals of repute both national and international. The Central library of the university also supplements the information requirement of students/faculty. Soft skills have assumed importance much more than what was in past and with World Wide Web (WWW) shrinking the global community transcending boundaries. Computer facilities with internet broad band connectivity are available to students. A centralised hostel facility is available to students of all courses of the university. In addition large number of accommodation arrangements such as paying guests and private hostels are available close to the premises of the university.

Eminent and well-experienced faculty is a pre requisite to ensure quality of the programme. Training and development at regular intervals help them to update with recent developments in the field of education and subject matter. The course includes learning methodologies like classroom lectures, interactive sessions, presentations and seminars, assignments and practical and laboratory sessions. Students are exposed to multitude of applications in addition to creating theoretical awareness in the subject, which help in tackling real life situations in their career. Evaluation system in for the programme includes both internal and external (university level) examination. While internal examination carries about 40 per cent of the total marks, rest is earmarked for external assessment.

Excellent placement facilities are offered to students successfully completing the programme. Campus placements are conducted every year and during the past 2 years students of this programme have been absorbed by leading recruiters offering a salary range of Rs. 1,20,000/- to Rs. 4,48,000/- per annum. Recruiters include leading players in industrial and commercial ventures.

OBJECTIVE

Assess the stakeholders' perspective of quality of education received in terms of physical facilities, educational process and outcome

Materials and Methods

As earlier stated, there are several stakeholders, directly and indirectly associating with educational programmes. This study focuses on the students as primary stakeholders in the educational process. Secondary information was collected from the website of the university and other relevant publications. Primary data were collected from students of the engineering wing of the university. A pre-structured questionnaire was served randomly amongst 15 final year students pursuing the programme. Focus group discussions also were held to get an overall assessment. Data collected were tabulated and analysed using simple statistical tools like percentages and averages.

The questionnaire covered major areas such as evaluation of physical facilities, learning process and outcomes. The facilities, process and outcome were rated on Likert's scale. The five point ratings were Excellent, Good, Satisfactory, Poor and Very Poor. Scores were analysed by assigning values to the ratings as Excellent = 5, Good = 4, Satisfactory = 3, Poor = 2 and Very poor = 1. Mean scores were taken for all questions and overall rating of physical facilities, learning process and outcome were arrived. Satisfaction indices were worked out for overall evaluation.

$$\text{Satisfaction} = \frac{\text{Mean score} \times 100}{\text{Maximum score}}$$

The criterion for assessment on the basis of Satisfaction Index is as follows. A score of 80 to 100 is rated as Excellent, 60 to 79 is rated as Good, 40 to 59 as Satisfactory, 20 to 39 as Poor and 19 and below as Very Poor. Significant results are shown below .

RESULTS AND DISCUSSION

Evaluation of Physical Facilities

Majority of the respondents (35%) rated that the physical facilities available in the University supporting education is good while 30% found it satisfactory (Figure 1). A few of them found it excellent (4%).

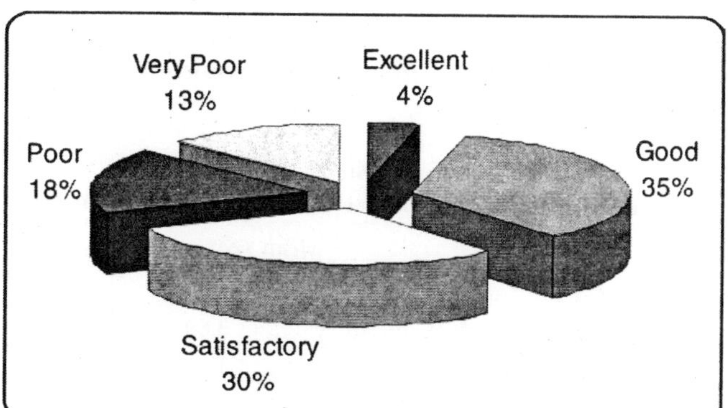

FIGURE 1: STAKEHOLDER'S OVERALL PERSPECTIVE OF PHYSICAL FACILITIES

Of the facilities provided, library and classroom facilities were found satisfactory and even above satisfactory by all the respondents. The laggards are the hostel facilities to students where majority (53 %) found it very poor, while only 14 per cent found it above satisfactory. Regarding computer terminals/student, 33% opined that the ratio was below their expectation (Table 1.)

Table 1
Perceived Value of Physical Facilities Available to Students (n=15)

Facility	*Excellent*	*Good*	*Satisfactory*	*Poor*	*Very Poor*	*Total*
Library	0	47	53	0	0	100
Lecture Halls/ Teaching Aids/Laboratory	13	40	40	7	0	100
Hostel facility	0	7	7	33	53	100
Computer Terminals/student	0	47	20	33	0	100

Source: Survey conducted among stakeholders.

The average scores of the facilities were worked out for each facility and satisfaction index was calculated. The overall satisfaction index was 59 indicating satisfactory performance with respect to physical facilities provided by the university (Table 2). While Lecture Halls/Teaching Aids/Laboratory was rated as Good scoring highest in the category, hostel facilities to students was rated as poor with the lowest index of 32. It is imperative on the part of authorities to provide sufficient hostel facilities.

Table 2
Average Scores of Physical Facilities Available to Students

Facilities	*Mean scores*	*Satisfaction Index*
Library	3.47	69
Lecture Halls/Teaching Aids/Laboratory	3.60	72
Hostel facility	1.60	32
Computer Terminals/student	3.13	63
Overall rating	2.95	59

Source: Survey conducted among stakeholders

LEARNING PROCESS EVALUATION

The learning process evaluation revealed that majority of the stakeholders found it satisfactory or above satisfactory (84%). Only 16 per cent rated these facilities below their expectations.

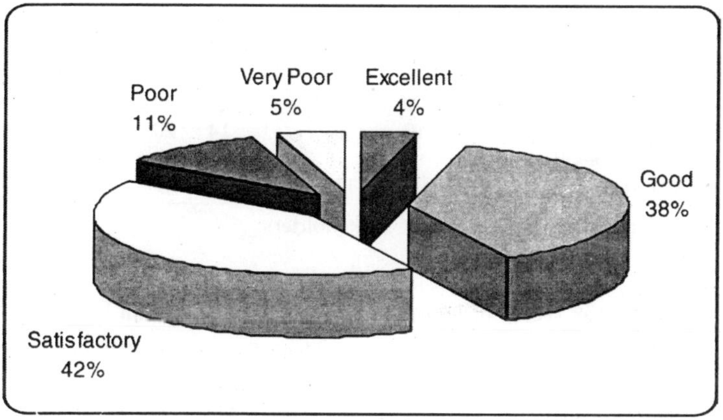

FIGURE 2: STAKEHOLDER'S OVERALL PERSPECTIVE OF LEARNING PROCESS

All the respondents rated the learning processes including lecture sessions, seminars/conferences, assignments, practical sessions and fees structure as satisfactory or above satisfactory. Exceptions was found in case of rating of examination system, in which internal evaluation was rated as poor by 20 per cent and 20 per cent rated external evaluation to be poor while 13per cent found it very poor (Table 3). Personality Development Programmes was rated as below satisfactory by majority (74%) of the respondents.

Overall Satisfaction Index of the learning process in the university evaluated by stakeholders was rated as good (65). Variation of satisfaction indices ranged between 43 (satisfactory performance) for Personality development programmes to 75 for practical/laboratory sessions (Table 4). The students in the university seek improvement in existing personality development programmes in addition to introducing new ones.

Table 3
Evaluation of Learning Process by Stakeholders (n=15)

Learning Process	*Excellent*	*Good*	*Satisfactory*	*Poor*	*Very Poor*	*Total*
Faculty/Lecture Sessions	7	46	47	0	0	100
Seminars/Conferences	7	13	80	0	0	100
Practical and Laboratory Sessions	7	60	33	0	0	100
Assignments	0	53	47	0	0	100
Fees structure	0	20	80	0	0	100
Internal Evaluation System	0	60	20	20	0	100
External Evaluation	13	40	14	20	13	100
Personality Development Programmes	0	13	13	47	27	100

Source: Survey conducted among stakeholders

Table 4
Average scores of learning process and satisfaction index

Learning Process Evaluation	*Mean Scores*	*Satisfaction Index*
Faculty/Lecture sessions	3.60	72
Seminars/Conferences	3.27	65
Practical and laboratory Sessions	3.73	75
Assignments	3.53	71
Fees structure	3.20	64
Internal Evaluation System	3.40	68
External Evaluation	3.20	64
Personality Development Programmes	2.13	43
Overall Rating	3.26	65

Source: Survey conducted among stakeholders

LEARNING OUTCOME EVALUATION

Learning outcome evaluation aims to analyse the stakeholders' perspective in skill set achievement. Evaluating of the end results of the learning programme, 9per cent found that existing system and facilities could provide excellent outcome while 17per cent rated it as good. Majority of the stakeholders felt that the university education could provide improvement in skill sets to a satisfactory level (Figure 3).

Break up of the skill set improvement among the stakeholders showed that subject knowledge improvement and placement facilities were rated as satisfactory and

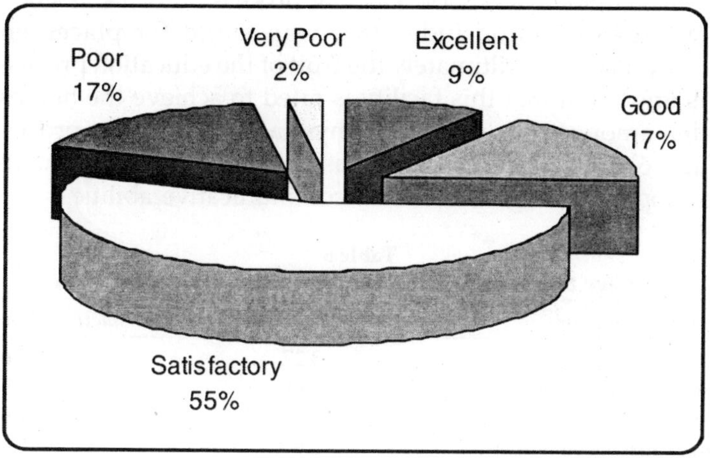

FIGURE 3: STAKEHOLDER'S OVERALL PERSPECTIVE OF LEARNING OUTCOME

above. It was noted that 53per cent of the respondents rated the placement facilities as excellent. Poor performance was reported by respondents in development of communication skills and personality development (Table 5). However majority of the stakeholders find the subject knowledge improvement and application orientation in the university satisfactory which is a pointer towards quality of faculty/ teaching. It is essential on the part of the university to introduce/improve personality development programmes.

Table 5
Evaluation of Learning Outcome by Stakeholders (n=15)

Learning outcome	*Excellent*	*Good*	*Satisfactory*	*Poor*	*Very Poor*	*Total*
Subject knowledge	0	27	73	0	0	100
Communicative abilities	0	6	47	47	0	100
Soft skills	0	27	60	13	0	100
Personality Development	0	0	67	27	6	100
Application Orientation	0	20	60	13	7	100
Placement facilities (on the basis of placement to previous batches)	53	20	27	0	0	100

Source: Survey conducted among stakeholders

Stakeholders assessed learning process outcome as good. Highest satisfaction index (88) was found for placement facilities, which is ultimately the fruit of the education process. It is important that this facility is rated to achieve the highest index amongst evaluation of physical and learning process (Table 6). Lowest mean scores was found in case of personality development programmes and communicative abilities.

Table 6
Average Scores of Leaning Outcome and Satisfaction Index

Learning Outcome	*Mean Scores*	*Satisfaction Index*
Subject knowledge	3.27	65
Communicative abilities	2.60	52
Soft skills	3.13	63
Personality Development	2.60	52
Application Orientation	3.20	64
Placement facilities (on the basis of placement to previous batches)	4.40	88
Overall rating	3.20	64

Source: Survey conducted among stakeholders

CONCLUSION

Quality is the buzzword in every spheres of activity. Academia has increasingly being aware of quality in education inspite of being introduced, of late. Accreditation ensures quality of educational providers, providing benchmarks for variables of assessment. In India accreditation has assumed importance in the context of mushrooming growth educational institutions and is carried out by NAAC and NBA constituted under UGC and AICTE. This warrants development of a quality conscious system of technical education where adequate emphasis is assigned to excellence, relevance to market needs and participation by all stakeholders. Recognising the need for quality assurance in education, the Tenth Plan has rightly set its objectives to promote sustainable human development via education.

Alternative approaches in quality of education points towards stakeholders' perspectives. While students are primary stakeholders in education, a case study of student fraternity pursuing technical education was taken up with the broad objective of assessment of perception of service quality in terms of physical facilities, educational process and outcome. Physical facilities were rated as satisfactory or above by 69 per cent of the respondents. The overall satisfaction index was 59 indicating satisfactory performance with respect to physical facilities provided by the university. The learning process evaluation revealed that majority of the stakeholders found it satisfactory or above satisfactory. Overall Satisfaction Index of the learning process in the university evaluated by stakeholders was rated as good. Evaluating of the end results of the learning programme, 9per cent found that existing system and facilities could provide excellent outcome while 17per cent rated it as good. Majority of the stakeholders felt that the university education could provide improvement in skill sets to a satisfactory level. Stakeholders assessed learning process outcome as good. Highest satisfaction index (88) was found for placement facilities, which is ultimately the fruit of the education process and Lowest mean scores was found in case of personality development programmes and communicative abilities. Regarding physical facilities, University has to concentrate on improvement of hostel facilities to students. Computer terminals/student also requires to be upgraded. Though subject specific learning process was found to be satisfactory, examination system requires reorientation and adequate emphasis should be placed on personality development programmes revealed as need of the hour. Learning outcome also reflected the weakness in the process, with students not satisfied of the development of communication abilities and confidence. The above suggestion holds good in this context also

Indian education system has serious problem of infrastructure .Standards are ignored and comprmises are beingf made with quality of education .presently education scenario faces challenging envionment similar to that of manufacturing sectors.Competition for excellence is rapidly going down. no doubt ,existing formal accrediation/affliations systems being operated .through various boards and councils do not provide a basis for implementing quantity system but do not address quality system needs . The challenge ,therefore before us is to provide satisfactory solutions to such issues.The only solution is to improvise upon the system and the processes that are being adopted to ensure quality education .Let us arise awake and act.

NOTE

We deeply acknowledge the constant encouragement, constructive suggestions and support from our Research Guide, Dr. M. Meerabai, Department of Applied Economics for preparation of the paper. Thanks are also due to School of Engineering faculty and students in participating in the survey.

REFERENCES

Birnbaum, R. (2000), The Life Cycle of Academic Management Fads', *Journal of Higher Education,* Vol. 71 No. 1, pp. 1-16.

Colder, (1994), Programme Evaluation & Quality, Kogan Page, London

Palihawadana, D. and Holmes, G. (1999), Modelling Module Evaluation in Marketing Education, Quality Assurance in Education, 7:1, pp. 41-46

Government of Kerala, 2005, *Economic Review.*

Harvey, L. and Green, D. (1993), Defining Quality, Assessment and Evaluation in Higher Education, Vol. 18 No. 1, pp. 9-34.

Henderikx P. (1992), Management and Promotion of Distance Education, Open Education cited in Negi, U.R and Bhalla, V (Eds)(1999), Effectiveness and Quality in Higher Education, Selections from University News-4, Association of Indian Universities, New Delhi, 1999.

Hira, D. S., and Mahesh Kumar (2000), Education For The Twenty-First Century, UNESCO Publications

Holdford, D and Reinders, T. P. (2001), Development of an Instrument to Assess Student Perceptions of the Quality of Pharmaceutical Education, *American Journal of Pharmaceutical Education* Vol. 65, Summer 2001.

Mukhopadhyay, S. and Anil Kumar K. (1999), Quality Profiles of Secondary Schools., Negi, U.R and Bhalla, V. (Eds) Effectiveness & Quality in Higher Education, Association of Indian Universities, New-Delhi, 1999.

Negi, U. R. and Bhalla, V. (1999), Effectiveness and Quality in Higher Education, Selections from University News-4, Association of Indian Universities, New Delhi, 1999.

Popli, S. (2002), Ensuring Customer Delight: A Quality Approach to Excellence in Management Education. Seventh International Seminar on Quality in Higher Education, Transforming Quality, RMIT, Melbourne.

Powar, K.B. (1999), Negi, U. R. and Bhalla, V. (Eds) (1999), Effectiveness and Quality in Higher Education, Selections from University News-4, Association of Indian Universities, New Delhi, 1999.

Seymour, D. *et al.* (Eds) (1996), High Performing Colleges. The Malcolm Baldrige National Quality Award as a Framework for Improving Higher Education. Volume I: Theory and Concepts, Prescott Publishing Co., Maryville, MO.

Sreekantan, G., and Dairymple, J. (2003), Developing Alternative Perspective for Quality in Higher Education, *The International Journal of Education Management*, 17/3(2003), pp. 126-136

The Hindu, Sept, (2006), Online edition of India's National Newspaper, Monday, Jan. 16, 2006.

Meera Bai M

21 Technical Education and Gender Needs A Keralite's View

Kerala is a region where everything is dynamic. With its beautiful land , educated people and rich culture Kerala is unique in all respects and aspects. The development experience of Kerala is noteworthy and a unique one. The major reasons for this is the advent of new technologies and all round innovations in Kerala. The developments in the information communication technologies have opened up both considerable opportunities and formidable challenges to the economy of Kerala.

Coming to the development experience of women in Kerala, they have a unique or special story to be shared with. No doubt, women's development has assumed greater significance in modern times. The status of women is relatively better in the State comparing with their counterparts in the other parts of the country. Women awareness, women movements at the grass root level, greater mobility, education, women and child health interventions etc. have led to the overall development of women in Kerala. Here comes the role of technology and the type of education they receive in general and technical education in particular. The present paper is written in this background.

WHAT IS TECHNOLOGY?

Technology plays an important role in the development process. Here technology is considered as a potential aid that can help to fulfil needs. Technology has an instrumental character. It is the objects and processes that can help humans and mediate in human actions and enhance human capabilities (Stamp 1989). It is the human made artifacts/processes and their social contexts that are geared towards enhancing human capabilities (Sasika Everts 1998).

GENDER NEEDS

Gender needs are needs that women or men may develop by virtue of their social positioning through gender attributes. Both men and women have gender needs. The present paper focuses on gender needs of women only. By gender needs of women, the author includes needs for economic empowerment, for securing higher incomes, for reduction of drudgery, for improved health and suitable employment. In the present paper how technical education affect the above mentioned gender needs of women in Kerala are focused.

Like men, women are also users and producers of technology. Women, particularly in the third world have different roles to play (Moser). These can be divided into three categories. These are productive, reproductive and community management roles. The productive role comprises of work done for payment in cash or in kind. But the reproductive role comprises of child bearing/rearing responsibilities and domestic tasks undertaken by women, required to guarantee the maintenance and reproduction of the labour force (Moser 1993).

The community management role comprises of activities undertaken primarily by women at the community level like the provision and maintenance of scarce resources of collective consumption such as water, health care and education. In this role women are influnenced by technologies and the level and type of technical education they received like water supply, medical technologies and technologies that impinge on the environment. On the one hand, technology inputs raises the expanding horizons of opportunities and on the other hand, it acts as potential threat. The type of technical education imparted by the various institutions should be capable of avoiding or at least reducing the potential threats and using its potential opportunity to meet the gender needs of women.

Coming to Kerala the State is blessed with the positive impacts of technology inputs, though there are certain negative impacts.

Regarding the female life expectancy , it is the highest in the state over the years. Similarly, the proportion of the aged females is the highest in Kerala compared with other State. Regarding the fertility indices like general fertility rate, total fertility rate and gross reproductive rate, it is favourablefor the State. Also infant mortality and death rates are least in Kerala, comparing with other States. The health status of Kerala women is better. This is mainly due to the high literacy status and employment . In all these the role of education is vry significant. The literacy rate of women in Kerala is the highest in the country and the difference between female literacy and male literacy rates in Kerala is the second lowest in the country. But a very important factor is to be mentioned here. The numberb of girl students in engineering colleges is low, contributing only around 30 per cent.

In the earlier part of the paper, it has been discussed that the important gender needs of women are for economic empowerment , for securing higher incomes , for reduction of drudgery, for improved health and suitable employment. What technology and technical education can do in achieving these needs?

TECHNICAL EDUCATION AND ECONOMIC EMPOWERMENT

The level and type of technical education received by women help them meet their gender needs as it enhances their opportunities in the labour market. The technology input approach prevailing globally in the labour market supports this situation. This is very relevant in the case of women enterprises. Many of the characteristics of women enterprises are common world-wide. Some of these are:

1. Most of the women enterprises are small in size
2. These have low profit margins.
3. Little opportunity for investment

4. They are part-time or seasonal in many cases
5. These are run from the home often
5. These units supplement other sources of income.
6. They are security oriented rather than growth oriented
7. These units have limited mobility and
8. They have limited accessibility to resources.

Regarding women enterprises, many of these units have only stories of success to tell. The major responsible factor for this is the technology support. The security and stability of these units depend mainly on the technology support. This help the units to attain economic empowerment by getting free time, broadening their economic opportunities, breaking through stereotypes of women and technology as antipodes and increasing their income.

TECHNICAL EDUCATION, SUITABLE EMPLOYMENT AND HIGH INCOME

One of the important gender needs of women is to secure suitable employment and high income. Technical education expands the horizon for getting better jobs with higher salaries to women as their male counterparts. In Kerala ,technically qualified women are ready to go outside the state or country for well paid jobs. These women are more self confident and ready to face risk and uncertainities than their counterparts in other parts of the country.

TECHNICAL EDUCATION AND REDUCTION OF DRUDGERY

Kerala is a region where 70-80 per cent of its female workers are engaged in the unorganized or informal sector . This sector is characterized by low employment, low income , high discrimination and high drudgery. Studies have revealed that the situation of high drudgery has a serious negative impact on their productivity. This can be reduced by the adoption of new technology in the different manufacturing stages and imparting technical education and training to these workers.This is very true in traditional industries like coir, cashew etc.

The developments in technical eduction have opened up both considerable opportunities and formidable challenges to all especially to women. Manufacturing , service and tertiary sectors provide wide opportunities to women especially service and tertiary sectors have become important sources of employment for women in the country. This is very true in the case of Kerala. This is because (1) women are ready to do the simpliest, repititive and least skilled jobs (2) technological changes have greater impact on service jobs and (3) employers prefer appointing women who are less resistant, flexible and easily dispossible.

The above being the case, technology centers and institutes can do a lot for the betterment of women's conditions both at home and wok places. In many cases these centers and institutes are away from villages. These must be linked to universities and established in and around the campuses. But in many cases it difficult to interact with poor rural and urban women from these centers and institutes and they don't have connections with women especially rural women.

In many cases, the various technology centers and institutes are technically oriented rather than socially oriented.So these centers and institutes fail in understanding the gender needs of women.

Another important point to be noted is the male dominance in the arena of technical education,technology centers and technical institutes. This leads to gender barriers in understanding women's needs. Here comes the need for effective research, the results of which can be transferred to women through appropriate intermediaries and agencies.

In today's globalised era, technology and technical education play important roles in satiating their gender needs for empowerment, higher wages and stable employment . This depends on factors like (1) information, (2) financimg, (3) training, (4) organization and (5) availability of technology. Technology centers especially meant for women can do a lot in these directions.Central and state governments should take steps in providing all these under one roof which will be of great use to women.

REFERENCES

Saski Everts (1998), Gender and Technology: Empowering Women, Engendering Development; Zed Books Ltd., London.

Stamp, Patricia (1989), Technology, Gender and Power in Africa, IDRC, Ottawa.

Moser, Caroline O. N. (1993), Gender Planning and Development; Theory, Practice and Training Routledge, London.

PART-3

Valliammai A

22 E-Learning–Emerging Trend in Modern Education An Overview

We are living in an era of instability, insecurity and constant change. The knowledge acquired by a person during the formal education becomes obsolete at a very rapid rate in the digital environment. Lifelong learning is the only way to survive and thrive in the rapidly changing environment. Internet has revolutionized the concept of education and changed the way the information is processed, stored, transmitted, retrieved and disseminated. It holds large volumes of electronic information in almost all fields of human knowledge.

In forming now Information Age economy knowledge and skills become the key factor of competition.. Internet and Global Information Infrastructure (GII) development in the world changes the main paradigm in Education and Research. Education should respond on global challenges of forming Information Society in providing necessary background for successful people living in this new knowledge based formation with following objectives:

Forming base knowledge and motivation for constant improvement of knowledge and skills

Forming moral principles of coexistence in open IS accepting of majority of truths and inadmissibility of harmful actions because of its possible global impact in information environment.

Setting up lifE-Long learning self-motivation.

Provide free access for learning and training matérials.

Education becomes a conductor and promoter of new technologies and area where new approaches and new social imperatives are forming now. New approaches in education and training should increase the assistance-to-contributive effect, i.e., education and training organisations should become the knowledge based organisations themselves. Classroom integration into Internet will demand special approach for curriculum design and instructional methodology used that should be focused on reaching main educational goals.. Curricula have to take into account existence of such global information environment as Internet. One of that emerging trend technology is E-learning.

E-LEARNING

What is E Learning

It is an all-encompassing term generally used to refer to computer-enhanced learning. It may include the use of web-based teaching materials and hypermedia in general, multimedia CD-ROMs or web sites, discussion boards, collaborative software, e-mail, blogs, wikis, text chat, computer aided assessment, educational animation, simulations, games, learning management software, electronic voting systems and more, with possibly a combination of different methods being used

Basically E-Learning is the online delivery of information, communication, education, and training. E-Learning can be in stand-alone form also like CD, DVD, etc. E-Learning provides a new set of tools that can add value to all the traditional learning modes-classroom experiences, textbook study, CD-ROM, and traditional computer based training. It is characterized by speed, technological transformation, and mediated human interaction.

AIM AND OBJECTIVE OF E LEARNING

Old-world learning models don't scale to meet the new world learning challenges such as quick and up to date information, geographically scattered information.

NEED OF E LEARNING

This new mode of learning promises to transform the experience of the classroom in a number of fundamental ways

- By augmenting traditional textbook materials with online resources;
- Lectures through the use of rich multimedia and interactive content;
- By extending student discussions beyond the walls of the classroom via a wide range of new communications platforms supporting inter classroom collaboration.

CHALLENGES MET BY E LEARNING

E-Learning will not replace the classroom setting, but effectively enhance it, taking advantage of new content and delivery technologies to enable learning. With E-Learning we can empower learners as well as instructors. Digital media provides a variety of contents and delivery vehicles for diverse nature of learners to meet their requirements.

ADVANTAGES OF E LEARNING

Advantages of E-Learning often include flexibility and convenience for the learner especially if they have other commitments, facilitation of communication between learners, greater adaptability to a learner's needs, more variety in learning experience with the use of multimedia and the non-verbal presentation of teaching material. Video instruction provides visual and audio learning that can be paused, and reversed for watching again. For organizations with distributed and constantly changing learners , E-Learning has huge benefits when compared with organizing classroom training. Some are critical of E-Learning in the context of education, because the face-to-face human interaction with a teacher has been removed from the process, and thus, some argue, the process is no longer "educational" in the highest philosophical sense. Supporters of E-Learning claim that this criticism is largely unfounded, as human interactions can readily be encouraged through audio or video-based web-conferencing programs, threaded discussion boards, live chat, blogs, wikis, email, or other synchronous or asynchronous means.

SUITABLITY OF E-LEARNING

E-Learning is not only suited for *distance learning,* it can also be used in conjunction with face-to-face teaching.

How to E-Learn

- Virtual Class Room
- Managed Tele Education
- Learning Course

Compnents of E-Learning

E Content

E book

E journals

E CONTENT

E-content is a digital content that can be transmitted over a computer network such as the Internet. The content is based on any electronic format. It is facilitated by the use of digital tools and content. Typically, it involves some form of interactivity. It is cost effective and time saving. It should be user friendly. The content of the information can be obtained by the individual according to their convenience and digested slowly. The presence of the individual is not required. Infinite number of users can be targeted by an individual. In E-Content photographs and video clips are inserted wherever necessary. The individuals are able to retrieve all the information necessary from one place. Users should be targeted. The E-Content should contain Frequently Asked Questions and their relevant answers .Adequate provision will be made so that the users can provide suggestions and feedbacks. References about E-Journals and E-Books Links should be provided.

The main component in e learning is development of E content that is courseware development The comparison between education tools used in convention and modern technology i education are given below.

Conventional Tools	*Modern Tools*
Lecture+Black Board	White board+Marker
Circulation of notes	Web notes/Hand outs
OHP Projector	LCD/DLP projector
Slide Projector	Guest Lecture/Educational Tour
Field/Inst. Visit	Development Films
Documentary films	Assignments-www.
Assignment	Manual and Online info.
Reference Books	

Various Steps Followed in E Content Development are

- Identification of Subject or Content
- SME or High Level Document
- Instructional Document
- Presentation
  - Document Format (ex. Word, PowerPoint, etc.,)
  - HTML
  - Flash Format
  - Multimedia
  - Application (Java, VB, etc.,)
- Implement & Maintain

Some of The Software Used for Developing E Content are Courseware Software

- A Tutor
- Moodle
- Reload Editor

Animation Software

- Macromedia Flash
- Macromedia Director
- 3D Animation
- Maya
- Studiomax
- Adobe Illustrator
- Visual Design

Video and Audio Conferencing

- Adobe premiere
- Visual Design
- Sound Forge

E CONTENT

Development of E Content in Web Page

A web page is a resource of information that is suitable for the World Wide Web and can be accessed through a web browser. This information is usually in HTML, DHTML or XHTML format, and may provide navigation to other web pages via hypertext link. Web Pages with limited content can be hosted on the Intranet. Web pages are requested and served from web servers using Hypertext Transfer Protocol (HTTP). Web pages include instructions as to the colors of text and backgrounds and links to images. Other media such as sound or video files may also be embedded within web pages. Insects, animations and other computer-generated material can also be embedded.

A dynamic web page is one that is created server-side when it is requested, and then served to the end-user/. The web page should be user friendly. The web page design should be simple. The web page should be simple in appearance without over usage of text, graphics and color. The web page should maintain clarity in the layout of text, graphics and links. Each page in a Web site should be linked to others. We need to take care in the layout of the graphics in a web page and the choice of the graphics. We should avoid using large sized bitmaps because they take a long time in downloading and opening a web page. We should choose a proper format for the graphics.

We can design the web page using various web-authorizing tools.

- HTML (Hyper Text Markup Language)
- DHTML (Dynamic Hyper Text Markup Language)
- XML (Extended Markup Language)
- Front Page
- Flash
- Dream weaver
- ASP

POINTS TO REMEMBER IN DEVELOPING E CONTENT IN WEB PAGE

We can develop E-Content in Web Pages using HTML.The designer should have a good knowledge in HTML. Individuals who are not familiar with HTML can use Microsoft Front Page to develop E-Content.Mandate and topics should appear in the front page of the web page. Subsequent pages should be in a linear format. Pages linked to references should appear in a hierarchical format. Every page should have minimum content so that the page can be opened or downloaded easily. Necessary pictures and Video clips should be inserted wherever necessary.If file document is large it should be converted into PDF format and then uploaded. Scanned images should not be used as it would occupy large space.Only images of GIF or TIF format should be used. The size of the image should be smaller so as the page can be opened quickly

DEVELOPMENT OF E CONTENT BY USING MULTIMEDIA

What I hear, I forget. What I see, I remember. What I do, I know" is a well known peasant proverb. Ability to present the information in an integrated way and in interactive way.The Media applications that allow users to actively participate instead of just sitting by as passive recipients of information Aeron (1998) indicated that, if you are stimulated with audio, you will gain about 20 per cent retention rate, that of audio visual is up to 30 per cent and in an interactive multi media presentation, the retention is as high as 60 per cent .

Among all the means of mass communication, multimedia is one of the most versatile audiovisual mediums of communication (Brun & Mangstl, 2001). Multimedia instructional material allows the learner actually to see, hear, and use the content to be learned (Roden, 1991). Interactive Multimedia Compact Disks can be used as an effective tool for the transfer of technology (Senthil, *et. al.*, 2003). Hooper (1986) also stressed the utility of multimedia in education. It would be an ideal tool to transmit information to the huge illiterate section of the

Indian population, especially students,on whom such an audiovisual medium could have a profound impact. It is also an effective tool for the students studying at college and school level. It can reproduce an experience with its sound and motions simultaneously and thereby creates an excellent learning effect.

MULTIMEDIA

Refers to the integration of multiple media-such as visual imagery, text, video, sound, and animation-which together can multiply the impact of your message. The interactive multimedia refers to the ability of the user to control these components and interact with them as needed.

METHODOLOGY AND DEVELOPMENT OF MULTIMEDIA

During this electronic era video plays a major role in awareness creation, education and transferring the technology among different category of audiences. Video can be effectively used for multi various purpose. The video as a mass medium can be used to telecast the technologies, as a group medium may be used as video shows and as an individual medium may be used as one of the media in multimedia interactive CD preparation. The video can be effectively used provided they are produced with utmost care.

CAUTIONS

1. Video is an AUDIO VISUAL medium. It's best use is for the dissemination of a message that must be SEEN AND HEARD to be understood and implemented effectively.
2. Using video requires a completely different technique from using radio. Too often where a radio writer/ producer is expected to be able to transfer to video there is tendency to write a script that is really "radio with picture". The secret of video is to allow the picture to carry most of the message.
3. If you choose a visual medium, you must be sure you have something to SHOW throughout the full length of the program time.

4. You need a wide range of talented people for a video production; writes; producers; cameraman; sound engineers; on air talent; lighting engineers; possibly make-up artists; graphics designers; editors; etc.
5. Video is a much more time consuming production process than radio. Be sure that you have the necessary time available before you decide the use video.
6. Video is a much more expensive medium to produce than radio. Be sure that you have necessary budget before you use video.

PREPARING THE VIDEO FOR E-COURSEWARE

In a video program for a E-courseware three things must be matched up the audio, the video and the message objectives. Objectives must come through clearly but most not misuse the medium in other words, you should not be so concerned with "getting the message across" that you simply sit people in front of the camera and have them lecture on the message. You have to decide which component or technology to be highlighted with video in your courseware.

On the other hand, you must avoid letting the medium over ride the message. Don't become so carried away with creating an interesting film that you allow the message to be swamped.

The creation of a good video program for a development message is a delicately balanced affair, particularly when you remember that you finished message also must be sufficiently culturally sensitive to appeal to your target audience, and that almost inevitably-it will have to be made within a limited time frame and budget.

Components of a Good Video Program

A good video program must: attract the audience's attention hold the audience's attention.

It will do this by being:

- Relevant to the audience
- Understandable
- Believable

- Technically well made
- Attracting the Attention of the Audience

It is a good idea to give some thought to what it is that attracts an audience to a subject-particularly a subject with which they are not already familiar. Here are some suggestions you might consider:

Generally, people are attracted to something for one or more of the following reasons:

- It affects their lives.
- It affects their health.
- It affects the welfare of their families.
- It offers an immediate (or near immediate) chance of improved income.
- It offers an immediate (or near immediate) chance of improved life style.
- It allows them to make use of natural talent.
- It provides them with a feeling of self-worth
- It gives pleasure
- It is funny, odd or bizarre.
- They are introduced to it by a person they respect or like.

On the other hand, people are generally NOT interested in or attended to a subject.....

- Affects only OTHER people
- Is beyond their personal control
- Will bring results only at some unidentifiable time in the future.
- Is difficult, confusing or expensive to carry out.
- Is offensive to their personal beliefs.
- Is too abstract or esoteric in nature
- Is dull and boring and repetitive.
- They are introduced to it by some one for whom they have neither respect nor liking.

With these considerations in mind, you can begin to prepare for using television as part of your project. Start by asking yourself these questions.

1. What are the special characteristics of video that make it worth considering as a major medium for your project?
2. What are the advantages of using video as a major medium for this project?

Television Program Types

1. Entertainment
2. News
3. Instructional/Informational Television Programs.

Good Design

Purpose, objectives and message will be strong and clear throughout, and will be based on through planning. There will be an effective balance of visual and rural presentation of the message, so that the visuals are not used as "decorative additions" to the spoken message.

Good Script

The messages will be presented in a format suited to the medium and attractive to the chosen audience. At all times the script will acknowledge the importance of finding and maintaining the balance between message and medium.

Good Production

The finished program will be good, cleanly produced television, adhering to all the rules of good presentation-both technically and artistically. The "instructional" nature of the program will not detract from the importance of first class production.

Instructional/Informational Program Types

Exposure and Information (Awareness)

The audience will be informed about something new and will gain new knowledge from which they can build new attitudes and awareness.

Skill Teaching

The audience will be given specific instruction in how to accomplish a certain task (or tasks) and they will gain the ability to respond to the programs with new behaviour.

Support/Reinforcement

The audience will be reinforced to continue and or change existing behaviours and attitudes.

STAGES IN VIDEO PRODUCTION

I. Pre Production

This is nothing but a planning stage. Here we plan for story/ subject matter, talents, location and equipments

Subject Matter

Subject matter is a key variable in any video production. It is essential to decide the components of the E-courseware to be converted in the form of video. The following points to be considered in subject matter area while planning.

1. Budget
2. Select the subject matter
3. Finalyse the title
4. Collect literature
5. Decide your audience
6. Decide mode of presentation : The concept of mode of presentation refers to treatment of the message to give it a particular form for the purpose of communication. There are different modes of presentations like drama, straight talk, documentary, interview, quiz, question answer, method demonstration and so on. It is very much essential to decide the mode of presentation before writing script.
7. Editing of literature
8. Preparation of preliminary script

Points to be considered for writing preliminary script

- Use simple sentences
- Use short concrete and familiar words
- Be direct, personal and straight forward
- Avoid technical terms and difficult words
- Avoid academic style
- Express the idea clearly and briefly
- Avoid contradictory ideas
- Avoid too many data
- Use local dialect
- Active voice
- Direct to the subject
- Reinforce salient points

VIDEO SCRIPT WRITING

The script writing for video is different from that of script writing for radio and print. A script is not like writing an essay or an article and not even just questions and answers. It is much more than that and follows its own particular grammar. In video script writing we visualizing the content written in the preliminary script. The whole content should be transferred in video script with suitable visualization.

Types of Video scripts

Basic Production Script

Topic .... Duration ....Scripted by............

Basic Production Script

Shot No.	*Shot Description*	*Approximate Duration*	*Description of script/ Narration*	*Sound Effect*	*Remark*
1.	L.S of TNAU building	15 Seconds	TNAU is one of the oldest institutions	Music	

Story Board Script

All are same that of basic production script. But the shot description will be highlighted with illustrations.

Camera Script

If you use more than one camera, you have to go for camera script. But the visual shot description, open new sub columns based on number of camera used.

Production Stage

The shooting to be carried out as per the video script

Post Production

The important activities in this stage is editing the the shots as per the video script.

E BOOK

It is an electronic text of a book and electronic text simulating the layout of a book.It is portable reading device. The e-book is a challenge to the ergonomic perfection of printed books. The enhancement in E book are Resizing, rotating, automatic scrolling of book is possible and Zooming is also possible

Some of the software used to create E book and methodology are as follows.

E Book Builder 2.00.333

There is no installation or setup. EBook Builder will not update or alter any existing computer files or libraries.prides itself on this respect function. EBook Builder is perfect for the budding author or seasoned writer. Compile your valuable penship to Chapters/Book format, using Rich Text Format (RTF) or plain text, into standalone, independent EBooks (.exe), requiring no supportive software

E Book Maker 2.0.3.2.2

EbookMaker is a professional Ebook compiler software. It can compile all HTML files and their included image, JavaScript, Flash, MP3, and video files in a specific folder into a standalone .EXE file. Such file is easy to distribute via CDROM, Email, and Internet. Ebook uses Internet Explorer to display its HTML pages, so readers don't have to install any other software to open Ebook for reading. Simple and easy to use, EbookMaker provides a variety of features to meet any custom need which an Ebook author may have for user interface, functions, and content protection, etc.

EBook Pack Express 1.7 build 0375

eBook Pack Express is a professional ebook creation software. It is very user-friendly and has all the features needed for professional ebook creation. It converts HTML, JavaScript, Flash, MP3 and video files into stand-alone eBooks, eZines, catalogues, reports and multimedia presentatións. The compiled ebook can be easily distributed via CDROM, email or Internet.

Natata eBook Compiler 2.2.1/Natata eBook Compiler 3.0.3

Natata eBook Compiler is an powerful software that packs and compresses multiple files including HTML, CSS, WAV, TXT, GIF, JPG, MID, JavaScript, DHTML, Flash, PDF, etc and converts them into a single compact executable file which contains a small viewer that launches the selected start document in an e-book like interface. You can use it to compile e-books, offline web pages, HTML photo albums, presentations and more. The interface uses a step-by-step approach that guides you through the process of creating your compiled file.

NeoBook v 5.5.0

NeoBook 5 allows you to produce royalty-free, professional quality, electronic publications. It easily integrates text, images, sound, music,animation, interactive controls, color and other graphical elements to create stunning multimedia productions. NeoBook can be used to produce electronic magazines (e-zines) that can be distributed over the Internet,interactive educational and training materials, CD-ROM interfaces, electronic books, reference works, brochures, catalogs, entertainment titles, and much

Text2exe 1.00.161

Convert plain text or RTF document into tiny standalone .exe Windows program.

Document capacity limited to approximately 1Mb capacity. The Features are Compact.exe header 53Kb, Definable Title/

Author details ,Definable background color with screen color grab ,Definable border width ,Password protect ,Information dialog Sizeable.

Multilingual interface-see our Select Language ,No installation.

Webexe 1.55

WebExe lets you convert your HTML pages into a stand alone, self-running EXE file.This file contains a built-in browser, so that no additional software for starting and viewing the file is required.

WebSiteZip Packer 1.3.0.1

It is a powerful and easy-to-use application which will help you to turn a single HTML page or a group of pages into a solid executable file (.exe) with an integrated HTML browser. After using our WebSiteZip Packer you can conveniently transport your HTML page or a complete web site as a single file embodying all necessary components (graphics, sounds, linked pages, etc.) and present it successfully independently of the type of HTML browser installed at the destination computer.

Writers Dream 32 bit 6.0.2

Writer's Dream presents text you have created with your favorite word processing program as a super-easy-to-use electronic book. You can display images and play sounds along with your chapters.

X-exe 1.7 Full

X-EXE is an easy-to-use, but powerful program for encrypting and protecting your data. With X-EXE, you can encrypt files of any type using secure RC6 algorithm. Your self-extracting encrypted files can be viewed on any Windows PC without needing to install any special software. Besides, X-EXE supports steganography, thus allowing you to use digital data hiding technology to encrypt and hide files within other files (carriers) such as pictures or audio files. Carrier files are not damaged after they are used to hide secret information.

ELECTRONIC JOURNALS

Libraries function as an essential integral component in higher education system. Without a proper information and knowledge infrastructure, no education system can sustain and achieve its laid down goals and objectives. The library environment is currently undergoing a rapid and dynamic revolution leading to new generation of libraries with an emphasis on e-resources. On one side, there is an increasing demand for good library collection in terms of large amount of data/information and on the other hand, the publishing media is striving hard to support this demand at lightning speed by way of e-publication as well as online access. As a result, a large number of e-resources are published on all subject areas. Therefore, libraries need to adopt electronics media for its collection developments in a better way to fulfill the requirements of users.

India has a large educational system comprising thousands of Colleges and hundreds of Universities along-with several Institutes of higher learning and Centers of excellence. The college and university libraries, being the nerve centres of the higher education and learning, play a vital role in support of all the activities such as teaching, research and publication. Our higher education system is passing through lot of problems due to economic recession and cost-recovery concepts. The college and university libraries in India are faced with the challenges to meet the user requirements due to various reasons such as exponential growth of knowledge, price escalation, budget restrictions. The increasing growth in the enrollment of students and researchers, lack of proper and adequate infrastructure further aggravates the overall problems and challenges for the college and university libraries. This situation has paved the way for serious thinking on the capabilities to compensate for reduced budgets. E-subscription is one of the emerging tool kit for libraries to survive in the present circumstances.

What is an E-journal?

Electronic journal may be defined broadly as any journal, magazine, e-zine, webzine, newsletter or type of electronic serial publication which is available over the internet and can be accessed using different technologies such as World Wide Web (WWW), Gopher, ftp, telnet, e-mail or Iistserv.

The University of Glasgow defines the term 'Electronic journal' as "Any journal that is available over the Internet can be called an 'electronic journal'. In some cases, print equivalents exist; in some cases, not. Some electronic journals are freely available; other has charging mechanisms of different types.

In simple words it is said that the electronic journals are the one where the text is read on, and l or printed from, the end-user's computer rather than as print-on-paper. In the online journal, the data is downloaded directly from the host computer rather than via an intermediate medium such as CD-ROM.

ELECTRONIC JOURNALS

From the year 1998, a few publishers namely Elsevier, Academic, Springer etc had offered access to their Online Journals free of cost against subscription to print version as an additional gesture. The library made use of this facility by registering such free online journals officially. Thus, the library entered the second phase towards the e-resource collection development without much of budget constraint.

The goal of E-Journals is to provide desktop access to freely available electronic version of journals subscribed by IISc Library and free e-journals of relevance to IISc. To this end a web-accessible directory was developed containing a database of all journals subscribed by IISc. The directory also contains several free peer-reviewed electronic journals. Thus the database stores a variety of information such as holding details, internet addresses, user IDs and Passwords etc about each journal including links to the journal's website. Using these links, users can visit the journal site and access the full text of articles.

What are E-Resources?

Any electronic product that delivers a collection of data, be it text referring to full text bases, electronic journals, image collections, other multimedia products and numerical, graphical or time based, as a commercially available title that has been published with an aim to being marketed. These may be delivered on CD-ROM, on tape, via the Internet and so on.

ABSTRACTING AND INDEXING SERVICES AND OTHER BIBLIOGRAPHIC SOURCES

The ability of the computer to store information in the form of records, and allow quick searching of these has long been recognised. Therefore it is understandable that one of the most important electronic reference tools used in libraries worldwide is the bibliographic sources. Both major bibliographic resources and numerous Abstracting and Indexing services with the ability to search vast collections of Table of Contents (TOC), Conference Proceedings and data from Books and Serials are offered. The benefit of these large sources is that they cover many subjects and thus facilitate a multidisciplinary approach.

As a first phase in e-resource collection development process, library embarked into subscribing e-version of following Abstracting and Indexing periodicals along with the back files and stopped print subscription of the same from 1994. The amount saved by stoppage of print version was diverted for purchasing e-version (CD-ROM) of the following.

Why to Buy E-Resources?

The reasons for actually embarking on the purchasing of electronic resources are generally accepted because of the ease of usability, readability, affordability and accessibility and in addition to these, the following are the advantages of e-resources over the print media.

- **Multi-access:** A networked product can provide multiple points of access (in the campus) at multiple points in time (24 hours a day, 7 days a week) and to multiple simultaneous users.
- **Speed:** An electronic resource is lot quicker to browse or search, to extract information from, to integrate that information into other material and to cross-search or reference between different publications.

- **Functionality:** E-resource will allow the user to approach the publication to analyse its content in new ways by click of the mouse on search mode.
- **Content:** The E-resources can contain a vast amount of information, but more importantly the material can consist of mixed media i.e. images, video, audio and animation which could not be replicated in print.

The electronic resources are basically divided into two types:

Full text electronic resources,

Electronic resources available through on-line databases. For the purpose of shared subscription of electronic journals following journals can be marked as the natural choice as they are most widely used and demand e-journals in the field of science and technology.

1. IEEE Journals
2. Elsevier's Science Direct
3. Springer Verlag's Link
4. Applied Science and Technology Plus etc.

Advantages of E-journals

Following are the worth mention advantages of the e-journals.

1. Speed of access to the latest information
2. Ability to implement multimedia elements
3. Quick searching
4. Linking from one and to other resources
5. Security
6. Single user or location restrictions do not apply
7. Downloading an article to a personal computer for later use or printing is easier than photocopying or scanning.
8. The e-information are minimizing the labour & time of the resources and other users with the following effect.
9. Easy and effective retrieval search
10. Downloading the text image, audio with the MM concept
11. Quick access thro' efficient search engines,

12. Teaching & learning process in a live manner
13. Teleconferencing
14. Retrieval thro' web indexing/Mete data
15. Meet the people of the subject specialization
16. Vast statistical data

FORMULATING POLICY FOR ELECTRONIC RESOURCES COLLECTION DEVELOPMENT

The collection development refers to collection of different types of library materials keeping in view the changing requirements of the users. Collection development, being a planning function is carefully designed and executed in three levels.

1. Collection development policy decisions are made at the highest level (Senate Library Committee).
2. Selection of resources is the second level of decision making and acquisition of materials (Division and Department Chairmen).
3. The third level is the process by which library acquires various materials, implementing selection decision and collection development plan (Librarian).

The single most important message is the e-resources should be considered alongside printed resources (such as e-journals, books, databases etc.) and the library formulates an overall "Quality" collection development policy covering all material. Such as

1. Outline the present collection's strength and weaknesses.
2. Identify the reader community that the collections are aimed at and recognize their needs, which will be met by the policy.
3. Make the policy decisions available to all involved in purchasing activities.
4. Most importantly the policy should be open to changes and constantly reviewed and updated.

It was only during the late 1990s that E-resources were made available to various subscribers. Attention was brought to these E-resources through the distribution of catalogues, personal marketing promotion and free online trial access. The evaluation of trial access revealed that there was a great scope for the development of a collection of books and journals in soft copy. The two main advantages of this media of resources include sizeable cost effectiveness compared to print version and time efficiency as data may be acquired within a short span of time thus increasing the speed and ease with which one acquires information from a resource collection.

ON-GOING E-RESOURCES COLLECTION DEVELOPMENT ACTIVITIES

To overcome the lacuna in e-resources collection and to develop a comprehensive e-resources collection, which will reasonably meet the core information resource access requirements of the faculty and researchers in the Institute, library has planned e-resources development programs in category wise as follows:

1. Extending online access facility to e-resources for which already limited access is available by purchasing back files to access archival data for current and future use. This has complemented the INDEST consortium subscriptions and enhanced the access facilities.
2. Purchase of back-files of core e-resources for perpetual access.
3. Subscribe to online version of core resources for which currently no online access is available particularly Society and Institutional publications.
4. Collection developments of e-resources other than journal such as Books, Reference Works, Standards, Factual Databases etc.

DIGITAL RESOURCE ORGANIZATION

The library should develop an information resources collection and development policy consistent with the objectives of its institution or community. These information resources should satisfy through content, currency format organization and quality, i.e., OPAC, Electronic text and journals, Electronic books, Internet wave, email, bulletin board, database (CD ROM and DVD- ROM database).

The digital information services personnel should, beyond in house collections and in house expertise, draw on the resources of other organizations, collect and provide information, by consulting individual experts and by tapping external information sources. The digital library should provide access to the most current reference source available in order to assure the accuracy of information.

Challenges facing the E-information sources management

1. Preservation
2. Legal issues
3. Lack of professional skills key skill for digital librarians
4. Lack of co-operation amongst librarians
5. Lack of resources
6. Lack of expertise
7. Lack of manpower training
8. Information explosion on the Internet
9. Technology change
10. Political & social constraints

PRESERVATION

Digital data does not have a long enough natural lifetime for us to wait for better medias to come along Even today we have not achieved stability in data storage technology. Effects should be made for survival of digital data for longer duration right from its birth. This is known as the 'retention-intention' Data preservation cannot and must not be left to chance.

CONCLUSION

In modern education,especially, the increasing tendency is to create a Virtual Learning Environment (VLE) in which all aspects of a course are handled through a consistent user interface standard throughout the institution. A growing number of physical universities, as well as newer online-only colleges, have begun to offer a select set of academic degree and certificate programs via the Internet at a wide range of levels and in a wide range of disciplines. While some programs

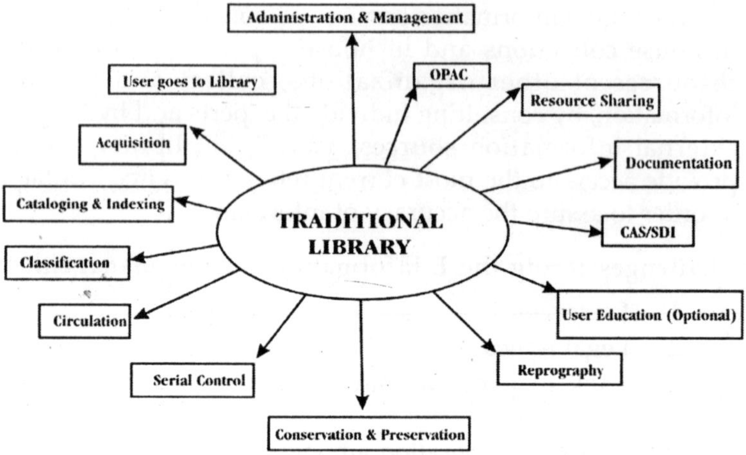

Figure : Traditional Library

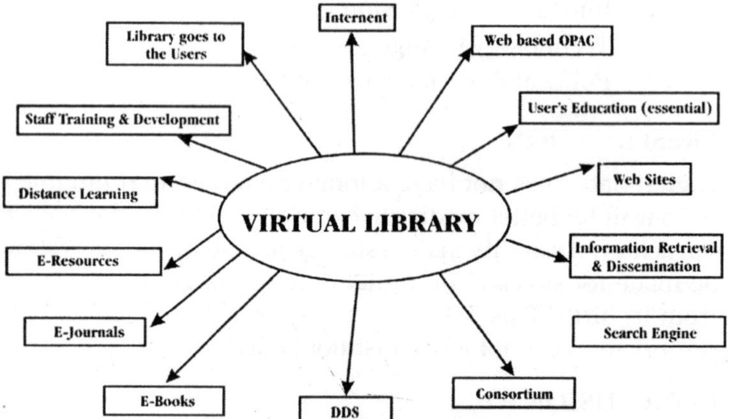

Figure : Virtual Library

require students to attend some campus classes or orientations, many are delivered completely online. In addition, several universities offer online student support services, such as online advising and registration, e-counselling, online textbook purchase, student governments and student newspapers.

There is a need to develop a policy for consortia-based subscription to electronic resources which should clearly indicate the terms and conditions favoring and protecting the academic interest of the college and university students.

REFERENCES

Designing World Class E-learning, Roger C. Schank, Publisher: McGraw-Hill Education-November, 2001.

E-learning Tools and Technologies, by William Horton, Katherine Horton, Publisher: John Wiley & Sons Inc, February, 2003.

Advances in Web-based Learning-icwl 2004: ICWL 2004: Third International Conference, Beijing, by Wenyin. Liu, Yuanchun. Shi, Qing. Li.